Mastering Enterprise Platform Engineering

A practical guide to platform engineering and generative AI for high-performance software delivery

Mark Peters

Gautham Pallapa

Mastering Enterprise Platform Engineering

Portfolio Director: Kartikey Pandey

Relationship Lead: Preet Ahuja

Project Manager: Sonam Pandey

Content Engineer: Apramit Bhattacharya

Technical Editor: Simran Ali

Copy Editor: Safis Editing

Proofreader: Apramit Bhattacharya

Indexer: Pratik Shirodkar

Production Designer: Deepak Chavan

Growth Lead: Marylou De Mello

First published: July 2025

Production reference: 1041125

Published by Packt Publishing Ltd.

Grosvenor House

11 St Paul's Square

Birmingham

B3 1RB, UK

ISBN 978-1-83588-048-7

www.packtpub.com

*To my wonderful wife, who makes every endeavor possible
and contributes to reviewing all the words written.*

– Mark Peters

*To my wife and son, whose unwavering support and daily inspiration have made every step of this
journey possible. Your belief in me fuels my continuous growth and success.*

– Gautham Pallapa

Foreword

Even after a decade of fulfilling work in the Platform Engineering space, the productivity magic of great platform teams continues to inspire me. Just recently, a customer delightfully shared how their developers cut timelines by 80% thanks to the unexpected ease of moving their applications to their first deployment. What might have taken weeks of highly skilled human effort, made effortless by the convenience of a resilient, secure, and intuitive self-service interface.

During my five years working with Gautham Pallapa, we helped ignite and extend Platform Engineering transformations across some of the world's largest enterprises. Our customers consistently relied on his thoughtful and analytical insights not just to make the initial decision to embark on their journey, but more importantly, to continually benchmark their progress against both their potential and their peers. Gautham's rare blend of technical depth, cultural awareness, and business acumen accelerated their progress at every stage. Now, readers have a remarkable opportunity to draw from that proven experience throughout this book.

As we enter the era of AI-enabled development and operations, the need for standardized platforms, patterns, and infrastructure is more critical than ever. Two significant forces are driving this shift:

> First, the time pressure to deliver AI-enabled features is once again highlighting software engineering's core responsibility to deliver outcomes and value for the organization. Executive sponsors today have little patience for multi-year transformations, and nothing accelerates delivery like a well-designed platform.

> Second, for all its breakthroughs, AI remains a probabilistic technology. Integrating and debugging AI-enabled capabilities will be far more manageable within the same simplified interfaces and standardized environments that already enhance human productivity.

If the benefits of Platform Engineering are so clear and enduring, why haven't more organizations adopted it at scale? It's worth briefly considering the alternative—the inverse of a proactive platform approach. In this text, you will find a helpful summary of Platform Engineering:

> *The evolution of Platform Engineering is a narrative of adaptation and foresight.*

Foresight is the primary barrier to adopting a platform-centric approach. Intuitively, we all understand that if we wait until we are already late for the airport, it's too late to build the highway to get there. The same principle applies to organizational design, tooling and automation scope, and consistent infrastructure architecture. For a platform approach to succeed, someone in every organization must possess and champion foresight across these domains.

Since you are picking up this important book to study Platform Engineering today, perhaps with a bit of passion, study, and persistence, that person will be you!

James Watters

Senior Director of R&D, Tanzu, Division, Broadcom

Contributors

About the authors

Dr. Mark Peters works as senior director of solutions architecture, responsible for constructing innovative technological solutions for government and commercial customers. He has worked on four different DevOps DoD programs and is a DevOps Institute Ambassador. He has integrated intelligence processes with operational delivery in the USAF, retiring as a LtCol. He has double doctorates in strategic security and information technology and has analyzed cyber-attacks for a decade. A cybersecurity expert, he holds CISSP, PMP, CGSCL, and other certifications. In his spare time, he likes to read and write, as well as speak at conferences. He enjoys fitness, drawing, and spending time with his family. Dr. Peters is passionate about working with individuals on their unique DevSecOps implementations. A full-on DevOps junkie, he maintains unbounded optimism about incorporating DevOps across multiple industries. He has authored *Cashing in on Cyberpower* and hundreds of technical reviews, articles, and presentations.

Dr. Gautham Pallapa, a globally recognized thought leader and award-winning author of *Leading with Empathy*, has a distinguished 24-year career in IT. He's spearheaded enterprise transformations at Fortune 500 and Global 2000 companies, utilizing his expertise in cloud-native technologies, AI/ML, and DevOps to drive substantial business value. His ethos, Transform with Empathy, underpins Transformity, a thought leadership forum he founded to transform organizations with empathic leadership and technology. As a sought-after keynote speaker and executive advisor, Dr. Pallapa's contributions to application modernization and business value acceleration have earned him numerous accolades, making him a pivotal figure in empathic leadership, innovation, and organizational transformation.

About the reviewers

Bryan Ross is an accomplished leader, seasoned technologist, and public speaker. With over 15 years of industry experience as a senior IT leader, he now helps customers realize business value from IT faster. Equally comfortable speaking with executives and engineers alike, he bridges the gap between technical and business stakeholders through compelling storytelling and real-world examples.

Outside of work, Bryan finds balance in the non-digital world, immersing himself in the beauty of Scotland's shores through his love for sailing and scuba diving. He lives with his wife and three rambunctious boys on a smallholding on the outskirts of Edinburgh, Scotland.

Arun Pandiyan Perumal, an accomplished technology infrastructure specialist working as a site reliability engineer at Adobe, boasts over 11 years of experience in cloud infrastructure management, DevOps, and site reliability engineering. His career at top organizations has been marked by leading teams and projects in building secure cloud infrastructures, designing highly scalable systems, integrating DevOps tools for automation, enforcing cloud security practices, and managing globally distributed multi-cloud infrastructures for hosting several critical business applications. Arun has been deeply involved in the research and technical communities, sharing his knowledge and collaborating with experts on various research initiatives.

Table of Contents

4

Part 2: Execute Run Enterprise Platforms with Precision   91

5

6

Engineering Platform Data Management   119

7

Security, Compliance, and Risk Management   143

8

Real-World Applications and Case Studies   161

11

From Vision to Reality: Mastering Enterprise Platform Engineering 237

12

Preface

Platform Engineering signifies the next seismic shift in DevOps development by connecting ongoing improvement to long-term automation. It condenses many years of valuable knowledge into a unified framework to evolve how organizations construct, oversee, and expand their digital platforms. In today's fast-paced business environment, bringing products to market quickly can make or break a company. Creating organic custom platforms often wastes time and misses chances. Platform Engineering offers a straightforward, powerful solution: concentrate on innovation and value while entrusting infrastructure and transformation intricacies to experts. The road to effective Platform Engineering is not a straight line; it is fraught with challenges that demand a deep understanding of technology and strategy.

Many organizations embark on this journey with the best intentions but find themselves trapped in an inefficiency cycle, taking 12–18 months or longer to escape, if ever. The truth is that what you need already exists; the challenge lies in knowing how to harness, integrate, and delegate platform responsibilities.

This book is more than just a compendium of theories; it is a practical guide offering actionable insights, best practices, and real-world tested tools. You'll learn how to configure scalable, secure, and reliable platforms with precision, ensuring your organization stays ahead of the curve. By the end, you'll feel fully prepared to lead your organization's Platform Engineering implementation.

This comprehensive guide covers everything from laying the cultural and architectural foundations to incorporating the latest advancements in AI-driven platforms. Through practical tutorials, hands-on projects, and insightful self-assessment questions, you will grasp Platform Engineering and be empowered to spearhead its adoption within your organization. Key features include the following:

- Designing and building an effective platform.
- Establishing platform infrastructure metrics and integration, including AI solutions.
- Maximizing platform success through accelerated delivery and continuous revenue.

By the time you finish reading, you won't just be ready for the future—you'll be prepared to shape it. This book will be your ally on the path to creating a DevOps-compatible, AI-powered platform that is not only a technical marvel but also a strategic asset, positioning your organization at the forefront of digital innovation.

Who this book is for

This book is crafted for professionals across IT, product, and business functions who are at the forefront of enterprise transformation. It speaks directly to business leaders, transformation change agents within IT departments, software developers, and IT operations teams responsible for ensuring the stability, reliability, and overall health of platforms. Whether you're leading the transformation, developing the platforms, or ensuring operational efficiency, this book is designed to equip you with the knowledge and tools you need to succeed.

This book offers a better path for software developers who are weary of the relentless cycle of building and maintaining their own platforms. The time spent on platform construction (often lasting 40–60 weeks) is time diverted from creating the applications that drive ROI and sharpen your competitive edge. If your goal is to build applications that succeed in the marketplace, the smart move is to leverage a platform engineered by experts, allowing you to focus on what truly matters: innovation and delivery. Similarly, for IT operations teams, Platform Engineering can reduce the burden of platform maintenance, allowing you to focus on strategic tasks that enhance the overall health of the platforms.

This book is an indispensable guide for the C-Suite, managers, and directors of engineering, security, platform, and operations teams, as well as the software developers and platform operators ready to elevate their organizations by adopting a strategic approach to Platform Engineering.

What this book covers

Chapter 1, Introduction to Modern Platform Engineering, offers a foundational explanation for why platforms are essential, some of the basic problems faced by platforms such as speed to market and resource costing, and some of the software solutions that exist. The chapter continues through a comparative analysis of existing tools. Understanding what DevOps is allows one to see the expansion of DevOps through using platforms to concentrate on the important aspects of flow, feedback, and delivery.

Chapter 2, Architectural Foundations and Strategy, helps you understand platform standards starting with the basic cloud migration, the cloud format from AWS to Azure or Google, and the cloud structure, as well as setting up Kubernetes clusters. The basic standards lead one to design and implement custom architectures within those spaces, but architectures also arrive with their own standards.

Chapter 3, Cultural Transformation and Leadership, shows that platforms aren't just about making technical changes to a production system but about aligning the cultural changes that support implementation. Cultural change requires acknowledging what exists and building a path to organizational changes. As leading-edge innovation, the chapter shapes technical leadership decisions to reach the platform marketplace through effective changes, delivering user value.

Chapter 4, The Platform Engineering Ecosystem, explores the idea that Platform Engineering is not just about installing a single software fix or implementing configuration as code but adjusting the entire delivery ecosystem. Good platforms incorporate a number of different tools to achieve success. Integrating those tools within different aspects of the platform is a key element of effective platforms. Furthermore, those tools should be incorporated into CI/CD outcomes through a DevOps methodology.

Chapter 5, Incorporating Artificial Intelligence into Platform Engineering, talks about how ingesting large amounts of data from different locations can be aided by using generative AI models both in coding and automating operations for software development. The chapter highlights several different off-the-shelf tools that can be integrated to support AI-based outcomes that enhance overall capabilities. Users must recognize their own approach to AI, as well as what other competitors may have done with AI and their lessons learned.

Chapter 6, Engineering Platform Data Management, shows you that platforms don't just need the initial formation but require managing data throughout multiple applications. One must implement effective strategies, optimize those strategies, and then manage data. Data management tools are described along with methods to handle all data, from user input to streaming solutions.

Chapter 7, Security, Compliance, and Risk Management, explores how DevOps has been recharacterized as DevSecOps, but any operational solution requires security. Platforms emphasize secure-by-default solutions for vulnerability tracking, software bills of materials, and patching solutions before deployment. Security goes beyond the platform itself to managing those who connect to the platform, especially in PaaS and SaaS-type solutions with AI tools.

Chapter 8, Real-World Applications and Case Studies, allows you to review case studies showcasing successful platform transformations and the integration of platforms with business strategies. It explores failed platform transformations to highlight the value of strategic planning and disruption in the enterprise. A DevOps success model is used to capture previous lessons and incorporate them to support current operations. This chapter also examines potential future lessons from those technologies and solutions that are not yet fully implemented.

Chapter 9, Testing, Quality Assurance, and Operations, highlights that platform solutions build beyond the basics to offer standardized pipelines and testing processes. Successfully implementing these processes generates repeatable bodies of evidence, allowing all software to be measured against the same standard. Implementing these standards creates quality across the product and allows for continual success.

Chapter 10, Building High-Performance Platform Teams, shows that central to the platform is having effective platform teams. Using optimal buy versus build strategies allows organizations to minimize dedicated platform individuals while maintaining scalability and reliability. High-performing teams can be designed within a DevOps framework without specialized knowledge based on platform benefits generated from standardized tooling, generative AI solutions, and modernized observability.

Chapter 11, From Vision to Reality: Mastering Enterprise Platform Engineering, emphasizes the importance of visionary leadership, strategic planning, and continuous improvement in driving platform success. It explores articulating platform initiative value to stakeholders, measuring and tracking progress against key performance indicators, and adapting strategies in response to evolving business and technological landscapes. It includes real-world examples and practical advice to maintain platforms as adaptable, resilient, and continuously evolving assets that drive business value.

To get the most out of this book

The following table outlines the key software and tools covered in this book, along with the recommended operating systems to ensure optimal compatibility and performance.

Software/hardware covered in the book	Operating system requirements
Robot Framework	Windows, macOS, or Linux
Grafana, Prometheus	
Open Telemetry (OTEL)	
Python	
StarUML	
ChatGPT, Microsoft CoPilot, Google Gemini, Perplexity AI	
Terraform, GitLab, GitHub Actions	
Large language models	

Conventions used

There are a number of text conventions used throughout this book.

`Code in text`: Indicates code words in text, database table names, folder names, filenames, file extensions, pathnames, dummy URLs, user input, and X/Twitter handles. Here is an example: "The next step is running command lines for `terraform init` and applying and configuring `kubectl` with AWS to react to the individual cluster."

A block of code is set as follows:

```
Module "eks" {
  Source = "terraform-aws-modules/eks/aws"
  Cluster_name = "deployment-target1"
  Subnets = ["subnet-1", "subnet-2"]
  vpc_id = "vpc-54321"
 workers_desired_capacity = 10
Instance_type = "t2.large"
}
```

Any command-line input or output is written as follows:

```
terraform init
terraform apply
```

Bold: Indicates a new term, an important word, or words that you see onscreen. For instance, words in menus or dialog boxes appear in **bold**. Here is an example: "A common example is to use **Lightweight Directory Access Protocol (LDAP)** for the platform, which then shares authentication across all the tools."

> Tips or important notes
> Appear like this.

Get in touch

Feedback from our readers is always welcome.

General feedback: If you have questions about any aspect of this book, email us at `customercare@packtpub.com` and mention the book title in the subject of your message.

Errata: Although we have taken every care to ensure the accuracy of our content, mistakes do happen. If you have found a mistake in this book, we would be grateful if you would report this to us. Please visit `www.packtpub.com/support/errata` and fill in the form.

Piracy: If you come across any illegal copies of our works in any form on the internet, we would be grateful if you would provide us with the location address or website name. Please contact us at `copyright@packt.com` with a link to the material.

If you are interested in becoming an author: If there is a topic that you have expertise in and you are interested in either writing or contributing to a book, please visit `authors.packtpub.com`.

> The authors acknowledge the use of cutting-edge AI, in this case Grammarly, with the sole aim of enhancing the language and clarity within the book, thereby ensuring a smooth reading experience for readers. It's important to note that the content itself has been crafted by the authors and edited by a professional publishing team.

Share Your Thoughts

Once you've read *Mastering Enterprise Platform Engineering*, we'd love to hear your thoughts! Scan the QR code below to go straight to the Amazon review page for this book and share your feedback.

`https://packt.link/r/1-835-88049-5`

Your review is important to us and the tech community and will help us make sure we're delivering excellent quality content.

Free Benefits with Your Book

This book comes with free benefits to support your learning. Activate them now for instant access (see the "*How to Unlock*" section for instructions).

Here's a quick overview of what you can instantly unlock with your purchase:

PDF and ePub Copies   **Next-Gen Web-Based Reader**

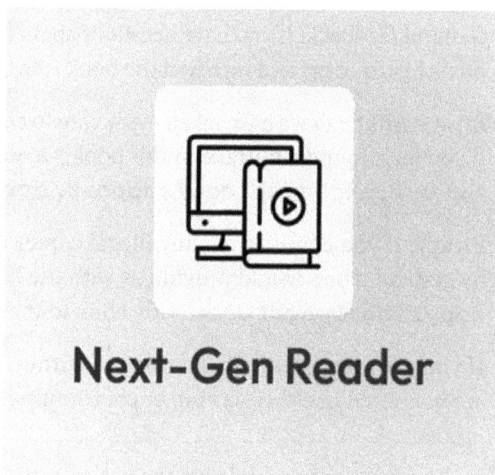

📄 Access a DRM-free PDF copy of this book to read anywhere, on any device.

📄 Use a DRM-free ePub version with your favorite e-reader.

🔄 **Multi-device progress sync**: Pick up where you left off, on any device.

📝 **Highlighting and notetaking**: Capture ideas and turn reading into lasting knowledge.

🔖 **Bookmarking**: Save and revisit key sections whenever you need them.

☀ **Dark mode**: Reduce eye strain by switching to dark or sepia themes

How to Unlock

UNLOCK NOW

Scan the QR code (or go to packtpub.com/unlock). Search for this book by name, confirm the edition, and then follow the steps on the page.

Note: Keep your invoice handly. Purchase made directly from packt don't require one.

Part 1: Build Establish the Enterprise Platform Foundation

This part sets the groundwork for mastering Platform Engineering at scale. We will define strategic intent, align platforms with business outcomes, and design architecture built for resilience and growth. By the end of this part, we will have built a strong foundation, ready to handle enterprise complexity and long-term impact.

This part has the following chapters:

- *Chapter 1, Introduction to Modern Platform Engineering*
- *Chapter 2, Architectural Foundations and Strategy*
- *Chapter 3, Cultural Transformation and Leadership*
- *Chapter 4, The Platform Engineering Ecosystem*

1

Introduction to Modern Platform Engineering

In this book, we will dive into the transformative world of Platform Engineering, where cutting-edge technology and innovative processes converge to accelerate software development and delivery, creating business value at an unprecedented velocity. This field has emerged as a pivotal force shaping the digital landscape, empowering organizations to be more agile, efficient, and competitive. Here, you will gain a deep understanding of the strategic importance and technological underpinnings that make Platform Engineering an indispensable part of modern IT strategy. This chapter takes you on a stimulating journey through the evolution, principles, and strategic significance of Platform Engineering, providing actionable knowledge to enhance your operational and developmental capabilities.

In this chapter, we'll explore three pivotal areas that shed light on the rise and relevance of Platform Engineering. First, we'll trace its evolution and defining moments—charting the historical developments that have positioned it as a transformative force in modern tech organizations. Next, we'll examine the interplay between Lean, Agile, and DevOps, uncovering how these methodologies work in concert to enhance the value and impact of Platform Engineering. Finally, we'll delve into its strategic business importance, highlighting the competitive advantages and compelling business case for adopting Platform Engineering principles at scale.

We will be covering the following main topics:

- What is Platform Engineering?
- Transforming the digital landscape through the DevOps revolution
- Evolution of DevOps to Platform Engineering
- A brief analysis of existing technologies
- Actionable takeaways

Prepare to be equipped with the knowledge and insights needed to navigate the complexities of Platform Engineering in enterprises, setting the stage for a transformative impact on your organization's approach to software development and business value generation.

Technical requirements

There are no technical requirements for this chapter. A baseline understanding of Lean, Agile, and DevOps principles, along with an insight into your organization's customer value proposition and software development life cycle, will be advantageous in contextualizing the strategic discussions and insights presented in this chapter.

> **Free Benefits with Your Book**
>
> Your purchase includes a free PDF copy of this book along with other exclusive benefits. Check the *Free Benefits with Your Book* section in the Preface to unlock them instantly and maximize your learning experience.

What is Platform Engineering?

At the dynamic intersection of technology and customer demands, a powerful new paradigm has emerged that is fundamentally redefining the contours of software development and operations: **Platform Engineering**. This innovative discipline heralds a transformative shift, reimagining the digital landscape by enabling organizations to harness technology with precision, scalability, and efficiency.

At its core, a **platform** is a cohesive set of digital tools and shared infrastructure designed to deliver value through repeatable and standardized processes. Platforms incorporate core components such as **Internal Developer Platforms** (IDPs), which provide developers with self-service tools for managing their workflows; **Infrastructure as Code** (IaC) for consistent, declarative infrastructure management; and automated CI/CD pipelines, which enable secure software supply chains and accelerate the delivery of high-quality applications.

Platform Engineering builds on these foundations by unifying developers and IT operations teams around a shared, standardized, and scalable infrastructure, ensuring faster and more reliable software delivery. This discipline emphasizes automation, consistency, and self-service capabilities, reducing operational friction and empowering teams to focus on innovation rather than managing complexity.

Much like generative AI, which adapts and learns from vast datasets to deliver tailored, context-aware outputs, Platform Engineering thrives on iterative feedback and responsiveness. Both disciplines create environments that foster innovation, efficiency, and agility, enabling organizations to meet dynamic demands with precision and speed.

For instance, generative AI has been instrumental in revolutionizing personalized content creation, where it learns from vast datasets to generate tailored, context-aware recommendations for users. Similarly, Platform Engineering has been applied in the creation of scalable cloud platforms, evolving its systems, tooling, and processes to empower teams to meet shifting demands with precision and speed.

Like generative AI, which abstracts complexity to deliver intuitive solutions, Platform Engineering simplifies intricate development workflows, making it easier for teams to focus on innovation rather than operational hurdles. Both thrive on continuous feedback—generative AI refines outputs through iterative learning, while Platform Engineering actively seeks and utilizes ongoing feedback loops to optimize developer experiences and operational outcomes.

By filling gaps, easing transitions, and enhancing performance, Platform Engineering creates a synergistic relationship with DevOps, where their combined strengths amplify human creativity and productivity. In today's fast-paced digital landscape, this shared adaptability is critical. Just as generative AI quickly produces solutions tailored to specific challenges, Platform Engineering equips teams with the flexibility to pivot and recalibrate strategies in response to technological and market changes, ensuring businesses remain resilient, relevant, and competitive.

Businesses worldwide are facing significant challenges in keeping up with the fast-paced digital era. Platform Engineering, like generative AI, offers the ability to learn and adapt, which is crucial in such a hyper-dynamic environment. The flexibility provided by Platform Engineering allows teams to quickly pivot and adjust their strategies in response to market demands and technological advancements, ensuring that they remain relevant and competitive.

This approach to creating and maintaining software is based on a few fundamental principles, the most important of which is ensuring the platform is simple and easy to use. That simplicity is the key to unlocking the full potential of software development. The real beauty of a platform lies not in how complex it is but in how well it meets the needs of the people who will be using it. Understanding and addressing these needs is at the heart of effective software development. For example, a well-designed platform should demonstrate measurable improvements in developer productivity, reduce cycle times for delivering software, improve deployment frequency, and maintain low **mean time to recovery (MTTR)**—clear indicators of its effectiveness in meeting user needs. Metrics such as platform adoption rates and developer satisfaction scores can also provide valuable insights into how well the platform serves its intended purpose.

When choosing the right tools for the job, being selective is essential. Not every tool is suitable for every job, and having too many options can make it hard to choose the best one. Platform Engineering recommends carefully selecting a small number of tools that are well-suited to the task at hand and that align with the goals of the enterprise. This targeted approach ensures that the platform meets functional requirements while optimizing resource utilization, achieving operational excellence, and fostering a culture of continuous improvement and collaboration.

The effective implementation of Platform Engineering calls for a culture that values feedback and emphasizes continuous improvement. This approach fosters a collaborative environment where developers have the necessary tools and workflows to create and deploy applications that resonate with the users. However, it's essential to note that the success of these platforms is essentially dependent on proper utilization, regular updates, and openness to feedback.

Enterprises that adopt this approach can create an architecture that not only simplifies the creation and maintenance of software but also propels them forward on their digital journey. Therefore, organizations must understand that the tools they employ are only as effective as the individuals wielding them. By empowering developers to use these platforms to their fullest potential, businesses can achieve their goals and stay ahead of the competition.

> **Our foundational definition of Platform Engineering**
>
> Platform Engineering is the discipline that bridges the gap between value creation and value management. It provides developers and IT operations teams with a shared, standardized, and scalable infrastructure platform, enabling faster and more reliable software delivery.
>
> It involves creating and maintaining self-service tools, services, and platforms that support the entire software development and deployment life cycle, from coding through building, testing, deploying, and operating.

In the following sections, we will delve into the impact of Platform Engineering on technological progress. This narrative is characterized by collaboration, automation, and an unwavering commitment to efficiency, all aimed at improving the software development and operation experience. By understanding Platform Engineering, we can orchestrate a digital transformation that is profound in its impact and generous in its benefits, democratizing innovation and accelerating the journey to excellence.

As we explore the intricacies of the DevOps revolution, we will also examine the evolution and strategic significance of Platform Engineering and how it relates to DevOps. By doing so, we will uncover the layers that make this discipline an essential element of modern enterprise strategy. Through comparative analysis and actionable insights, we invite you to reimagine the possibilities of your technological infrastructure and embrace the principles that will usher in a new era of digital mastery.

This is more than just a chapter; it's an invitation to embark on a journey that promises to redefine the boundaries of software development and operation. In doing so, it will redefine what it means to be truly Agile in the age of digital transformation.

Transforming the digital landscape through the DevOps revolution

The annals of technological progress are punctuated by defining moments that redefine the process of business value creation. In software development and operations, DevOps represents a seminal shift in philosophy that drives cultural and technical transformations. It is not just about streamlining processes but fundamentally changing how we experience and interact with technology. DevOps is a powerful tool that enhances productivity, innovation, and user experience. It is a vital component of modern business strategy and a key driver of success in the digital age.

In an era dominated by rapid technological advancements, the emergence of DevOps stands as a watershed moment, reflecting a paradigm shift in how software is developed, delivered, and maintained. At its heart, DevOps is more than a set of practices or tools; it represents a cultural and professional movement that embodies a philosophy of integration, communication, and collaboration between software developers and IT professionals. By embracing DevOps, businesses can unlock noteworthy benefits, including faster time-to-market, improved software quality, and enhanced customer satisfaction.

Central to the success of DevOps is the **CALMS** model, which defines the core principles of DevOps as a combination of **Culture**, **Automation**, **Lean** practices, **Measurement**, and **Sharing**. This model emphasizes the importance of fostering a collaborative culture, automating repetitive tasks, optimizing workflows through Lean principles, and using metrics to drive continuous improvement. Sharing knowledge and tools across teams creates a foundation of transparency and collective responsibility, ensuring that every part of the organization works toward common goals. The CALMS model has revolutionized the digital landscape by embedding these principles into the fabric of DevOps transformations, enabling businesses to adapt rapidly to changing demands.

In addition to CALMS, practices such as **Continuous Integration** (**CI**) and **Continuous Deployment** (**CD**) serve as pillars of DevOps. CI enables developers to frequently integrate their code into a shared repository, where automated testing ensures quality at every step. CD extends this automation, seamlessly deploying changes to production environments, reducing human error, and ensuring a faster time-to-market. Further enhancing the DevOps toolset, IaC has revolutionized configuration management by treating infrastructure as programmable code, fostering consistency, scalability, and repeatability across environments.

These practices, combined with the CALMS principles, epitomize DevOps's technical and cultural excellence, fundamentally reshaping how software is developed and delivered. Together, they have created a framework that accelerates innovation, enhances collaboration, and drives measurable business value, setting the stage for Platform Engineering as the next evolutionary step in this transformative journey.

History of DevOps – A cultural and technological renaissance

DevOps emerged as a result of the pressing need for greater collaboration, incremental progress, and adaptability in the operational aspects of software development. Despite the success of the Agile software development movement, a disconnect persisted between creation and implementation, leading to inefficiency and delays. The term *DevOps* was coined by Patrick Debois, an IT consultant from Belgium, during the first DevOpsDays conference in 2009. This event served as a catalyst for a global renaissance in the IT industry by promoting a culture where collaboration is paramount and silos are dismantled. DevOps sought to create an environment where software building, testing, and release could occur rapidly, frequently, and reliably. By bringing developers (Dev) and IT operators (Ops) together under a unified philosophy—and, importantly, within the same team— DevOps aimed to foster a culture of continuous delivery, innovation, and reliability. The significance of DevOps lies in its ability to bridge the gap between developers and IT operations, paving the way for organizations to realize their full potential.

Beyond its cultural impact, DevOps has profoundly shaped modern technological architecture. The movement's emphasis on rapid, iterative delivery paved the way for adopting microservices architecture, enabling teams to develop and deploy modular components of applications independently. Complementing this is the rise of containerization technologies, such as Docker and Kubernetes, which ensure consistent deployment across environments and streamline the scalability of cloud-native systems. These innovations illustrate how DevOps has reshaped workflows and redefined how software systems are designed and operated.

The principles of Agile software development profoundly influenced the foundations of DevOps. Agile introduced the idea of iterative progress and cross-functional collaboration, which DevOps expanded into the operational domain. This interplay between Agile and DevOps would lay the groundwork for transforming how organizations approach the entire software development life cycle.

The Agile Manifesto

The inception of DevOps dates back to the early 2000s, when the Agile Manifesto sought to transform traditional software development practices. Initially, Agile practices became the norm, but the operational aspect of software development needed to catch up, leading to a significant disparity in business value delivery. While developers enjoyed newfound flexibility, operators still used outdated methodologies that were incompatible with the Agile ethos. Most critically, operations teams often lacked visibility into how their efforts contributed to overarching business goals, resulting in a misalignment between operational execution and the strategic value businesses sought to deliver. This caused a misalignment between what was built and what the business needed. This growing gap underscored the urgent need for a more cohesive and comprehensive approach to software life cycle management.

Agile frameworks such as Scrum and Kanban were pivotal in shaping early software development practices, emphasizing adaptability and the power of team collaboration. Scrum introduced structured processes such as sprint planning, daily standups, and retrospectives, enabling teams to plan and deliver work in manageable increments iteratively. Kanban complemented this by providing a visual approach to managing workflows, promoting continuous delivery, and reducing bottlenecks through work-in-progress limits. These frameworks empowered development teams to respond swiftly to changing priorities and deliver value incrementally, highlighting the power of teamwork in software development.

However, while Agile revolutionized development practices, it initially failed to address the operational aspects of IT. Now proficient at delivering frequent releases, development teams often handed off their work to operations teams still bound by traditional, rigid processes. As you can imagine, the increased frequency of deployments overwhelmed the operations teams significantly, as they were not equipped to handle such rapid change. This disparity in velocity created bottlenecks and misalignment, as operations teams became the gatekeepers of stability while developers pushed for continuous innovation.

The need for a unified approach to software development and operations became increasingly apparent. This dynamic of clashing priorities highlighted the importance of bridging the divide between developers and operators, fostering collaboration, and establishing workflows that could seamlessly integrate both domains. The challenges of this disconnect catalyzed the emergence of DevOps, a transformative approach that would bridge these gaps, redefine software life cycle management, and set the stage for a new era of efficiency and alignment.

Bridging the divide – The birth of DevOps

The divide between development and operations teams highlighted critical inefficiency that Agile practices alone could not resolve. While Agile empowered developers to iterate rapidly and deliver frequent updates, operations teams often grappled with systems that were unprepared for such rapid changes. This misalignment and a lack of shared goals created bottlenecks, delayed releases, and undermined the ability to deliver consistent customer value. Addressing these challenges required a transformative approach that unified development and operations into a cohesive and collaborative workflow.

DevOps emerged as this transformative solution, bridging the gap by aligning development and operations under shared objectives. At its core, DevOps represents a cultural shift that fosters collaboration, empathy, and shared accountability, enabling cross-functional teams to own the software delivery life cycle collectively. This unified philosophy eliminated silos and redefined workflows, empowering teams to deliver high-quality software rapidly and reliably while maintaining system stability.

Beyond culture, DevOps introduced a new focus on measurable performance improvements through key metrics. Deployment frequency became a central indicator of agility, reflecting how quickly teams could deliver code to production. MTTR highlighted operational resilience, measuring the time required to restore service after an incident. These metrics provided organizations with tangible benchmarks to assess and refine their DevOps practices, ensuring alignment between technical performance and business outcomes.

The first DevOpsDays conference, held in 2009 and spearheaded by Patrick Debois, marked a pivotal moment in shaping the DevOps movement. It brought together practitioners to share ideas, tools, and experiences, fostering a sense of community and catalyzing the adoption of DevOps principles. At the heart of this philosophy lies the principle of *"fail fast, learn quickly,"* which reframes failure as an opportunity for growth. By embedding practices such as automated testing, CI, and proactive monitoring, DevOps empowers teams to identify and resolve issues early, minimizing disruption and accelerating delivery cycles.

DevOps is more than a set of practices; it is a mindset that transforms how teams approach software development and operations. By combining cultural change with automation and measurable success, DevOps has become a critical enabler of agility, scalability, and innovation in modern software delivery. As organizations continue to navigate the complexities of digital transformation, DevOps serves as a vital framework for driving operational excellence and achieving business goals.

Milestones and growth

We can trace the DevOps journey through significant milestones that demonstrate its growing maturity. The adoption of CI/CD pipelines marked the beginning of the DevOps methodology. The automation framework provided by CI/CD pipelines enhanced the consistency and speed of deployments. With the advent of cloud computing, DevOps practices were further amplified, and microservices architectures became viable. The agility and scalability of cloud platforms enabled organizations to become more granular and responsive in their development strategies. Over the years, DevOps has not only scaled new heights but also woven itself within the fabric of IT culture. The evolution of DevOps has had a profound impact on IT operations, and it has become a critical enabler for organizations seeking to achieve business agility and innovation.

The adoption of DevOps has been marked by a series of milestones that highlight the maturation of its practices:

- **CI/CD**: The integration of CI/CD practices was one of the first steps in the DevOps evolution. By enabling automated testing and delivery, CI/CD helped to minimize manual errors and accelerate release cycles. CI/CD pipelines improve deployment frequency, ensuring faster and more reliable updates, and provide automated testing to catch issues early, reducing defects and improving overall software quality.

- **Automation**: Automation extended beyond CI/CD, incorporating IaC, configuration management, and proactive monitoring. Tools such as Jenkins, Puppet, and Ansible became mainstays in the DevOps toolkit, streamlining the deployment and management of IT infrastructure. IaC enables teams to define and manage infrastructure through code, ensuring consistent configurations across environments and making infrastructure changes traceable and repeatable. Proactive monitoring tools such as Prometheus and Nagios empower teams to detect and address issues before they impact users, enhancing system reliability. Together, these practices reduce manual intervention, accelerate provisioning, and enable rapid failure recovery, significantly improving operational efficiency.

- **Cloud computing**: The adoption of cloud computing was a significant milestone for DevOps. It provided the flexibility to scale infrastructure on demand and supported the DevOps ethos of rapid, iterative development. Cloud-native technologies such as serverless architectures and Kubernetes offer exceptional elasticity and self-healing capabilities. Serverless solutions allow teams to focus on deploying applications without managing infrastructure, while Kubernetes, as a container orchestration platform, optimizes resource utilization and automates failure recovery to reduce downtime. These advancements also enhance cost management with pay-as-you-go models, allowing organizations to adjust resources dynamically based on real-time demand.

- **Microservices architecture**: DevOps practices have also been closely aligned with the rise of microservices architecture. Organizations have achieved greater agility and resilience by breaking down monolithic applications into smaller, independently deployable services. This architecture enables teams to develop, test, and deploy individual services independently, reducing deployment times and minimizing the impact of changes or failures on the overall system. Coupled with containerization technologies such as Docker and orchestration platforms such as Kubernetes, microservices architecture supports scalability and fault isolation, allowing applications to handle dynamic workloads more effectively. This modular approach empowers organizations to deliver features faster and maintain high system availability.

- **DevSecOps**: As cybersecurity threats escalated, integrating security practices into DevOps, known as **DevSecOps**, became essential. This evolution underscores the need to bake security into the software development life cycle from the start. DevSecOps automates security tasks such as vulnerability scanning, compliance checks, and static code analysis, ensuring potential threats are identified and mitigated early. Tools such as Snyk, Black Duck, and Aqua Security integrate seamlessly into CI/CD pipelines, enabling security to become integral to development without slowing down delivery. This proactive approach ensures that applications remain secure while maintaining the speed and agility of modern DevOps practices.

The impact of DevOps on business has been transformative. Companies that have implemented DevOps practices have experienced significant improvements in deployment frequency, lowered change failure rates, and reduced MTTR after failures. DevOps has enabled businesses to be more agile and responsive to market demands and customer needs by fostering a culture that prioritizes collaboration and accountability. DevOps is more than just a methodology; it's a mindset that challenges businesses to reimagine and rethink their approach to software development and delivery. In today's fast-paced digital landscape, embracing DevOps is critical to staying competitive and delivering value to customers.

The interplay between Lean, Agile, and DevOps

Lean methodology provides a foundation for maximizing value delivery by eliminating waste and fostering a culture of continuous improvement. Lean practices such as Kaizen emphasize incremental, continuous improvement, encouraging teams to identify and address inefficiency in their workflows. The use of Kanban, a visual management system, helps teams maintain clarity on work-in-progress, prioritize tasks, and ensure a steady flow of value delivery. Metrics such as cycle time (the time it takes to complete a single task) and lead time (the time from task initiation to delivery) are essential tools for measuring process efficiency and identifying bottlenecks. These practices and metrics align with Agile and DevOps principles and provide actionable insights that drive better decision-making.

Lean lays the groundwork by eliminating waste and optimizing flow, ensuring that every process step delivers value to the customer. Agile builds on this by breaking work into manageable increments and focusing on adaptability and customer feedback. Together, they dismantle traditional rigidity and create an environment where DevOps can thrive.

DevOps combines Lean's efficiency and Agile's flexibility, bridging the gap between development and operations to encapsulate the entire software life cycle. By emphasizing automation, CD, and collaboration, DevOps accelerates the Agile feedback loop while maintaining Lean's focus on flow, enabling faster and more reliable value delivery.

In practice, integrating Lean's focus on value and flow, Agile's iterative development, and DevOps' culture of collaboration leads to a transformative business impact. Organizations that successfully merge these three can expect a significant acceleration in their ability to respond to market changes, deliver high-quality products, and achieve customer satisfaction.

Figure 1.1 illustrates how Lean, Agile, and DevOps intertwine, highlighting a cohesive, collaborative relationship that accelerates business value. This unity is embodied in a continuous cycle, a virtuous circle of efficiency, innovation, and adaptability that enhances each stage of software development and delivery. Lean's principles of eliminating waste and optimizing flow create the foundation by streamlining processes and prioritizing value-driven activities. Agile builds on this by fostering adaptability through iterative feedback loops, which refine and shape development to meet evolving customer needs. DevOps operationalizes these efforts, embedding automation and collaboration to ensure seamless delivery and scalability. These practices reinforce one another, forming a dynamic system that continuously drives improvement and innovation.

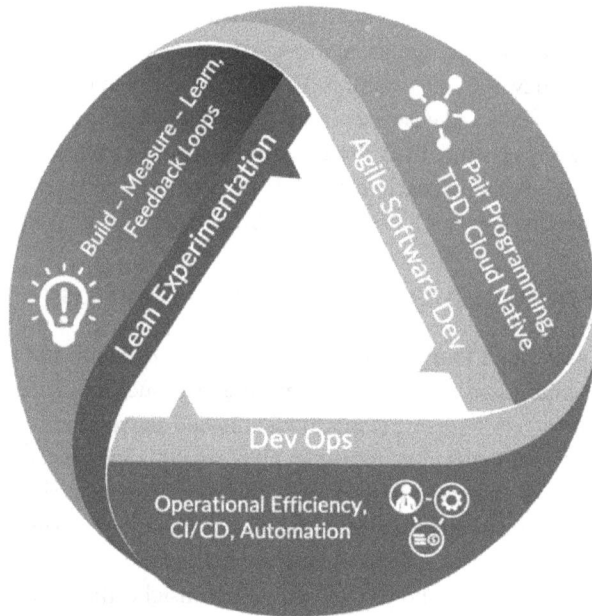

Figure 1.1: The interplay between Lean, Agile, and DevOps

The Lean methodology is at the core of this continuous value delivery cycle. It is based on the principle of Lean Experimentation, which involves the *Build-Measure-Learn* process, emphasizing feedback loops. The driving force behind Lean is making informed decisions based on customer feedback and data to ensure every effort contributes meaningfully to the end goal. It focuses on creating more value with fewer resources, eliminating waste in production, and streamlining all aspects of the business.

Next, Agile software development requires implementing vital practices such as pair programming, **test-driven development** (**TDD**), and cloud-native approaches. Agile software development relies on collaboration, iterative progress, and adaptability to change. Agile methodologies remove barriers to change by promoting adaptive planning and continuous improvement. Customer needs and user experience take center stage, with human communication and feedback valued over rigid processes and extensive documentation.

DevOps closes the loop, representing the culmination of Lean and Agile through its focus on operational efficiency, CI/CD, and automation. It takes Agile's collaboration and iterative nature and scales it with Lean's focus on efficiency. It streamlines the transition from development to operations, reducing the time it takes to bring changes to production. By automating repetitive tasks, DevOps frees human talent to focus on innovation and problem-solving, leading to faster and more reliable software delivery.

Each methodology feeds into the next in this integrative model, creating a self-enhancing feedback loop. Lean informs the principles of Agile, and Agile shapes the practices of DevOps. DevOps, in turn, enables Lean principles to be applied more broadly and effectively. This synergy leads to an organizational capability that is more than the sum of its parts—capable of delivering exceptional value at speed and scale. The cyclical nature of this relationship becomes a powerful model for delivering continuous value and adapting to the rapid pace of change in technology and business.

Notable case studies

The following case studies illustrate the impact of DevOps on various industries, highlighting its transformative power and effectiveness in improving efficiency, security, and delivery speed. Examining these examples provides valuable insights into the challenges and benefits of implementing DevOps and its potential to revolutionize business operations:

- **Global healthcare transformation**: The COVID-19 pandemic significantly impacted the world, causing a fundamental shift in how we interact with our environment and each other. The global healthcare industry has faced unprecedented challenges, affecting healthcare providers, payers, and medical device manufacturers. Organizations that were considering a digital transformation strategy had to quickly adapt to comply with new health protocols and provide a contactless, digital-first patient experience. The healthcare industry underwent a DevOps transformation to improve its processes and digitize healthcare services. The challenge was to integrate DevOps into a non-software-centric environment, but organizations have succeeded in creating custom software applications for data analysis in precision medicine. This case study highlights the potential of DevOps to accelerate software delivery and improve service quality, even in organizations not traditionally focused on software development.

- **Financial services sector's DevOps adoption**: The financial services sector, including FinTech and traditional financial companies, has made significant progress in adopting DevOps, overcoming challenges related to legacy infrastructure and cultural resistance. The sector's adoption of DevOps practices has been recognized for its maturity, with benefits such as better release cadence, faster deployments, and improved security and compliance. This case study highlights the sector-wide impact of DevOps in addressing the unique IT demands and constraints of financial services.

- **Flickr**: One of the earliest adopters, Flickr's development team famously illustrated the potential of DevOps with their ten deployments per day mantra, demonstrating the agility that DevOps could bring to software development.

- **Netflix**: Netflix's move to a DevOps model supported its transition to a microservices architecture and the cloud, enabling it to scale rapidly and become the streaming giant it is today.

- **Etsy**: Etsy's DevOps transformation improved their deployment frequency from twice weekly to multiple times per day, enhancing their ability to iterate on their product quickly.

These case studies collectively illustrate the transformative impact of DevOps across various industries, highlighting the methodology's adaptability and effectiveness in addressing unique challenges and driving significant improvements in service delivery, operational efficiency, and product quality.

Evolution of DevOps to Platform Engineering

The evolution of Platform Engineering is a narrative of adaptation and foresight, emerging as a natural progression from the practices and philosophy pioneered by the DevOps movement. As organizations sought to scale their DevOps practices, they encountered significant challenges. While integrating development, testing, security, and operations within single teams improved agility and collaboration, this approach became increasingly costly and unsustainable at scale. Additionally, as each team optimized for its local environment, inconsistencies arose at a global level, leading to fragmented tooling, disparate workflows, and isolated silos of DevOps teams. Here is a high-level comparison of DevOps and Platform Engineering:

Focus Area	DevOps	Platform Engineering
Primary focus	Bridging the gap between development and operations to enable continuous delivery	Providing standardized platforms that enable teams to build, deploy, and operate software efficiently
Ownership	Shared responsibility between development and operations for the entire software life cycle	Centralized ownership of platforms, ensuring consistency, reliability, and scalability across teams
Team structure	Distributed teams with cross-functional roles combining Dev, Ops, QA, and sometimes Security	Dedicated platform teams focused on creating self-service capabilities for product teams
Key responsibilities	<ul><li>CI/CD pipelines</li><li>Infrastructure automation</li><li>Monitoring and observability</li><li>Incident response</li></ul>	<ul><li>Building and maintaining self-service platforms</li><li>Standardizing infrastructure and tooling</li><li>Automating workflows</li><li>Supporting multi-team collaboration</li></ul>

Focus Area	DevOps	Platform Engineering
Scope	Team or project specific, often focused on delivering a single product or service	Organization wide, aimed at supporting multiple teams and products with unified platforms
Challenges	Scalability issues due to cost and siloed team optimizations for local needs	Addresses scalability with centralized, reusable solutions that minimize redundant effort
Key metrics	Deployment frequency, MTTR, lead time, change failure rate	Platform adoption rate, developer satisfaction, system availability, operational cost-efficiency
Tools and practices	CI/CD (e.g., Jenkins and GitLab CI), IaC (e.g., Terraform), observability tools (e.g., Prometheus)	Container orchestration (e.g., Kubernetes), platform APIs, GitOps for declarative deployments, progressive delivery tools (e.g., Argo Rollouts), and advanced monitoring tools (e.g., Grafana)

Table 1.1: Comparison of DevOps and Platform Engineering

Understanding this evolution from DevOps to Platform Engineering is crucial; it highlights why simply scaling DevOps practices is insufficient to meet the demands of modern software development. Platform Engineering addresses these challenges by providing centralized, standardized platforms that enable consistent, scalable, and cost-effective development and operations. This shift equips organizations with the robust infrastructure and tooling necessary to thrive in today's fast-paced digital economy.

From CI/CD to automation and cloud technologies

The initial forays into CI and CD represented the early stages of what would become Platform Engineering. These practices, foundational to DevOps, highlighted the need for systematic automation across the **software development life cycle** (**SDLC**). As CI/CD became more ingrained, the focus expanded to include GitOps, IaC, configuration management, progressive delivery, and proactive monitoring, setting the stage for the comprehensive automation of infrastructure management. This evolution from CI/CD to broader automation practices underscored a pivotal shift in IT's role—from gatekeepers of infrastructure to enablers of innovation. Tools such as Terraform, Ansible, and Kubernetes became synonymous with this new era, empowering teams to manage complex systems more efficiently and with greater reliability.

Platform Engineering builds on foundational DevOps practices such as CI/CD by incorporating advanced approaches such as progressive delivery, enabling gradual and safe rollouts through techniques such as Canary or Blue-Green deployments. Additionally, **GitOps** has become a cornerstone of Platform Engineering, allowing teams to manage infrastructure declaratively through version-controlled repositories, ensuring consistency and automated deployments. These innovations, coupled with container orchestration tools such as Kubernetes, have elevated Platform Engineering's ability to deliver scalable, reliable, and efficient solutions across complex systems.

The ascent of cloud computing marked another significant milestone in the evolution of Platform Engineering. With their inherent scalability, flexibility, and variety of services, cloud platforms provide the perfect environment for DevOps practices to flourish. The cloud's ability to abstract away the underlying infrastructure complexity was a boon for developers, allowing them to focus on building software without being encumbered by operational concerns.

The adoption of cloud technologies catalyzed the shift towards microservices architectures, enabling organizations to develop, deploy, and scale applications in more granular, independent components. This architectural style further exemplified the principles of Platform Engineering, emphasizing agility, resilience, and the decentralization of application development.

As cloud computing and automation landscapes matured, the need for a disciplined approach to managing these complexities led to the formalization of Platform Engineering. We define Platform Engineering as the discipline that provides developers and IT operations teams with a shared, standardized, and scalable infrastructure platform, enabling faster and more reliable software delivery.

At its core, Platform Engineering bridges the gap between software development and infrastructure management. It entails designing and managing self-service tools, services, and platforms that support every stage of the software development and deployment lifecycle—from coding and building to testing, deployment, and ongoing operations.

Central to Platform Engineering is the focus on the human element—enhancing developer experience and operational efficiency. Platform Engineering strives to reduce or remove friction from the development process, making it as seamless as possible for developers to bring their work to production. This not only accelerates the pace of innovation but also fosters a culture of collaboration and shared responsibility.

By providing a robust, scalable, and developer-friendly platform, Platform Engineering enables organizations to harness the full potential of their technology stack, driving operational efficiency and enabling faster time to market for new features and products.

Platform Engineering – The *mise en place* for business transformation

Platform Engineering, in its essence, parallels the culinary principle of *mise en place*—a practice as disciplined as it is creative. It involves the meticulous preparation and organization of ingredients and tools necessary for cooking, ensuring that the chef can focus on the art of creation without the interruption of searching for resources. Similarly, in Platform Engineering, this preparation involves establishing self-service capabilities, creating standardized infrastructure and tooling, and automating workflows. These practices ensure that the necessary tools, environments, and processes are readily available, enabling developers and operators to focus on delivering high-quality software efficiently.

Platform Engineering builds on these principles in the cloud-native era to streamline software development and deployment. By meticulously organizing tools and workflows, it eliminates operational bottlenecks and allows developers to concentrate on writing innovative, high-quality code without being encumbered by infrastructural complexity.

Just as a chef preps their ingredients and arranges the kitchen for optimal flow, Platform Engineering curates technology stacks and streamlines operations. This preparation is about more than just convenience; it's about creating a space where creativity can flourish, and software engineers can achieve a state of *flow*, thus accelerating productivity and innovation.

Through the meticulous discipline of Platform Engineering and the strategic application of Lean, Agile, and DevOps, enterprises are equipped to face the ever-accelerating pace of technological change. This approach ensures that, like in the finest kitchens, everything is in its place, empowering teams to efficiently and effectively deliver business value and delight customers.

Platform Engineering plays a crucial role in scaling and operationalizing the principles of agility, automation, and collaboration. It provides the framework within which DevOps practices can be applied across large organizations and complex systems, ensuring that the agility promised by DevOps does not become bottlenecked by infrastructure and operational complexity.

The strategic importance of Platform Engineering for enterprises

Platform Engineering has emerged as a critical driver of enterprise innovation. Its strategic significance permeates modern businesses, serving as an operational asset and a crucial competitive differentiator. An organization's platform engineering capabilities determine its agility and resilience in rapid technological changes.

Platform Engineering accelerates experimentation cycles by automating infrastructure provisioning and deployment. Practices such as automated testing, rollback mechanisms, and A/B testing empower teams to validate ideas quickly and safely, reducing time-to-feedback and ensuring more reliable outcomes. Cloud services such as AWS Lambda, Google Cloud Build, and Azure DevOps amplify these capabilities, enabling seamless scaling and integration with CI/CD pipelines. By fostering a culture of experimentation, Platform Engineering allows businesses to innovate faster while mitigating risks.

This foundation of streamlined processes and rapid iteration enables enterprises to shift their focus to what matters most—delivering customer value. As infrastructural complexity fades into the background, organizations gain the agility required to thrive in a competitive landscape. In order to do this, enterprises must prioritize a strategic approach to Platform Engineering. This entails a multitude of benefits, including the following:

- **Driving agility and innovation**: Platform Engineering is a game-changer for businesses. It empowers companies to integrate agility into their DNA, allowing them to pivot quickly and continuously innovate. By abstracting the complexities of infrastructure and software delivery, Platform Engineering simplifies the development process, allowing companies to shorten the time from idea inception to execution. The platforms engineered for DevOps serve as launchpads for new products and services, giving companies a competitive edge in the market. In today's fast-paced business environment, the ability to pivot quickly is essential to success. Platform Engineering provides businesses with the agility to move fast and stay ahead of the competition.

- **Fostering a culture of efficiency and collaboration**: The philosophy of Platform Engineering fosters a collaborative culture that dismantles silos, encouraging teams to build and maintain platforms that anticipate and scale according to future demands. Promoting shared ownership over these platforms cultivates a sense of unity, purpose, and efficiency that is essential for the DevOps model to thrive. This approach enables teams to work together towards a common goal, ultimately leading to increased innovation and agility in the face of ever-evolving business needs.

- **Enhancing developer experience**: Platform Engineering is vital in optimizing developer experience by creating an environment that fosters creativity, productivity, and innovation. Providing standardized tools, **role-based access control** (**RBAC**), and streamlined API integrations reduces cognitive load, allowing developers to focus on creating innovative software. The self-service nature of these platforms empowers developers with autonomy, enabling them to procure resources, deploy applications, and access standardized workflows without the bottlenecks traditionally associated with IT operations. This empowerment translates into increased efficiency and productivity, delivering tangible business benefits. The result is a developer experience that is seamless, efficient, and designed to maximize productivity, ultimately leading to better software products, faster time-to-market, and increased customer satisfaction.

- **Ensuring resilience and reliability**: A robust Platform Engineering strategy prioritizes resilience and reliability above all else. This means creating systems that can withstand increased demand, recover from failures quickly and automatically, and maintain high availability of services. Continuity and reliability are essential for ensuring uninterrupted operations and upholding customer trust, which are critical factors for any successful business. Achieving these qualities requires a well-planned and executed Platform Engineering strategy that can anticipate and mitigate potential issues, ultimately leading to a more stable and efficient infrastructure.

- **Streamlining compliance and security**: As the regulatory landscape continues to evolve and the threat of cyber-attacks grows increasingly prevalent, Platform Engineering has become a cornerstone of modern business. By implementing compliance checks and security protocols at the platform level, organizations can ensure that these critical considerations are not an afterthought, but instead, are integrated into the development process from the outset. This proactive approach to compliance and security not only protects enterprises from potential breaches and fines but also reinforces their reputation as trustworthy entities. In today's environment, it is imperative for businesses to understand that taking a comprehensive approach to Platform Engineering is no longer optional but essential for survival.

- **Driving economic efficiency**: The importance of Platform Engineering is multi-fold and underpinned by its significant economic implications. By optimizing resource utilization and automating routine tasks, it drives cost savings and operational efficiency. It also converts capital expenditure into operational expenditure, providing a more Agile and scalable financial model that aligns well with the variable nature of digital services consumption. As a result, Platform Engineering emerges as a strategic force that empowers businesses to improve their bottom line while simultaneously enhancing their competitive edge.

Platform Engineering is the backbone of modern enterprise agility and innovation, providing a scalable foundation for businesses to adapt and excel in a digitally driven market. It goes beyond operational support, becoming a crucial ally in pursuing market relevance and customer satisfaction.

By embracing Platform Engineering as a strategic imperative, you create robust, resilient infrastructures that accelerate your journey from ideation to delivery, ensuring your enterprise survives and thrives in the digital age. Unlock efficiency, enable seamless collaboration, and foster an environment where developers and operations work together, driving your enterprise toward a future where adaptability and speed are synonymous with your brand.

Next, let's examine some of the technologies that can help drive business value and become a strategic driver of enterprise innovation.

A brief analysis of existing technologies

The technological ecosystem supporting Platform Engineering and DevOps is rich and varied, with each tool and platform carrying its own set of strengths and trade-offs. In this analysis, we will scrutinize the key technologies, their functionalities, ease of integration, and alignment with DevOps principles. This analysis is by no means comprehensive, and one only needs to look at the **Cloud-Native Computing Foundation (CNCF)** landscape (`https://landscape.cncf.io`) to appreciate the complexity of the digital ecosystem.

However, adopting and managing a vast array of tools introduces significant challenges. Dependency management becomes increasingly difficult as tools interconnect in non-standardized ways, often leading to integration complexity and operational inefficiencies. Organizations frequently encounter issues such as fragmented workflows, lack of interoperability, and tool sprawl, which can hinder efforts to scale and standardize practices. Addressing these challenges is central to Platform Engineering, which emphasizes building cohesive platforms that abstract and unify these tools under standardized processes.

To navigate this complexity, we establish a set of criteria that reflect the goals and challenges of Platform Engineering in a DevOps context. These criteria serve as a framework for assessing and selecting technologies that can drive operational efficiency and innovation while minimizing complexity.

Criteria for effective Platform Engineering

To objectively assess the myriad technologies, we establish a set of criteria that mirror the goals and challenges of Platform Engineering in a DevOps context. These criteria draw inspiration from the CNCF Platform Engineering Maturity Model (`https://tag-app-delivery.cncf.io/whitepapers/platform-eng-maturity-model/`), which provides a robust framework for evaluating the maturity of Platform Engineering practices across organizations. Building upon this model, we have extended its foundational principles to encompass key criteria that ensure a platform's effectiveness in real-world enterprise scenarios:

- **Integration and compatibility**: How well does the technology integrate with existing tools and platforms? Compatibility is critical for seamless workflows and minimal disruption.

- **Scalability**: Can the technology grow with the enterprise? Scalability ensures that the technology can accommodate that growth as the organization evolves without significant overhauls.

- **User experience**: How intuitive and accessible is the technology for the various stakeholders involved? A positive user experience is vital for adoption and productivity.

- **Automation capabilities**: To what extent does the technology automate processes? Automation is the cornerstone of DevOps, aiming to reduce manual toil.

- **Security and compliance**: Does the technology facilitate or hinder compliance with security best practices and regulations? Security and compliance fortify the enterprise's defense systems, ensuring adherence to stringent regulatory standards and best practices.

- **Community and support**: Is there a robust community and support framework around the technology? Community strength can be indicative of the technology's resilience and potential for evolution.

Now that we know the criteria for effective Platform Engineering, let's look at a few popular technologies that drive enterprise innovation and elevate Platform Engineering.

Popular technologies

With these criteria as guideposts, the following technologies are frequently at the forefront of Platform Engineering and DevOps environments:

Version Control Systems (VCSs): Version control is the linchpin of any development process. Tools such as **Git** (**GitHub** or **GitLab**) have become ubiquitous for their distributed architecture and branching capabilities, fostering collaboration and flexibility. Alternatives such as Bitbucket, **Subversion** (**SVN**), and **Mercurial** offer different version control models, catering to varied preferences and project needs. The choice between these tools often hinges on the project's scale, the team's familiarity, and specific workflow requirements. In recent years, the rise of **GitOps** has marked a significant paradigm shift, extending the role of version control into infrastructure management. By leveraging Git-based workflows to define and manage infrastructure as code, GitOps ensures declarative configurations, traceable changes, and automated deployments, aligning version control directly with modern DevOps practices. This approach enhances operational consistency and bridges development and operations through a shared, Git-centric workflow.

- **CI/CD tools**: CI/CD tools form the arteries of the DevOps workflow. **Jenkins**, with its extensive plugin ecosystem, stands out for its adaptability. **GitLab**, **Github Actions**, and **CircleCI** offer integrated solutions for Git-based workflows, catering to teams seeking streamlined, out-of-the-box experiences. Modern tools such as **ArgoCD** extend CI/CD by incorporating GitOps principles, enabling declarative application deployments and seamless configuration management across Kubernetes clusters. The choice of CI/CD tools depends on pipeline complexity, customization needs, and integration requirements with broader development and infrastructure workflows.

- **IaC platforms**: IaC has revolutionized how infrastructure is provisioned and managed. **Terraform**, with its declarative language, excels in multi-cloud environments, whereas **AWS CloudFormation** is often the go-to choice for AWS-specific resources. These tools differ in syntax, cloud service provider focus, and the extent to which they manage state—critical factors in their selection. IaC is pivotal in enabling scalable and reproducible environments. However, managing security is equally essential; best practices include using secure secret management tools (e.g., **HashiCorp Vault**) to avoid hardcoding sensitive information in IaC files and ensuring access to infrastructure is properly restricted to authorized entities. Adopting these practices aligns IaC workflows with DevOps security standards, mitigating risks while maintaining agility.

- **Configuration management tools**: For configuration management, **Ansible** provides a simple, agentless setup that uses YAML for its playbooks. **Chef** and **Puppet**, while more complex, offer a more mature solution with a stronger emphasis on state and the idempotency of system configuration. The decision to use one of these tools over the others often comes down to the team's expertise, the need for scalability, and the complexity of the infrastructure.

- **Container orchestration systems**: **Kubernetes** (or **K8s**) has emerged as the de facto standard for container orchestration due to its robust scaling and self-healing capabilities. Every hyperscaler and cloud virtualization company has its own flavor of Kubernetes. Alternatives such as **Docker Swarm** and **Apache Mesos** present simpler, albeit less feature-rich, options. The choice among these technologies will typically be influenced by the organization's scalability needs, the existing container ecosystem, and the required level of control over container orchestration.

- **Monitoring and logging**: Effective monitoring and logging are crucial for maintaining visibility into applications and infrastructure. **Prometheus** provides powerful monitoring capabilities and works particularly well with Kubernetes, while the **Elasticsearch, Logstash, and Kibana** (**ELK**) stack offers comprehensive logging solutions that excel in data visualization and analysis. Selecting between these options often involves considering the ease of setup, the scalability of the solution, and integration with existing systems.

This analysis does not prescribe a one-size-fits-all solution but rather emphasizes the importance of aligning technological choices with organizational needs, goals, and capabilities. It's a delicate balance that requires a strategic vision aligned with practical execution capabilities. The right mix of technologies can empower Platform Engineering and DevOps practices, driving efficiency, innovation, and resilience. In Platform Engineering and DevOps, every technology is a vital component in a well-oiled machine. It's not just about individual strengths but how they come together to form a cohesive and efficient platform. Optimal technology combinations can produce greater results, leading to improved operational efficiency and increased innovation.

Actionable takeaways

As we come to the end of this journey of exploring modern Platform Engineering, we find ourselves at a crossroads of contemplation and execution. Our voyage took us through the DevOps revolution, the progress of Platform Engineering, its significance to the enterprise, the interdependent connection with DevOps, and the evaluation of technologies. Here are some insights gleaned from this exploration that offer a roadmap for enterprises to harness the transformative power of these practices:

- **Embrace the Platform Engineering mindset**: Establish a culture that values preparation, efficiency, and continuous improvement. Create a center of excellence for Platform Engineering to champion best practices and share knowledge across teams.

- **Strategically select your tools**: Perform a comprehensive analysis of your organization's needs and select the appropriate mix of tools that enhance your DevOps practices. Look for tools that provide the right balance between functionality, ease of use, and integration capabilities.

- **Prioritize automation**: Identify repetitive, error-prone, or complex tasks within your SDLC and target these for automation. Automate your infrastructure through IaC, utilize CI/CD for automated deployments, and implement monitoring and logging for continuous feedback.

- **Foster an Agile and collaborative environment**: Break down silos by promoting cross-functional teams. Encourage collaboration and sharing of tools, experiences, and challenges to build a cohesive and Agile environment.

- **Focus on security and compliance**: Integrate security practices throughout your SDLC. Conduct regular security assessments and ensure compliance with relevant regulations from the outset.

- **Measure, learn, and improve**: Implement metrics to measure the effectiveness of your DevOps practices, using data to identify areas for refinement and optimization. Focus on performance and outcome-driven KPIs such as MTTR, deployment frequency, and change failure rate, as these metrics provide actionable insights to guide continuous improvement.

- **Test for resilience**: Adopt Chaos Engineering as a proactive method for resilience testing. By deliberately injecting failures into systems, Chaos Engineering See *Chapter 2* helps identify vulnerabilities and ensure that infrastructure and applications can withstand unexpected disruptions. This practice fosters confidence in your platform's ability to maintain reliability and uptime under adverse conditions.

- **Prepare for the future**: Stay informed about emerging technologies and evolving best practices in Platform Engineering and DevOps. Encourage a culture of learning and experimentation to stay ahead of the curve.

- **Incorporate the *mise en place* philosophy**: Just as chefs prepare their stations for efficiency, set up your development environment to maximize productivity. Organize your tools, workflows, and infrastructure to support swift and efficient software development.

By internalizing these takeaways, enterprises can embark on a path to enhanced agility, reliability, and competitiveness in the digital era. When aligned with DevOps, Platform Engineering is not merely an operational model but a strategic asset that drives continuous value delivery in a world where the only constant is change.

Summary

In this chapter, we demonstrate the transformative power of merging Lean, Agile, and DevOps principles to enhance organizational efficiency and agility. We explore the strategic significance of Platform Engineering and its impact on creating competitive advantages. We emphasize the importance of selecting the appropriate technological foundation to achieve these benefits.

In the next chapter, *Architectural Foundations and Strategy*, we delve deeper into designing resilient, future-oriented platform architectures that align with business outcomes. By doing so, we prepare your enterprise for future growth and innovation.

Further reading

For further reading on the foundations of DevOps and its evolution, we highly recommend the following resources:

- *The Phoenix Project* by Gene Kim, Kevin Behr, and George Spafford, which offers insights into applying DevOps principles in practice.

- *Accelerate: The Science of Lean Software and DevOps: Building and Scaling High Performing Technology Organizations* by Nicole Forsgren, Jez Humble, and Gene Kim, which provides statistical evidence of the effectiveness of DevOps practices.

- *The DevOps Handbook: How to Create World-Class Agility, Reliability, & Security in Technology Organizations* by Gene Kim, Jez Humble, Patrick Debois, and John Willis, often the first one most DevOps professionals start with, provides a great overview of DevOps and imparts a good, generalized knowledge of the field.

- *Continuous Delivery: Reliable Software Releases through Build, Test, and Deployment Automation* by Jez Humble and David Farley, provides a solid foundation in continuous delivery and creating a great deployment pipeline.

- *Effective DevOps* by Jennifer Davis and Ryn Daniels, which covers the big picture of DevOps and provides some actionable suggestions for building up a DevOps organization.

- *What Is This Devops Thing, Anyway?* by Patrick Debois, which explains DevOps as a multidisciplinary approach to improve software development and delivery through communication and collaboration.

- *Manifesto for Agile Software Development* is a revolutionary call to embrace change, prioritize people over processes, deliver working solutions through continuous collaboration, and relentlessly pursue excellence through self-reflection and adaptation: `https://agilemanifesto.org/`.

- *The Lean Startup* by Eric Ries champions an iterative, customer-centric approach to building sustainable businesses through continuous experimentation and learning.

Get This Book's PDF Version and Exclusive Extras

UNLOCK NOW

Scan the QR code (or go to packtpub.com/unlock). Search for this book by name, confirm the edition, and then follow the steps on the page.

Note: Keep your invoice handly. Purchase made directly from packt don't require one.

2

Architectural Foundations and Strategy

Everything in software ascribes to specific standards, from security to operations, and running a platform is no different. Platforms use shared digital tools with a common infrastructure to maximize value. Understanding the standards applied to a platform starts with the essential cloud migration; the cloud format selected from **Amazon Web Services** (**AWS**), Azure, or Google; and then moves from the cloud structure into setting up clusters for Kubernetes. The basic standards allow us to design and implement custom architectures within those spaces, but architectures also have their own standards. The chapter explains how to set up a platform within a cloud with a practical, custom architecture, leading to success and meeting regulatory standards.

An analogy for building a good platform is asking someone else to build your workshop rather than doing it yourself. You need to build a shelf, so you travel to the hardware store and buy wood, tools, and screws. On returning home, you realize that you have forgotten something and return to the store. The project multiplies, taking more time and effort than you want to spend. The process requires grabbing multiple items, at different times, as the need arises. When building architecture, you plan what you need in the workshop so that the tools are available and safe, and you can complete projects without returning to the hardware store. The successful platform provides everything up front, without you ever needing to return to a marketplace, and keeps all the tools up to date. The architectural concepts in this chapter provide some options for designing the best platform to accomplish user needs, scaling to multiple projects, and eventually including multiple platforms.

In this chapter, we'll introduce key architectural concepts that form the foundation of modern platforms. We'll break down architecture into specific components to guide practical implementation, and examine how to scale and secure these models to ensure greater resilience. The chapter also explores the challenges that arise when balancing legacy systems with cloud-native applications, and concludes by outlining various architectural models that apply across different elements of a platform.

We will be covering the following main topics:

- Core concepts and components

- Designing for scalability, security, and resilience

- From legacy systems to cloud-native applications

Technical requirements

There are no technical requirements for this section. A minimal understanding of architectural diagrams and some basic Terraform knowledge could prove helpful.

Core concepts and components

At the beginning of an architectural design, it can help to start with a common framework. Regardless of where you build architecture, any cloud-based strategy incorporates four primary areas:

- **Cloud**: The cloud is the basic framework for later operations, a space where the potential exists for events to occur, such as AWS, Google Cloud, Azure, or a private cloud installation. Many take the cloud to mean that operations occur somewhere else, which is also valid. When you run private constructions, the virtual space is the cloud, just a private one on a personal server. The cloud contains all the requirements and standards to operate on someone else's server. The following three components are all contained within the initial cloud.

- **Cluster**: Clusters aggregate a collection of virtual machines that can work together to accomplish tasks. Clusters typically use a standard function such as a controller node to integrate the various tasks. Controller nodes manage tasks in a cluster to effectively determine compute and storage for various functions. Kubernetes and Docker are examples of shared services used to integrate clusters. Clusters are designed to act like a single system delivering parallel processing, high levels of availability, and balanced resources across a wide function base.

- **Container**: Containers are the next level down within the cluster. Each container, or group of containers, can operate independently or dependently with other containers in the cluster. Containers should be packaged programs that execute all the dependencies within a single instance. Another term for a container is a unit of capability.

- **Code**: The last level is code. Code describes the language used to provide instructions to the computer. Containers are written in code and then executed.

These areas are demonstrated in the following figure:

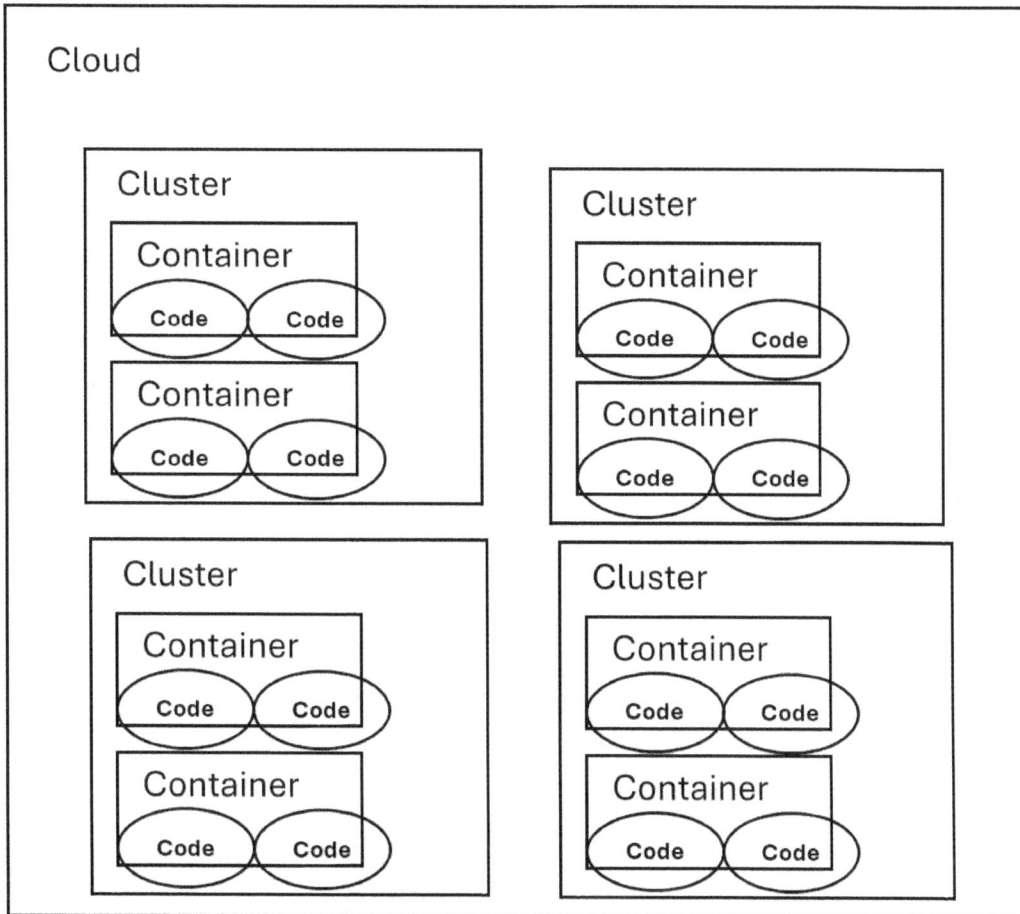

Figure 2.1: The four Cs of cloud computing

Multiple containers operate within a cluster, and multiple clusters can interact within the cloud. When designing a platform, the first architectural choice is picking a cloud. Since platform design optimizes streamlined functions, multi-cloud functionality can remain an issue. Within the cloud, platforms can operate multiple clusters and design them based on functionality. As a reminder, a platform is a set of digital tools using a shared infrastructure to create value. A good example is having a **collaboration function** within a cluster that interacts with other clusters designed for development, testing, and production. Separating clusters allows multiple functions to happen simultaneously. Each cluster will incorporate multiple containers to run specific functions like development environments, version control, security testing, or user management.

The **Open Systems Interconnection** (**OSI**) model for data interaction is another option to consider when designing a platform. Understanding what each tool requires within the platform allows structuring interaction to maximize value. The mnemonic for remembering these layers is *All People Seem To Need Data Processing*, standing for **Application**, **Presentation**, **Session**, **Transport**, **Network**, **Data link**, and **Physical**. When looking at the initial architecture for a platform, we are mainly concerned with the middle three layers (Session, Transport, and Network). We assume that Physical (raw data) and Data link (data format) are handled by the initial cloud. Our primary objective is to assess the network; move data within the system; transmission; review communication between clusters, containers, and sessions; and maintain working connections and ports within the platform. Presentation and Application are important but remain on the outside as the final interface of presenting usable data to the user in a format that allows simple interactions. These foundational considerations are often reflected in common architectural patterns, which provide a baseline for understanding how systems interact. Building on that, the chapter then introduces more specialized platform architectures that address the unique demands of modern, scalable environments.

A common architecture should provide guidelines to expand. The typical architectural guidelines are the **SOLID principles**. These principles are important as we build a platform architecture:

- **Single responsibility**: Each architectural object has only one reason to change.
- **Open-closed**: Every element is open for extension and closed for modification.
- **Liskov substitution**: All class elements can be derived from a parent class and will still provide the same results.
- **Interface segregation**: Users should not depend on unused interfaces.
- **Dependency inversion**: Objects should depend on abstractions rather than inversion.

These principles have guided much of the transition between monolithic systems and the microservices approach, but they remain an important guideline. Numerous research and materials appear across the internet on each principle and their combined effectiveness, but that is beyond the scope of this book; hopefully, the generic reference will either spark your brain or guide you to the necessary information.

The essential platform

When examining the principles in aggregate, they show important factors desired in a platform. A platform should support various applications, and when the SOLID foundation governs their interaction, it helps to create a resilient architecture.

When converting to a platform, we change our mindset from building an entire system to a partial one that enables the broader design to function. There are two important aspects to first consider within the platform architecture:

- How to design it
- Where to display or implement those designs

These aspects can be best defined as collaborative and deployment components. A collaborative environment generally uses a common cluster with multiple containers to provide functions. The deployment target will also be a cluster with a different set of containers depending on the purpose of that deployment target. Both can be scaled repeatedly to add resilience and expand operations, but discussing each in detail provides a starting point for a broader architecture.

The collaboration component is the first element to consider in architectural design for a platform. When we say collaboration, we mean the spot where cooperative work can happen. This work includes all elements short of the actual deployment of the application. From the DevOps perspective, these are the elements to plan, code, and build. Monitoring applications can also collaborate as they gather information from the deployment targets. The most essential part of any collaboration occurs in the discussion between the team and establishing a communication function. Essential support for this should include some asynchronous chat, such as Mattermost or Slack. These communication tools provide a way for the individual team and multiple teams to connect.

The second element of collaboration is an **Integrated Development Environment** (**IDE**). While an IDE could be as basic as a text editor or VSCode, you could provide options such as GitHub, GitLab, or Anaconda, depending on the later platform demands. Different IDEs specialize in different languages and enable platform customization even if plug-in software can make an IDE multi-language. One essential is that the connection chosen should be linked to the communication piece so that IDE commits and changes are visible to the broader team. IDEs should also include common security aspects such as fuzz testing, static analysis, linting, and dependency checks. Including these security aspects as a separate platform element is possible but most effective when directly tied to code.

Communication components and the IDE link to the third element of collaboration, **work management**. Some IDEs provide ways to track work as an embedded feature, but using an external tool such as the Atlassian suite or Aha can be beneficial. These tools allow high-level observability into elements through feature flags, essential tasks, and connections to releases. In addition, these work management tools should also provide knowledge management for the platform. Knowledge management includes various how-to guides and self-help pieces. Linking work and knowledge management provides a place for generative AI to excel, finding not only standard documentation but internal instances across chat, planning, and work execution. As an example, when searching for information about App A, you would find the how-to documentation, mentions in Slack, and tasks on a Jira board. These could be cross-referenced or time-linked to provide context.

Monitoring elements are a good addition to the collaborative environment but are not required. Monitoring means linking some operational tools to demonstrate which users are present and active, how the various deployment targets are running, current updates, and various other data. These tools link through functions and software such as Prometheus, Kibana, Grafana, Open Telemetry, and the Elastic Stack. These tools should provide those using the platform with observability.

All these collaborative elements are centrally managed by an integrated dashboard. This dashboard allows you to manage users within the platform, observe operational metrics, and manage permissions. The permissions element should integrate through a **Single-Sign-On (SSO)** application once a user establishes an identity. These pieces also provide separation between multiple teams to establish security. This application ensures that teams within the platform can only access approved data. Sometimes, you want all the platform teams to view everything, and sometimes, regulatory or compliance standards might require separation in either the coding or the data used in the deployment targets. With all those elements in mind, the following diagram gives an example of the collaborative architecture within the platform:

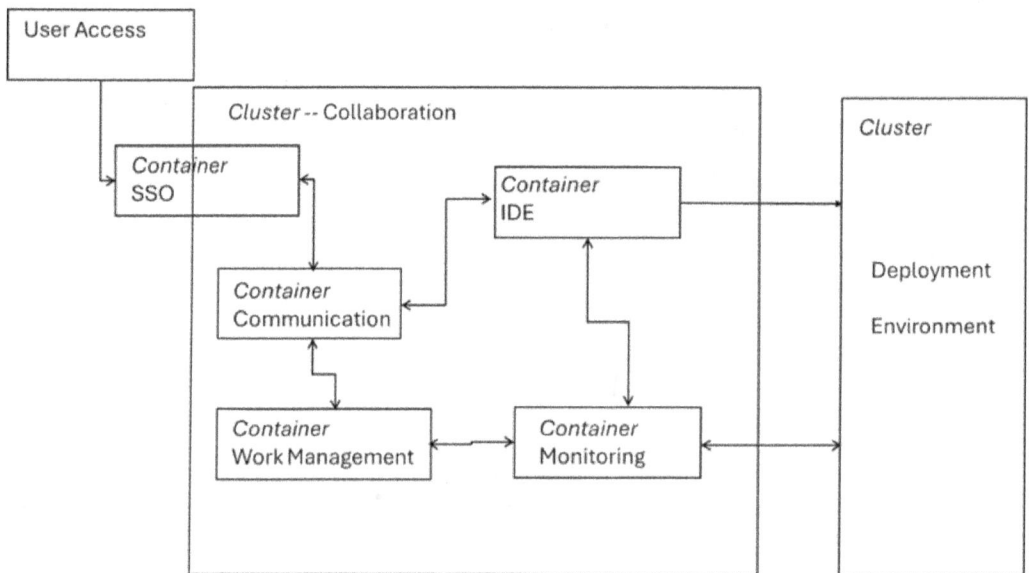

Figure 2.2: Collaboration components diagram

Each functional element is depicted as a single container, but they can be multiple containers or applications depending on the functional needs. For example, work management can include timekeeping, program progress, and business-level reporting, while an IDE might include security tools or alternate languages. Communication can also include knowledge repositories.

Monitoring responsibilities are shared between these tools throughout the collaboration element. Monitoring occurs for multiple reasons but should benefit observability through operational and developmental aspects. At the application level, systems can incorporate tools such as Prometheus, **Open Telemetry (O-TEL)** or the **ElasticSearch, Logstash, Kibana (ELK)** stack to provide adequate visibility. Cloud integration can also use tools such as AWS CloudWatch, Azure Monitor, or Datadog to combine the various pieces. Monitoring should provide details on which applications are being used, at what level, and how the platform performs during their usage.

Deployment components

Deployment components are those virtual spaces where you deploy code from the platform. These targets support the DevOps functions for testing, releasing, and deployment. Much like the initial element, these clusters are built from Infrastructure as Code with clear requirement definitions. Although these work functions follow the collaboration cluster, SSO should be enabled to allow direct, secure access to these clusters. Definitions provide a safe space to work. Common definitions include Kubernetes baselines, Docker configurations, Amazon Machine Interfaces, or specific Linux releases. Returning to the concept of the workshop metaphor, the deployment environment functions as a controlled space where teams can safely test and release their work. It offers the stability and isolation needed to validate changes before they move further down the delivery pipeline, reinforcing the platform's reliability and reducing risk during deployment.

Deployment cluster creation, which occurs through implementing a common baseline, typically includes two functions residing solely in that environment: the **continuous integration** (**CI**) and **continuous delivery** (**CD**) functions. CI/CD tools are the elements of the platform that test and publish software. Remember, the building piece appeared as a part of the collaboration environment. These tools communicate with that IDE to pull new code changes or receive pushes from the underlying platform. Some DevOps professionals see the initial pipeline as the final integration of CI; as we build common platforms, the pipelines we use in the platform are only the first step. Examples of commercially available CI tools include Jenkins, GitHub Actions, CircleCI, GitLab CI/CD, and Harness. I prefer GitLab CI/CD as it integrates smoothly with the GitLab IDE incorporated in the collaboration environment. The deployment environment architecture is shown in *Figure 2.3*:

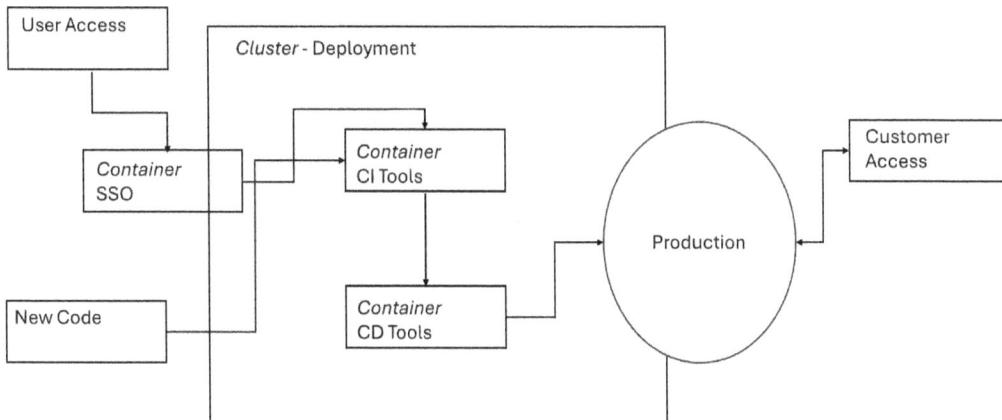

Figure 2.3: Deployment environment

Builders often select multiple tools to prevent vendor lock-in. Vendor lock-in can be difficult, but many of the GitLab functions are smooth enough to allow easy export between tools. Recently, one well-known vendor migrated from open source to a subscription model, requiring anyone using the model to pay license fees. At the same time, switching vendors frequently across the platform can lead to integration issues and is one reason why self-built platforms take such a long time to achieve profitability. The Platform Engineering goal is to build a common platform for various developers. Azure DevOps excels in allowing deployment to multiple environments regardless of where the code is built, or where pipelines are executed.

The CI tool ensures all new and approved code changes integrate into the new code. This integration provides productized version control in the applications available to the customer. The versions in the following sentences are generic and not connected to any particular tool. In the background, within the collaboration environment, you may be working on versions 7.16, 7.17, and 8, but the version released to the customer and supported might only be 7.15. This is because 7.15 is the full production version that has been tested and deployed. An effective CI tool in a Kubernetes implementation would allow the creation of distinct namespaces for each version to ensure the quality of changes.

The next step implements CD tools to expose the desired version, in this case, version 7.15 to the customer. The current version may have bug fixes or security concerns that do not require a new release. These implementations occur through CD. CD automatically readies submitted code for release into the production environment. These tools ensure those changes reach the customer immediately every time updates to the baseline code occurs. Standard tools specializing in CD include Jenkins, GitLab, Datadog, GoCD, and JBoss. ArgoCD and FluxCD are tools for the delivery of Kubernetes solutions.

In many cases, finding a tool delivering exclusively CI or CD can be challenging because many companies prefer to integrate CI and CD. These solutions work in broader applications but can create difficulty across a platform. In the platform, separating CI and CD functions creates the opportunity to work on multiple versions and features without slowing the development process. The decision to combine CI and CD in a single tool or split that functionality should be deliberate and based on resources, training, and cloud availability. DevOps methods frequently include CI and CD but cannot scale effectively beyond a single product or feature. Examples might include strictly controlled industries that require external testing, such as pharmaceuticals, or large companies with multiple legacy systems. Integration works well for a single team working on a single product or multiple teams working on different projects but proves challenging when you build to multiple teams supporting different aspects of a single project. The next section examines these challenges through the context of scalability, resilience, and security.

Designing for scalability, security, and resilience

Now that you understand the essential platform components, we can discuss how these items can adjust for scalability, security, and resilience. Scalability relates to how we can add users and platforms without changing the architecture. Security ensures that only the individuals who intend to use the platform are still benefiting from applications. Finally, platforms should demonstrate the resilience of the SOLID principles in allowing recovery while eliminating waste regarding unused cloud resources. These aspects should be essential drivers of initially architecting a platform. One thought framework I use in applying new systems is shown in *Figure 2.4*:

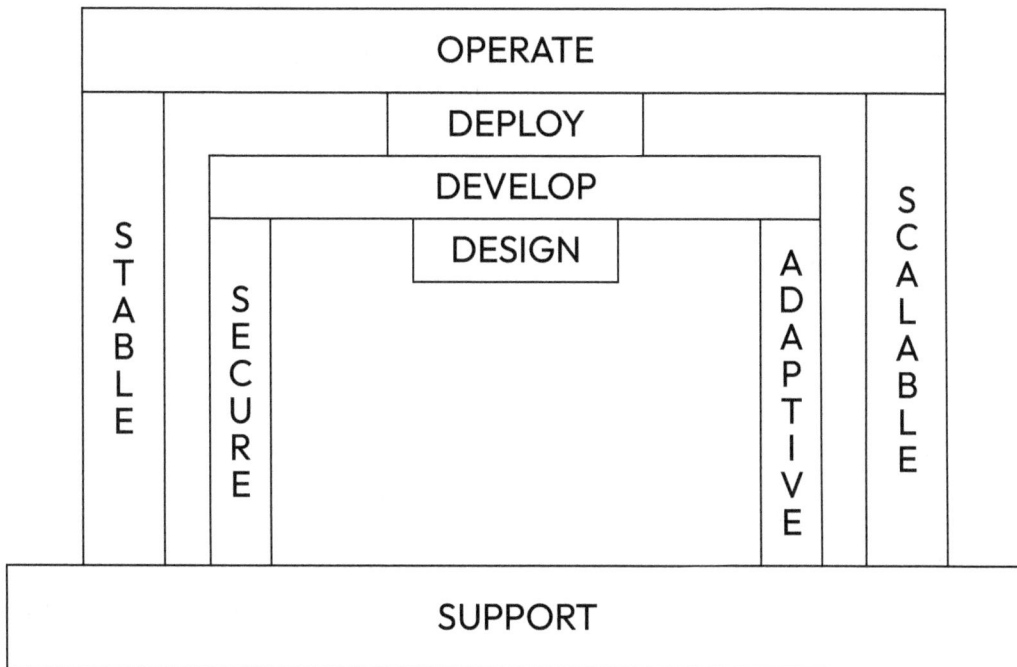

Figure 2.4: Thought framework

The framework appears as a table with operational elements down the middle and thought pillars around the side. Scalability and security are defined, while resilience forms the stable and adaptive pillars. The size of each operational element gives general trends for how much time users spend in those spaces. For example, teams should routinely spend three times as much work on development as design and four to five times as much work on operations as deployment. Following sound DevOps principles, all of these functions should be automated as much as possible.

Building for scalability

We can define **scalability** as the ability for the platform to continue to function well when it is changed in size or volume to meet customer needs. Typically, scalability applies upward to increased demands, but you can also think about downward trends when a function needs to contract. This scalability becomes especially relevant when considering a platform with a variable user base. You need to rapidly change to maximize high user numbers but implement auto-scaling to reduce cloud costs during off-hours or slow development periods.

Upwards scalability creates a more straightforward progression; you simply need more storage, compute, and functions. Functions such as databases, message queues, and analysis can complicate these progressions as well. Platform models support scalability as deployment clusters are eminently scalable. You can always add more clusters within the cloud to support additional app development. Internally, using Kubernetes namespaces allows the division between different applications, but configuration through resources such as Terraform makes life extremely easy. Generative AI support to provide coding elements can apply to any of these sections to supplement initial coding and solutions. If you have a Terraform basis for the deployment cluster, creating additional clusters is as easy as the following EKS sample:

```
Module "eks" {
  Source = "terraform-aws-modules/eks/aws"
  Cluster_name = "deployment-target1"
  Subnets = ["subnet-1", "subnet-2"]
  vpc_id = "vpc-54321"
 workers_desired_capacity = 10
Instance_type = "t2.large"
}
```

The next step is running command lines for `terraform init` and applying and configuring `kubectl` with AWS to react to the individual cluster:

```
terraform init
terraform apply
```

This initializes the Terraform instance within the environment so that tools can be used and the variables are assessed. It then applies the variables to the Terraform code and ensures all fields are supportable. If an error occurs in `apply`, it will mean the variables are not clear in the supporting field. The Terraform instance running those clusters will configure those instances with the previously referenced CI/CD functions for the deployment clusters.

Scalability for the collaboration cluster can be more difficult. In this case, the containers can scale by creating additional containers or changing CPU/memory limits rather than creating additional collaboration instances. If you add additional collaboration clusters, the challenge can be synching work across IDE, SSO, and work management instances. Many of those instances are designed to work separately. Integration becomes the prime challenge when multiple collaboration clusters are added with the same users. However, most of the referenced tools for those areas are designed to scale rapidly without changes.

The primary guideline for scaling should be that one collaboration cluster can support any number of deployment targets. Collaboration clusters should only be added when a security or user-based challenge exists. User-based challenge means that I may employ different contractors and do not want them to be able to observe code from the other teams. As a side note, these logical separation types can be just as easily scaled and managed through the SSO functions. In those SSO functions, you can create different permissions and, using RBAC, prevent certain users from interacting with certain elements or data within the collaboration node. These considerations lead to building security functions as an integrated part of the platform architecture.

Designing security

Security should be a primary feature of any platform design. Using SSO has been a continuing concept. SSO implements a session and user authentication service to allow users to use one set of credentials for multiple applications. While initial user credentials are frequently a username and password, modern designs should incorporate a **One-time Personal Identification Number** (**OTP**). OTP functions send a time-limited number to an external device to enter in conjunction with the username and password. After initial access, **Multi-Factor Authentication** (**MFA**) provides a viable alternative. This standard meets the security theory that verification emerges from something possessed, something known, and something intrinsic to the user, such as biometrics. All platform credentials should be stored in an encrypted account.

For commercial platforms, one SSO example is to implement **Open Authorization** (**OAuth**) as a framework to federate user information between third-party services. Google uses this approach, as a single Google account can be activated with multiple applications and sites. However, other site information is maintained internally rather than externally available when integrating with the platform. A common example is to use **Lightweight Directory Access Protocol** (**LDAP**) for the platform, which then shares authentication across all the tools. This implementation allows designing the platform so a user can either log in to a central collaboration point, or directly to the applications within the platform.

If you are integrating an existing SSO system rather than building one, some commercially available applications include Duo, Okta, AWS SSO, AuthPoint SSO, and Azure Active Directory. SSO is an area where benefiting from someone else's extensive security knowledge can be helpful. Some SSO functions might be limited to a certain type of cloud. Understanding the cloud limitations in communicating security is essential to the initial platform architecture.

Once users are signed in, there is another element to consider within the platform: how do we protect the data? To create integration, data must be available within multiple applications, but you should still retain some control over the various functions. Data is typically categorized as data at rest and data in transit. In either case, some type of encryption can be beneficial. You should encrypt access information, passwords, and usernames, with those functions being normally integrated within a good SSO system.

The other piece is that the data at rest, the code, and the work management details within the system should also be encrypted. One advantage to the platform is the majority of the work occurs within a single cluster. This cluster-based approach is an advantage because internal data can remain unencrypted until accessed from the outside. This may be slightly misleading since most internal data would reside in encryption layers, just not encrypted between users within the same key structure. This encryption model improves communication speeds and prevents delays. For example, all the data used during the day would be unencrypted after the user signed in but inaccessible without an approved sign-in. After operations, data would be backed up and stored in encrypted files. When users start the following day, they log in and continue to work as before, but any restoration would use the encrypted files. Security practices supplement backup and disaster recovery but ultimately demonstrate **resilience** within platforms.

Implementing resilience

The first example of resilience within the platform should be that an SSO links to a collaboration environment which, during the first sign-on, creates a working place within all the subsequent applications. With a quick return to *Figure 2.2*, the operations would be an initial sign-in asking a user for a name, password, OTP, and then linking the user to an organization and a team. The user account would then be approved to work within the platform's communication, IDE, work management, and deployment applications. A quick example is as follows:

- User – John Smith
- Password – XXXXXX
- OTP – Authenticator – six-digit time-limited number
- Organization – Ostrich
- Team – Egg1
- Applications – IDE, Communication, Work Management, CI

When the information is entered, John Smith would set up an OTP authenticator to verify access. The system would register him against the Ostrich organization and the Egg1 team for the IDE, communication window, work management tools, and CI. This system would ensure he can access team items in those areas. Additional areas might include roles that provide different sets of permissions within environments, as sometimes IDE systems distinguish between a guest who can view, a maintainer who can edit and create new work, and an owner who can merge work. The architecture should carefully detail each of these areas.

Building resilience between the platforms means laying out what each platform application requires and demonstrating parity between roles. For example, the role in the work management system might be a scrum master or team lead while the IDE role could be development lead or technical review. Understanding the limitations of those various pieces is critical for creating resilience when moving from one application to the next. The more understanding there is between those roles, the better the applications interact within the platform. The best solution would be the same roles across all applications, but that can be difficult with commercially available functions.

A critical aspect of resilience should be **recovery**. This recovery may be required because of a user error, a network outage, or a disaster such as a tornado or tsunami. Recovery involves having ready backups that can be quickly restored to provide functionality to the platform. Any resilient platform should conduct regular backups of the primary platform clusters and the data associated with those clusters. We must realize that there is a disconnect in operational performance between how you revert from an IDE upgrade, moving version 6.2 back to 6.1 to resolve a bug, and then how you restore data to that instantiation that users have committed. Versions are examples and do not reference any specific tool. These aspects towards to standard recovery practices that the platform must support.

A general backup process is the **three-two-one model**. Data storage should always occur in three locations, on two different media storage types, and with one copy offsite. This practice allows multiple places to verify crown-jewel data versus daily operations. An interesting real-world example is the NotPetya cyberattack against a significant international shipper. When they commenced restoration, the shipper had lost hundreds of systems and realized all their backup systems were also infected. Only one site for the company had safe data to conduct any recovery operations, and that was because they were offline for maintenance when the attack happened. You should avoid this scenario at all costs, hence the three-two-one model for generating resilience in any system, especially the platform in our use case.

Scalability, resilience incorporated with adaptability and stability, and security should all form the basis for expanding into platform architecture. These guidelines help shape those initial questions to build a comprehensive diagram. The next step is to agglomerate this conceptual understanding into a practical architecture to build or incorporate a platform within an organization.

From legacy systems to cloud-native applications

There are two main aspects to building a platform. The first considers whether you are using cloud-native systems, and the second provides ways to build the various deployment targets into an architecture. Cloud-native operations will be discussed briefly by reviewing the six Rs. The second half of this section explains how to design a permanent, transitory, or ephemeral design to support platform operations.

Any movement onto the cloud, or within clouds, depends on understanding the six Rs. As an experienced development professional, you should have already encountered many of them, although the full list is often new to many architects. A list is included here, and each R will be discussed in more detail:

- **Rehost**: Rehosting is sometimes called the *lift and shift* approach. It involves taking a full current environment and moving it to a similar location, except on the cloud. This can be a quick migration but often requires modifications to achieve cost-effectiveness or stability. While this can help with the basics of platforming, the amount of integration required means other strategies will also be needed. This strategy applies to organizations that simply want to be on the cloud without understanding the implications. Implications may include increased latency, suboptimal resource usage, and generally poor performance.

- **Replatform**: As a basic concept, re-platforming means adjusting to the cloud by integrating current processes with those provided by the cloud. As mentioned in this book, Platform Engineering takes a deeper look and assesses different types of platforms to cross-cut across multiple outputs. One DevOps concept involves using the thinnest possible platform for each section. This means that while platforms incorporate multiple technologies, they should build on stacks that potentially incorporate separate platforms. The primary platform assesses software development, but this can be platformed multiple times to integrate with platforms for operational output, security, testing, or other functions. Each platform should support those minimal functions to remain reliable and secure and help with scalability.

- **Repurchase**: The third alternative is repurchasing, buying another cloud alternative, or moving from local servers to someone else's server. This enforces what can be called the three As of migration:

  - **Access**: Having wider access to systems through cloud services.

  - **Awareness**: Being more broadly aware of everything occurring within a space due to cloud tools, and VM interaction.

  - **Abdication**: Abandoning all responsibility for elements within your platform by depending on cloud services to perform those functions.

  Repurchasing typically occurs when users want to gain access and awareness but want to abdicate management responsibilities.

- **Retain**: This is the opposite to the repurchase option; here, we keep what we have. Retaining practices can benefit the lower end but creates challenges when scaling platforms, mainly because the additional resources are not readily available. It is a different order of complexity between merely purchasing additional storage and computing through a credit card swipe and installing new server racks.

- **Retire**: Retiring means eliminating some of the services that are no longer needed. It also integrates with the next option.

- **Refactor**: This means redesigning and rebuilding needed functions. This can be used as a means to enhance performance through scalability and security changes. One common example of refactoring involves moving from legacy to more modern applications, which often involves containerizing software and applications.

Platform Engineering solves both challenges by focusing on what elements are needed for a particular platform, bringing them into a common framework, and eliminating waste within the process. Refactoring can be critical when building a platform but less so when buying or renting solutions. Most commercial platform solutions offer various available plugins supporting a constant software stream.

Essential platform architecture

After considering the six Rs, and the motivation for an initial cloud transition, the next step is designing a platform architecture. This architecture will inform subsequent design by creating a workshop with space to expand and having all the available tools within easy reach. There are three basic designs to begin or continue a platform design, each focusing on developing the thinnest possible platform and supporting the widest customer base. The difference between the designs lies largely in the permanence of the proposed design. The three designs can be labeled simply as follows:

- Permanent

- Transitory

- Ephemeral

The following figure demonstrates the construction of these three initial architectural models:

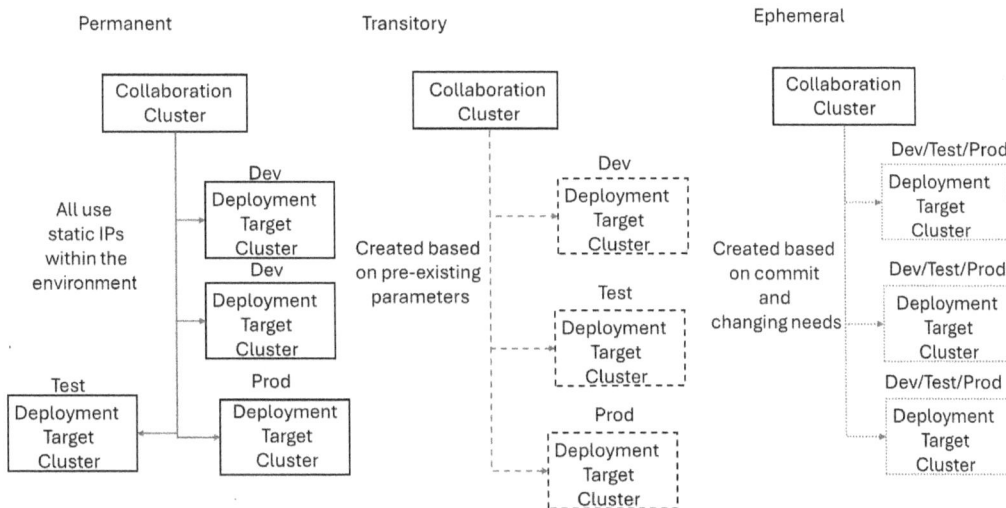

Figure 2.5: Platform architecture samples

Let's look at these architectures in more detail.

Permanent platform architecture

Permanent architecture is designed for the long term. The goal is to design and operate multiple clusters that are always there for the user. The system probably incorporates a primary collaboration cluster, at least one development cluster, and a production cluster. When designing a permanent approach, users would log in to the collaboration cluster and then promote work and design through the other clusters. This approach provides a highly stable environment for testing and deploying code. A permanent design deprecates load balancers on the primary tools by using pre-determined cluster sizes within the VPCs. Operational management allows us to add clusters if computing or storage becomes a concern. The primary advantage of this architecture is known configuration and easy maintenance. Establishing set clusters with defined namespaces early in the process creates an opportunity for set training approaches. These designs use pre-determined locations and known clusters for all operations. Companies with well-defined software needs or static concerns might prefer a permanent cluster. Well-defined and stable instances can help reduce public cloud billing costs by closing non-required cycles.

Permanent clusters work well for resources that are always required in set amounts. Building a testing platform with known resources or a security platform are excellent options. The permanent testing platform also has set resources that can be accessed to test operations or run functions across a cloud. A security cluster with this design provides a place to maintain security knowledge more restrictedly. A stable cluster design can prove more manageable to maintain RBAC permissions in the cluster, establish clear logs, and define some known metrics to manage operations.

Clusters designed in a permanent architecture incorporate advantages in **Representational State Transfer Application Programming Interfaces** (**REST APIs**), no-code applications, and strong relational databases. Since all the data is maintained, the cluster can have a wide range of potential implementations by relying on standing conversion and configuration across multiple toolsets. Examples include using Istio to manage container security across pods or a tool such as Crossplane. Crossplane extends existing APIs by translating all infrastructure calls into Kubernetes-native resources, allowing a consistent, declarative approach and reducing the need for developers to resolve infrastructure issues individually. This change reduces the endpoints users must manage during implementation. These permanent platforms tend to expand by maintaining known good pipelines and plug-in libraries that allow a large bench of additional applications. Open source tools can be rapidly integrated and used by everyone within the platform if a strong dependency library exists.

The disadvantage of permanent clusters is that they are difficult to change rapidly. Keeping these clusters aligned with new features and releases requires frequently using a different version of the same cluster. Feature upgrades for the platform that occur within the platform can be complex to access when facing a system crash or user issues. These issues normally result in the company maintaining the platform by owning a development and testing area that is distinct from the permanent platform. These crashes only become an issue if you are building and operating the platform in addition to working on the platform.

The other challenge for a permanent design is visualizing resource usage as fixed on the initial deployment. Although load balancers can help, in most cases, they are disabled to maintain stable operations across clusters. A design that rapidly increases the pipelines required or pulls large amounts of data on non-regular timelines can cause problems. For example, a system designed to find the best sale price on a given item might search numerous databases, including images and metadata. The massive pull for one application might create challenges within the cluster and slow other operations. The solution for these fixed designs is implementing a transitory design.

Transitory platform architecture

Transitory platform designs only call resources when needed. These designs incorporate auto-scaling at multiple steps but focus on creating a known cluster and then adjusting those clusters as needed. Another architectural element within the transitory design is to limit clusters, frequently by time and usage. The collaboration cluster serves as the primary, stable environment within a transitory platform design, but it also offers the flexibility for users to spin up additional clusters as specific needs or workloads arise. These clusters would have an expiration point, such as three months, below a certain compute usage, with inactive users or similar metric-based decision points. For example, when working in collaboration on a new design, I would reach a point where I needed to deploy a segment for testing. I would then use a cluster launch application to launch the CI/CD function for 72 hours. This type of launch could promote the development into a permanent location within those 72 hours, but if operations remained incomplete, the cluster would spin back down. That can be frustrating when you are facing numerous problems.

An advantage of transitory design is knowing the costs. You can implement a limit on initiated clusters and project costs through multiple quarters. Another advantage is that unused resources are always eliminated. These designs tend to be highly opinionated when creating clusters. The limited nature means fewer options are available for design, but it can be beneficial if you already know the defined workspace. Think about it as if you already know that the workshop only needs to produce shelves; there is no reason to maintain machinery capable of making bowls, birdhouses, or statues. These constraints can limit the cluster but also tend to make it more highly focused.

Transitory designs excel for items that are only required for a defined period, such as software supporting retail sales, event management, or support during a conference. A company may want to be able to launch many demos at a conference but no longer have those functions available afterward. This design ensures that those additional clusters will disappear when they are no longer needed. The first disadvantage is that everything constructed on those clusters will eventually disappear. While the code may be maintained, the specific aspects during operations will no longer be present. You may implement a transitory approach to a testing cluster; when you call a test, the cluster running those operations will run the tests, pass the data, and then shut down. These operational guidelines can be beneficial for managing resources.

A second disadvantage of a transitory cluster can be in managing operations. Although you know the cluster will eventually quit, setting those parameters can be difficult. If the parameters are set too high, you could just as easily use a permanent architecture; if the parameters are too low, then the needed work will remain incomplete. Users can become highly aggravated if all the required work disappears at the penultimate step, and they must return to the beginning of the process. This aggravation can also happen with transitory security platforms when the scans are designed to launch from those clusters. Sometimes, the artifacts are lost if the cluster quits before the security tool concludes.

Ephemeral platform architecture

A third architectural model is **ephemeral design**. Similar to transitory design, this sets up a cluster that will eventually disappear. Unlike the set guidelines for a transitory approach, ephemeral clusters take advantage of flexible load balancing. Ephemeral clusters are only designed to build on commit and then have a set expiration. Whether you are using a development, testing, operations, or security platform, these clusters spin up to complete a task and remove themselves. This cluster creation allows any user to create any number of clusters at any point as deployment targets but uses a metric like active users to decide when to terminate operations.

One key to using ephemeral clusters is ensuring that logging functions report to the collaboration cluster. Any data associated with that cluster disappears, so any long-term metrics or evaluations need to be reported elsewhere. You can see the advantage of running an operations platform ephemerally that spins up clusters to check performance, reports results, and then deprecates to minimize cloud usage. This is best suited to customers with tight budgets or those who are unsure what may be part of a future spending plan.

Ephemeral clusters are best suited for those at either end of the experience spectrum. For those with minimal experience, using a platform with an ephemeral design can allow you to explore platform properties without full commitment. Conversely, those who know exactly what they want, and for how long, can effectively use ephemeral platforms to control costs. One challenge is that each user must know exactly what they want. In the permanent approach, an operations team sets the deployment targets; in the transitory approach, a hybrid approach between an operations team and individual users probably exists; in the ephemeral architecture, each user sets their own needs. This challenge could be mitigated by having templates for various ephemeral clusters. However, setting templates too broadly leads us back into designing an ephemeral cluster and operationally running those functions in a transitory approach.

The ephemeral design maximizes many of the DevOps concepts in creating high availability, low coupling, and easy configuration changes. These designs are not suited to a production environment as they do not tend to last long enough. Low coupling emerges as every transitory environment contains all the elements necessary to move forward.

Each architectural design provides some benefits and some challenges. As a personal approach, I would use a permanent structure for internal development and operations, a transitory design for testing and security, and then an ephemeral platform for research and development. Each organization has its own needs and requirements. Understanding the difference between the structures allows you to quickly identify the tasks needed. These can be incorporated to consider the tools needed, ingress and egress pathways, and version changes.

When implemented through a platform, the other beneficial aspect of these architectures is the ability to structure for self-service. Understanding the base architecture and then working with a generative AI structure later allows each user to support their own needs through platforms at multiple levels. The more well-defined the architecture, the greater the capability for automated assistants to help. This increases the amount of work completed and reduces the toil from everyday tasks that must be accomplished multiple times.

Summary

This chapter began by explaining the key architectural concepts required to implement Platform Engineering. You start with the SOLID principles and then expand those functions as required for a platform. Platforms are relatively simple, with the basic architecture comprising collaborative clusters and deployment targets. Integrating those concepts allows you to maximize DevOps cultural constructions to obtain consistent and repeated quality.

An initial architecture can then be positioned to optimize scalability, resilience, and security. Scalability facilitates the adjustment of resource usage in either direction to maximize profit instead of spinning clusters without value. Resilient constructions ensure those platforms can perform when faced with external changes from buggy code, constantly changing dependencies, and even physical disasters. Secure platforms are a must for any operator in the modern digital landscape. Information may want to be free, but we must also prioritize protecting customer data from unethical use. We also must be able to secure our own intellectual property to protect long-term profits.

Finally, all the architectural concepts were integrated into moving to cloud-native solutions and then deploying a permanent, transitory, or ephemeral structure to our platform. Each option scales differently, incorporating resilience and demonstrating security. These platforms can be implemented for development functions, security tasks, operational needs, or testing various constructions.

These designs lead us to the next step: determining whether the existing culture can support a platform transformation. After all, DevOps is a cultural solution, not just a technical one, so the next chapter covers determining the best-fit cultures and leadership strategies to adapt fully to platform-engineered success.

Further reading

- Malik, U. (2024) *Provisioning an Amazon EKS Cluster with Terraform.*

Get This Book's PDF Version and Exclusive Extras

Scan the QR code (or go to packtpub.com/unlock). Search for this book by name, confirm the edition, and then follow the steps on the page.

Note: Keep your invoice handly. Purchase made directly from packt don't require one.

3

Cultural Transformation and Leadership

Embarking on a journey of cultural transformation and empathic leadership within the realm of Platform Engineering and DevOps requires more than just technical acumen; it demands a shift in mindset and the adoption of strategic frameworks that champion innovation, psychological safety, and a culture of continuous learning and improvement. This chapter delves into the essence of creating such transformative environments, offering insights into the principles and practices that can guide leaders and organizations through the complexities of modern enterprise. It's about cultivating a space where innovation thrives, challenges are embraced, and every team member feels valued and empowered to contribute to their fullest potential.

We'll explore the critical role of cultural transformation and empathic leadership in driving successful Platform Engineering initiatives. We'll examine how Platform Engineering can serve as a catalyst for innovation, empowering teams to build and deliver more effectively. Finally, we'll discuss how to incorporate and integrate strategic frameworks that support organizational change—enhancing business value, fostering psychological safety, and creating the conditions for sustained innovation.

Discover how these elements cultivate an organizational culture that drives technical excellence and human-centered workplaces in Platform Engineering and DevOps. By aligning leadership styles with engineering challenges—such as managing complex team structures, ensuring seamless collaboration, and navigating technical trade-offs—this transformation empowers leaders to foster innovation, enhance teamwork, and implement effective change management. These principles enable organizations to balance technical decisions with business goals while promoting employee engagement and well-being, ultimately creating resilient, adaptable, and successful organizations.

We will be covering the following main topics:

- The urgency of cultural evolution in a digital-first world
- Empathy – The core of organizational value
- Leadership as the catalyst for empathic change
- Orchestrating cultural transformation – The power of strategic frameworks

Technical requirements

While this chapter does not have specific technical prerequisites, a foundational understanding of organizational culture, leadership principles, change management, along with Lean, Agile, and DevOps, methodologies, will enhance the appreciation of the strategic insights and transformative strategies discussed.

The urgency of cultural evolution in a digital-first world

Businesses must reassess their approaches and organizational culture to ensure swift and efficient value creation and thrive in today's digital landscape. The tech industry, particularly Platform Engineering and DevOps, is driving this transformation. We urge businesses to adopt a more Agile, generative culture that aligns with the digital era and move away from hierarchical norms. This shift is essential for companies to excel in the new digital reality.

For instance, the *State of Agile Culture 2020-21 Report* indicated that organizations with strong Agile cultures experienced up to a 235% improvement in business performance. Similarly, companies fostering generative cultures report significantly higher employee morale and innovation. Pivotal Software's transformation is a powerful example—through Agile methodologies and a collaborative environment, Pivotal enhanced its development processes, enabling rapid responses to market shifts and customer needs. Another example is FREITAG, which implemented Agile management to boost flexibility and adaptability. These cases demonstrate how Agile and generative cultures drive technical excellence, foster innovation, and build resilience in a rapidly evolving digital landscape.

To effectively implement this transformative change, it is imperative to recognize and understand the existing organizational culture. Identifying where your organization currently stands will provide a clear starting point for fostering the generative culture required for business success.

Recognizing organizational culture

Organizations face a critical decision between clinging to outdated methods or embracing transformative change. **Westrum's Typology of Cultures** provides valuable insights into prevailing attitudes and behaviors that shape an organization's approach to teamwork, information flow, and innovation. The three distinct cultures—*pathological, bureaucratic*, and *generative*—help organizations make informed choices and create a culture that drives growth and innovation. For leaders, recognizing where their organization falls within Westrum's typology is the first critical step toward cultural evolution. It lays the foundation for a strategic shift towards a more open, dynamic, and collaborative organizational culture. Such a transformation is pivotal for leveraging the expansive capabilities of Platform Engineering and DevOps, methodologies that inherently thrive in adaptable, responsive, and generative cultures. Let's take a look at the different cultures:

- **Pathological cultures** breed fear, siloed functions, and a *blame* culture, stifling creativity and collaboration. Pathological organizations view messengers of bad news as problems and dismiss them before they can be heard. In such a culture, new ideas are suppressed with scapegoating and fear. This stifling of innovation can be disastrous in a technology-driven marketplace where adaptability is essential.

- **Bureaucratic cultures**, with rigid hierarchies and strict adherence to rules, provide structure but hamper agility and innovation. Bureaucratic cultures allow collaboration but within strict boundaries, leading only to opportunistic cooperation.

- **Generative cultures** are built on trust, open communication, and a shared purpose, creating an environment ripe for innovation, learning from failure, and collective celebration of achievements. Such cultures value messengers of bad news as they are crucial for quick problem-solving and continuous improvement. Generative organizations encourage collaborative effort and shared responsibility. Generative cultures embrace novelty and the innovative spirit.

The main aspects of the three different cultures explained in the list are summarized in the following figure:

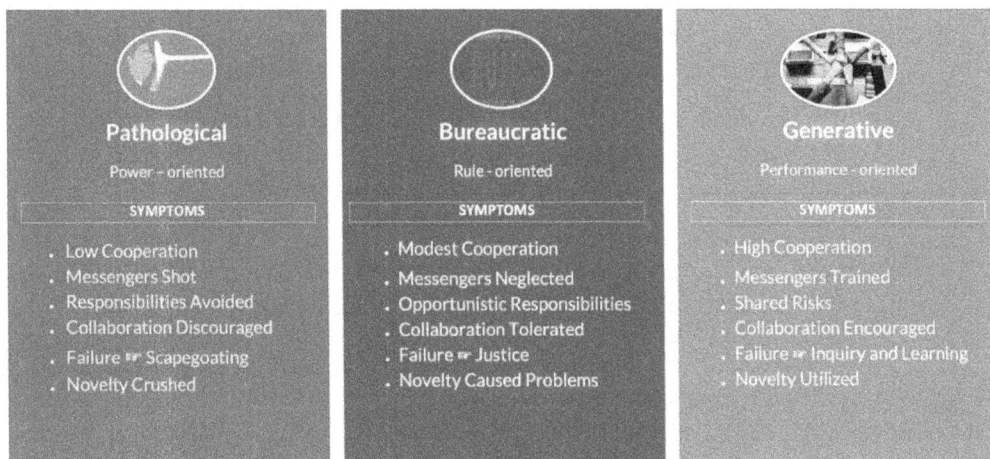

Pathological	Bureaucratic	Generative
Power - oriented	Rule - oriented	Performance - oriented
SYMPTOMS	**SYMPTOMS**	**SYMPTOMS**
. Low Cooperation	. Modest Cooperation	. High Cooperation
. Messengers Shot	. Messengers Neglected	. Messengers Trained
. Responsibilities Avoided	. Opportunistic Responsibilities	. Shared Risks
. Collaboration Discouraged	. Collaboration Tolerated	. Collaboration Encouraged
. Failure ☞ Scapegoating	. Failure ☞ Justice	. Failure ☞ Inquiry and Learning
. Novelty Crushed	. Novelty Caused Problems	. Novelty Utilized

Figure 3.1: Leaders must shift the organizational culture from pathological to generative

It is evident that a cultural shift towards the generative end of Westrum's spectrum is vital for organizations to remain competitive and forward-thinking.

Benefits of a generative culture

In the vanguard of competitive innovation, a generative culture is the ideal state for organizations looking to thrive in the digital age. Here, the collective focus shifts towards performance, adaptability, and the seamless integration of Platform Engineering and DevOps principles. The benefits of such a culture are not just additive; they are exponential:

- **Boosted innovation**: Generative cultures are fertile ground for innovation. The encouragement of risk-taking, coupled with a no-blame approach to failure, liberates creativity and allows new ideas to flourish. This environment allows rapid prototyping, iterative development, and a quicker transition from concept to market-ready solutions.

- **Enhanced collaboration**: These cultures break down silos, promoting an interdisciplinary approach where diverse skill sets converge. Such collaboration leads to holistic problem-solving, where collective expertise drives superior outcomes.

- **Increased agility**: A generative culture is synonymous with agility. With its flat hierarchies and streamlined decision-making processes, the organization can pivot swiftly in response to market shifts, technological advancements, and evolving customer needs.

- **Higher employee engagement**: When employees operate in a culture that values their contributions and fosters their development, engagement skyrockets. Engaged employees are not just more productive; they are advocates for the company and its objectives, driving forward with intrinsic motivation.

- **Resilience and sustainability**: Organizations with generative cultures can better withstand market turbulence and disruptions. The resilience built into their cultural DNA ensures sustainability, as they are adept at learning from experiences and emerging stronger from challenges.

- **Attracting and retaining talent**: A generative culture is a beacon for top talent. Professionals seek environments that promise growth, learning, and a positive impact. By championing such a culture, organizations become talent magnets, retaining and attracting the best in the field.

- **Customer-centric solutions**: With an empathic approach embedded in the culture, the products and services developed are inherently customer-centric. This alignment with customer needs often results in higher satisfaction and loyalty, translating to long-term success.

Transitioning to a generative culture is not a mere change; it's an evolution toward organizational enlightenment. It lays the foundation for a company not just to survive but to lead and set the pace in a rapidly evolving ecosystem where those who can adapt with speed and efficiency will define the future of technology and service delivery.

For instance, consider Netflix. Before its cultural transformation, Netflix operated with a more hierarchical structure, characterized by rigid management practices and limited employee autonomy. This environment often stifled innovation and responsiveness to market changes. Recognizing these limitations, Netflix underwent a significant cultural shift, embracing a generative culture rooted in trust and continuous feedback. This transformation empowered teams to innovate rapidly and make data-driven decisions, enabling Netflix to outpace competitors and redefine the entertainment industry with its Agile, customer-centric approach. By fostering a generative culture rooted in trust and continuous feedback, Netflix empowers its teams to innovate rapidly and make data-driven decisions. This cultural shift has enabled Netflix to not only stay ahead of its competitors but also redefine the entertainment industry.

Organizations must understand that adopting a generative culture demands reengineering the corporate ethos to replicate this success. Leaders must intentionally create a vision that embodies generative ideals and demonstrates trust while championing open dialogue. The following section outlines strategic steps to facilitate this transformation.

Strategies for transitioning to a generative culture

Transitioning to a generative culture is more than simply adopting a new set of policies; it's a fundamental reengineering of corporate ethos. It requires intentionality, unwavering commitment from leadership, and an actionable roadmap that empowers every tier of the organization.

Leaders must create a vision that encapsulates the generative ideals, making them tangible and relatable. They must exemplify the generative traits they wish to instill, demonstrating trust, championing open dialogue, and embodying the changes they advocate.

An actionable plan for transitioning must include the following strategic points:

- **Establishing open communication channels**: Cultivate an environment where information flows freely, encouraging transparency and fostering trust. Open forums and regular town hall meetings can democratize information and help dismantle the *need-to-know* barriers characteristic of pathological cultures.

- **Redefining failure**: Shift the organization's response to failure from scapegoating to learning. Introduce a *failure debrief* protocol akin to agile retrospectives, where lessons are extracted and celebrated as valuable intel for the organization's continuous learning cycle.

- **Championing collaboration**: Break down silos by promoting cross-functional teams and interdisciplinary projects. Use shared objectives to unify disparate groups, aligning them with common goals that reinforce the generative model's collaborative spirit.

- **Rewarding innovation**: Develop systems to recognize and reward innovation. Encourage experimentation by creating *innovation labs* or *hackathons* where novel ideas can be explored without the pressure of immediate ROI.

- **Leadership training**: Implement leadership development programs focused on generative behavior. Equip leaders with the skills to coach rather than command, to inspire rather than enforce.

- **Incremental change and quick wins**: Start with small, incremental changes to quickly demonstrate the benefits of a generative culture. These quick wins can build momentum and buy-in across the organization.

- **Measuring progress**: Define clear metrics to measure the cultural shift. Use surveys, feedback tools, and culture audits to gauge the organization's pulse and adjust strategies as needed.

This evolution is challenging. It demands perseverance, as cultural inertia can be a formidable adversary. Yet, the rewards—a nimble, resilient organization poised for innovation and growth—far outweigh the inertia of comfort zones.

To support this evolution, leveraging tools such as Jira, Linear, or Asana for transparent project tracking and Slack or Microsoft Teams for fostering open, real-time communication can help teams collaborate more effectively. Retrospective meetings offer continuous learning and process improvement opportunities, reinforcing psychological safety. However, adopting these strategies in a DevOps setting can face challenges, such as resistance to change from long-established teams. To overcome this, leaders should introduce incremental changes, highlight quick wins, and involve team members early in decision-making to build trust and reduce apprehension. Addressing concerns empathetically and demonstrating the value of these tools and techniques ensures smoother adoption and fosters sustained cultural transformation.

When executing these strategies, ensure they are not check-box exercises but part of a sincere effort to transform the organization's DNA. As the culture shifts from pathological to generative, Platform Engineering and DevOps practices will flourish, unlocking new horizons for growth and enabling the organization to thrive in the digital-first world.

Now that we've explored the benefits and strategies of a generative culture, it's time to delve into actionable steps to cultivate this transformative ethos within your organization, empowering you to lead with innovation and resilience.

Cultivating a generative culture – Strategic initiatives for leaders

To transition effectively to a generative culture, a strategic and sustained effort is required. The following actionable tasks and corresponding insights provide a framework for this profound transformation.

- **Educating and aligning leadership**: Begin by ensuring leaders are educated about the principles of a generative culture and aligned with the vision for change. Equip them with the knowledge and tools to champion this transformation and align their incentives with its success. This foundational step ensures leadership buy-in, creating a unified front to guide and inspire the rest of the organization through the cultural shift.

- **Developing an organizational culture roadmap**: Leaders must create a clear roadmap for a successful organizational cultural shift. This roadmap should outline specific objectives, assign accountability, and identify cultural indicators for each transition stage. It is imperative to communicate this roadmap widely so that every employee understands the destination and the journey ahead, fostering trust and buy-in. The roadmap should be a flexible, living document that can adapt to the evolving challenges faced during implementation. Key performance indicators such as employee engagement scores, cross-functional collaboration metrics, and innovation rates can be used to track progress toward a generative culture.

- **Creating a cultural change taskforce**: Establishing a cultural change task force is critical for leading the shift. This team, consisting of members from various levels and functions within the organization, serves as the cultural ambassadors. They facilitate open discussions, champion generative culture, and provide diverse perspectives. This inclusivity ensures that the shift resonates across the organization. Leaders can effectively diffuse generative principles throughout the organization by fostering ownership of the cultural transition.

- **Implementing a cultural feedback loop**: To truly evolve a company's culture, there must be a mechanism for ongoing dialogue and feedback that values input from all levels of the organization. Leaders can establish a cultural feedback loop through periodic surveys, open forums, or dedicated channels for continuous feedback. Tools such as Confluence for shared knowledge, Slack or Microsoft Teams for live discussions, and Pulse surveys integrated with collaboration platforms can be used to collect and act on feedback effectively, ensuring alignment across teams. Crucially, leaders must address feedback with responsiveness to drive culture forward and reinforce the principles of a generative culture: transparency, collaboration, and continual learning. This not only benefits the company but also inspires employees to participate and contribute to the company's growth.

These strategic initiatives pave the way for an agile, innovative, and resilient culture. The blueprint is actionable, driven by leaders committed to building a generative culture that can thrive in the fast-paced digital era. True cultural change is an iterative process that requires engagement and sustained effort rather than being imposed. Therefore, leaders must cultivate the culture with care, constant communication, shared experiences, and values. They must remain steadfast in their vision while demonstrating a willingness to adapt their strategy and approach in the face of challenges, ensuring that the cultural transformation remains aligned with evolving circumstances and goals. The ultimate result is a culture that champions innovation, agility, and a deep sense of community, positioning the organization to capitalize on the digital era's opportunities. Leaders should embrace these strategic initiatives to cultivate a generative culture that anticipates, and leverages change for continued innovation and growth.

Reflecting on these strategies, it is evident that fostering a generative culture is not only about processes and frameworks but also about the human elements that drive success. Understanding and incorporating empathy into organizational practices is vital for achieving this transformation. Let's explore how empathy serves as the core of organizational value, shaping successful and innovative workplaces.

Empathy – The core of organizational value

In today's fast-paced and intricately connected world, empathy is a crucial human trait that plays a significant role in organizational success and innovation. It is a cornerstone in shaping workplaces that foster collaboration, understanding, and a profound connection with their users. Empathy within Platform Engineering bridges the gap between technical solutions and the real-world needs of developers and users, guiding the creation of platforms that simplify workflows, enhance productivity, and solve everyday challenges faced by teams.

Empathy as the connective tissue of human interaction

Empathy is crucial to effective collaboration and innovation in Platform Engineering. It goes beyond a personal virtue, serving as an essential organizational principle that ensures platform engineers build systems aligned with the real needs of their users—developers, operations teams, and business stakeholders. Empathy connects platform engineers to the challenges their colleagues face, guiding decisions that prioritize usability and productivity over technical convenience, and is critical to meaningful human interaction.

Empathy plays a pivotal role in the creation of tools and systems in Platform Engineering. It guides the design process, ensuring that the solutions developed genuinely support developers and other stakeholders. This means understanding the unique challenges developers face and designing solutions that simplify their workflows, even if it introduces complexity for platform engineers. The end result is a platform that prioritizes the needs of developers, enhancing productivity, reducing toil, and fostering innovation.

Empathy is not a one-time consideration in Platform Engineering, but a continuous influence that impacts every stage of the life cycle. During the ideation phase, empathy drives the inclusion of developer feedback through UX research, stakeholder interviews, and collaboration sessions. Feedback loops and developer surveys help teams align their designs with actual needs. In code reviews, empathy ensures respectful, constructive feedback that builds trust within the team. In DevOps practices, empathy fosters a culture of shared responsibility by creating golden paths—optimized workflows that streamline delivery pipelines while minimizing friction.

Rather than assuming what developers might need, empathy requires platform engineers to build systems tailored to explicit developer pain points. For example, an **Internal Developer Platform (IDP)** might integrate features such as self-service provisioning for environments or a dashboard for pipeline visibility—features designed based on direct feedback from developer teams. This empathy-driven approach empowers developers to focus on building customer-facing applications rather than navigating infrastructure challenges.

Ultimately, Platform Engineering products—such as IDPs, golden paths, and secure software supply chains—become the backbone of developer success. These tools are not just functional but transformative, elevating the development process by addressing real-world needs. Empathy is the bridge that connects technical design with the human experience, ensuring platforms are intuitive, accessible, and impactful.

Platform Engineering teams foster a culture of empathy and enable continuous improvement and deeper collaboration. Feedback becomes valuable for understanding developer challenges, driving iterations that refine solutions, and establishing enduring partnerships between platform teams and developers. Empathy transforms Platform Engineering into an enabler of both technical excellence and human connection, setting a new standard for innovation and resilience.

To fully grasp the resounding impact of empathy, it is essential to explore its various forms and how they manifest within an organization. Understanding the spectrum of empathy can illuminate its pivotal role in shaping technology and business practices.

The span of empathy – Understanding its impact on technology and business

Empathy is an umbrella term and there are different kinds of empathy that one can experience. Within any organization, empathy manifests across a spectrum, encompassing cognitive, emotional, and compassionate empathy. This range represents varying degrees of understanding, feeling, and action that empathy can engender, each playing a distinct role in shaping business practices and technological advancements:

- **Cognitive empathy**, the intellectual understanding of another's perspective, is foundational to user-centric technologies. It enables designers and engineers to step into the users' shoes, anticipating needs and preferences without necessarily sharing their emotions. This form of empathy is crucial in tailoring **user experiences** (**UXs**) and **user interfaces** (**UIs**) that resonate with a diverse user base, making technology accessible and enjoyable for all. In Platform Engineering, cognitive empathy is critical when designing APIs or developer platforms. For instance, platform engineers might create an API that abstracts the complexity of multiple underlying tools into a single, well-structured, intuitive endpoint. Providing such an API simplifies workflows for developers, allowing them to focus on delivering value rather than wrestling with fragmented systems. Cognitive empathy enables platform engineers to anticipate developers' needs and design systems that align with their preferences and workflows.

- **Emotional empathy** involves sharing the feelings of another, creating a deeper, emotional connection. In the context of customer service and user support, emotional empathy can transform a standard interaction into an extraordinary one. Representatives with emotional empathy can genuinely relate to customers' frustrations or joys, leading to more satisfying and loyalty-building service experiences. It's the difference between a support call that resolves an issue and one that both resolves the problem and leaves the customer feeling truly heard and valued. Emotional empathy is especially relevant for Platform Engineering teams when managing developer frustration during incidents or escalations. Consider a scenario where developers face a critical outage caused by pipeline failures. A platform engineer with emotional empathy can engage with the team to address their frustrations, acknowledge the stress caused by the issue, and collaborate to resolve it. By doing so, they build trust and reinforce a sense of partnership between platform engineers and developers, fostering a positive and supportive work environment.

- **Compassionate empathy** goes a step further, moving individuals to take action to alleviate another's distress. For Platform Engineering, this translates into proactive problem-solving and innovation to reduce user pain points. Compassionate empathy drives teams to identify issues through feedback loops and eagerly devise and implement solutions that enhance user satisfaction and loyalty. This empathy moves beyond understanding and feeling—it involves taking action to address someone else's pain or challenges. A product manager within a Platform Engineering team exemplifies compassionate empathy by listening to developer feedback about cumbersome workflows and resource limitations and then advocating for solutions. For example, they might prioritize building self-service tools, such as provisioning dashboards, that empower developers to resolve issues independently without waiting for operational support. Even when faced with resourcing challenges, their ability to advocate for and implement such solutions showcases the actionable nature of compassionate empathy, directly improving developer satisfaction and productivity.

The following figure summarizes the aforementioned discussion:

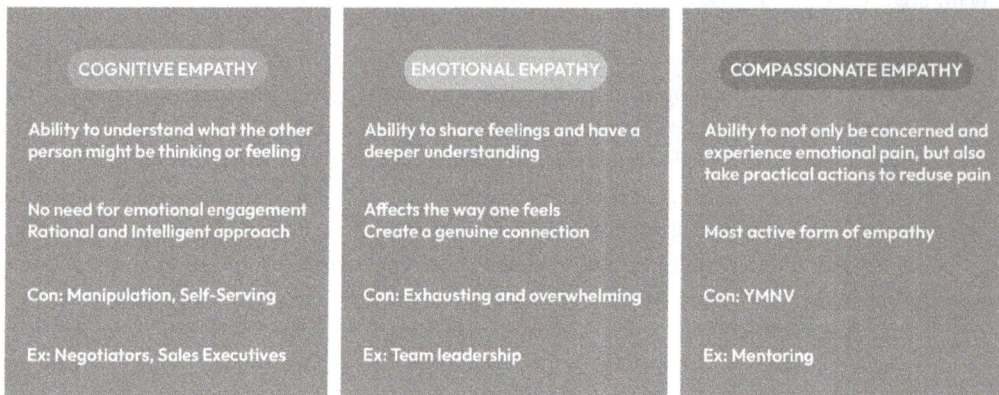

COGNITIVE EMPATHY	EMOTIONAL EMPATHY	COMPASSIONATE EMPATHY
Ability to understand what the other person might be thinking or feeling	Ability to share feelings and have a deeper understanding	Ability to not only be concerned and experience emotional pain, but also take practical actions to reduse pain
No need for emotional engagement Rational and Intelligent approach	Affects the way one feels Create a genuine connection	Most active form of empathy
Con: Manipulation, Self-Serving	Con: Exhausting and overwhelming	Con: YMNV
Ex: Negotiators, Sales Executives	Ex: Team leadership	Ex: Mentoring

Figure 3.2: Types of empathy

Understanding and leveraging this spectrum of empathy enables organizations to meet and exceed expectations, creating products and services that are not only technologically advanced but also deeply human-centric. Leaders can unlock unprecedented levels of innovation, customer satisfaction, and business value by recognizing and fostering empathy within their teams.

Empathy is not a static concept but a dynamic force that shapes how Platform Engineering teams interact, build, and deliver. By leveraging cognitive, emotional, and compassionate empathy, organizations can create platforms and processes that meet technical requirements and the deeper, human-centric needs of the teams that rely on them.

Platform Engineering is rooted in empathy

Platform Engineering thrives on empathy, bridging the gap between the systems it creates and those who rely on them—primarily developers and operations teams. Empathy drives platform engineers to design solutions that reduce complexity, streamline workflows, and empower teams to deliver value more effectively.

Empathy in Platform Engineering translates into practical benefits that drive business value, faster delivery, and reduced pain points, as illustrated in the following diagram:

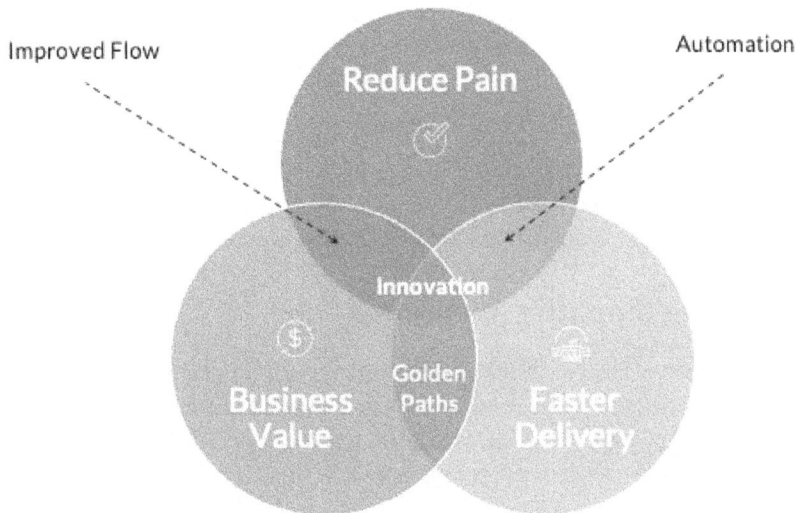

Figure 3.3: Platform Engineering is rooted in empathy

Empathy in Platform Engineering often focuses on minimizing pain points experienced by internal users, such as developers. For example, cognitive load is a common challenge for developers working across disparate systems. Empathy-driven initiatives such as creating **golden paths** help alleviate this. Golden paths are standardized, pre-optimized workflows or processes that guide developers to achieve everyday tasks—such as setting up CI/CD pipelines or deploying applications—quickly and reliably, without having to navigate unnecessary complexity. These paths reduce cognitive overhead, promote consistency, and free up developers to focus on writing code and experimenting with new ideas.

An empathetic approach also extends to automation. Platform engineers reduce manual toil and improve system reliability by automating repetitive and error-prone tasks. For instance, automating incident management processes with tools such as PagerDuty or integrating proactive monitoring with Prometheus can reduce **mean time to recovery** (**MTTR**), enabling teams to respond to issues faster and with less stress. This combination of automation and empathetic design ensures that developers can maintain momentum even in high-pressure situations.

Platform Engineering teams often rely on direct feedback from their users to drive these improvements. For instance, a Platform Engineering team implemented developer feedback loops at a major bank to refine their internal developer portal. By understanding the specific frustrations of their users—such as slow onboarding processes or insufficient documentation—they introduced features such as self-service provisioning and dynamic API catalogs. These changes empowered developers to resolve issues independently, improving satisfaction and productivity across the organization.

Empathy also fosters innovation by reducing the friction associated with experimentation. When developers know they have automated safety nets—such as robust version control and rapid rollback capabilities—they feel more confident trying new approaches. This minimizes the risks of failure and encourages creative problem-solving, which drives organizational innovation.

Ultimately, empathy in Platform Engineering isn't just about technical improvements—it's about creating an environment where developers feel supported and empowered to do their best work. By focusing on user-centric solutions, reducing cognitive load, and enabling seamless workflows, empathy becomes a catalyst for organizational growth and innovation.

Having established the transformative power of empathy, it's time to delve into its practical applications. Let's explore how compassionate empathy can be effectively implemented within Platform Engineering and DevOps to create meaningful and impactful technological solutions.

Compassionate empathy in action

The practical application of compassionate empathy within Platform Engineering and DevOps is not just theoretical—it's the heart of transformative technology that resonates with practitioners and end-users alike. By translating empathy into tangible actions, teams elevate their work from the mechanical to the meaningful, creating systems and solutions deeply attuned to human needs and experiences.

- **Empathic automation**: Automating repetitive tasks in Platform Engineering is an act of compassion that frees up creative energy. Streamlining processes allows colleagues to focus on innovation, problem-solving, and growth. Empathetic automation is not just about efficiency but about improving daily lives. It fosters a supportive environment where team morale and productivity thrive.

- **Golden paths – The empathetic highways of delivery**: Golden paths in Platform Engineering are optimized, predefined workflows that reduce stress and friction for developers during product development. By simplifying complex processes, such as CI/CD pipelines or infrastructure provisioning, they empower developers to focus on writing high-quality code rather than navigating operational challenges. While golden paths don't directly alter the software produced, they enable teams to work more efficiently and experiment confidently, leading to faster iterations and more innovative solutions. Their development reflects an organization's commitment to reducing cognitive load and valuing the time and skills of its teams.

- **Strategic disruption for organizational well-being**: Fueled by compassionate empathy, strategic disruption redefines how organizations approach change. It puts the well-being of individuals at the center of ambitious transformations. Platform Engineering teams transform internal tools and workflows, improving developer productivity and reducing intrinsic pain points. While these efforts may not directly shape the products paid customers consume, they enable developers to build higher-quality software faster, ultimately contributing to better end-user experiences and more innovative customer-facing solutions. In this regard, Platform Engineering revolutionizes products and work culture by improving happiness and reducing intrinsic pain points. This human-focused disruption leads to a productive and joyful organization where team members feel genuinely supported, and users feel deeply understood.

Platform engineers who approach each project with compassionate empathy demonstrate unparalleled skill and humanity. They drive transformation, turning technology into an art that enhances lives and reshapes experiences. Their empathetic craftsmanship transcends technical boundaries, becoming a beacon of human-centric innovation.

Platform engineers achieve this by crafting tools, frameworks, and workflows that amplify the productivity and creativity of their teams. Their efforts often manifest in internal developer platforms, self-service solutions, and automated processes that reduce friction in day-to-day operations. They embrace transparent communication, document best practices, and foster knowledge-sharing through regular collaboration sessions or internal tech talks to be recognized as models for others. By building an inclusive ecosystem where team members feel supported and empowered to contribute, platform engineers create a ripple effect of innovation and efficiency across the organization. These collective efforts demonstrate the profound impact of empathy in engineering, setting the stage for leadership to amplify these values further.

In the next section, we will explore how empathic leadership catalyzes this transformative change, merging human-centric management with technological innovation.

Leadership as the catalyst for empathic change

Empathic leadership is the perfect amalgamation of human-centric management and technological innovation. It is a leadership style that considers people's needs and business requirements equally. This approach transcends traditional paradigms by positioning empathy as the essence of a leader's efficacy and influence.

Empathic leaders possess a crucial ability to connect emotionally, fostering a culture of trust and value within an organization. It elevates leadership from a position of authority to one of profound impact and resonance. By cultivating empathic leadership, organizations can ensure that individuals feel valued and recognized, resulting in robust and sustainable people-focused enterprise growth.

In Platform Engineering and DevOps, leaders foster collaborative environments that drive continuous innovation by aligning team efforts with strategic goals. Empathy in Platform Engineering management is demonstrated by addressing developer pain points, promoting psychological safety, and creating tools that simplify workflows. These efforts impact measurable outputs such as developer productivity, system reliability, and time-to-market improvements.

At the executive level, empathy involves navigating the broader complexities of modern business with a strategic lens. Organizational leaders must balance market trends with the human factors underpinning corporate success, ensuring alignment between vision and execution. Their focus extends to fostering a culture that encourages innovation across all teams, bridging strategic goals with the organization's collective capabilities.

Both levels of leadership require empathy, but their scopes differ: Platform Engineering management drives tactical efficiency and innovation within the team, while executive leadership ensures the alignment of human-centric values with overarching business objectives.

Becoming an empathic leader

Becoming an empathic leader may seem like a journey marked with challenges, but it's an attainable transformation achieved through mindful practice. To demystify this process, we offer six accessible steps, each a straightforward action, to cultivate a leadership style that's both profoundly human and impactful.

- **Be authentic**: Credibility is earned through action, not words. As a leader, being genuine and authentic is crucial. Deliver on commitments with precision and timeliness, aligning words with deeds to build trust. Aim for a say-to-do ratio as close to one as possible, demonstrating a genuine commitment to your promises. True authenticity requires effort and action. Authentic leaders back up their words with actions, establishing a culture of keeping promises and building trust, which is the cornerstone of leadership.

- **Be vulnerable**: Effective leadership requires showing vulnerability with boundaries and embracing the courage to learn and grow from adversity. Authenticity and openness are essential traits of modern leaders, building deep connections and trust within teams. Personal anecdotes and team participation are not weaknesses but strengths that foster deep connections and trust. Leaders create genuine connections with their teams by cultivating openness, candor, and transparent communication.

- **Be approachable**: Leaders who engage directly with their teams gain firsthand insights into team dynamics, innovation, and impediments. To foster an environment of open communication, leaders should be approachable, breaking down barriers by hosting **Ask Me Anything (AMA)** sessions, organizing "Lean Coffees," and skip-level conversations. Encouraging open dialogue leads to valuable insights that can drive the organization forward.

- **Be attentive**: Any team member who seeks out a leader is displaying courage by overcoming their fears. Leaders must provide undivided attention and create an environment of open and honest dialogue to address their concerns. They must practice active listening to demonstrate their commitment to understanding their team fully. Instead of asking "Why," which can be judgmental, asking "How" helps uncover the root of challenges. In this way, leaders can create and foster psychologically safe environments in their organizations.

- **Be appreciative**: Show appreciation openly, letting the team know that their efforts do not go unnoticed. Provide feedback thoughtfully and privately, ensuring it's constructive and empathetic. Empathy in recognizing and evaluating outlier behaviors ensures that even when course corrections are needed, leaders can implement them with care and respect.

- **Be connected**: Stay in tune with your team, looking out for signs of overwork or burnout, and strive to reduce manual toil. A connected leader is proactive about their team's well-being, implementing measures to prevent burnout before it happens. By remaining engaged with your team's workload and stress levels, you demonstrate a commitment to their health and career longevity.

You do not need a leadership title to lead with empathy. Your actions to improve human quality of life in adverse times makes you a leader. The following figure outlines six essential steps leaders can take to develop empathy, nurture empathy within their teams, and drive transformational success.

Be Authentic
Say-to-Do Ratio close to 1
Helping can be hard
1

Be Vulnerable
Wear your heart on your sleeve
Vulnerability with boundaries
2

Be Approachable
Gemba walks, MBWA
Skip levels, AMAs, Lean coffees
3

4 **Be Attentive**
Active full-body listening
Ask "How" instead of "Why"

5 **Be Appreciative**
Praise in public. Feedback in private
Evaluate outlier behavior with empathy

6 **Be Connected**
Look for signs of overwork or burnout
Reduse manual toll

Figure 3.4: Six simple steps to become an empathic leader

Leadership is not about titles but the impact of your actions. Empathic leaders guide their teams through uncertainty, drive innovation, and create an environment that fosters transformative success. Committing to these simple steps can spark significant change in your professional domain. Building a culture of psychological safety is essential, and celebrating failure is crucial for innovation in Platform Engineering. The principles of empathic leadership are not just benevolent but strategic.

One of the critical components that support this approach is psychological safety. Let's explore why psychological safety is paramount for innovation and its pivotal role in Platform Engineering.

Psychological safety – The bedrock of innovation

Psychological safety is vital to modern organizational practices, especially in high-stakes functions such as Platform Engineering and DevOps. It encourages a collaborative culture that empowers individuals to speak up, share ideas, express concerns, and admit mistakes without fear of retaliation. This foundation is critical to fostering innovation and success in any business.

For example, Google's research on high-performing teams revealed that psychological safety was the most critical factor influencing team effectiveness. In a Platform Engineering context, the lack of psychological safety can lead to suppressed concerns about flawed code deployments, ultimately resulting in extended downtime or security breaches. Conversely, fostering psychological safety enables engineers to identify and resolve issues proactively, leading to measurable outcomes such as faster incident response times, reduced system downtime, and increased deployment frequency. By cultivating a safe space for open dialogue and collaboration, organizations can unlock the full potential of their teams, driving operational excellence and innovation.

Leaders play a pivotal role in nurturing this culture. It begins with their mindset: seeing the organization as a collective where every voice holds value, curiosity is championed over immediate judgment, and learning is celebrated as execution. The empathic leader recognizes that psychological safety is the fertile ground from which the seeds of innovation sprout. They understand that how they respond to failures, handle conflicts, and set the tone for communication directly shapes the team's comfort in taking intellectual risks.

By fostering an environment where team members can admit to not knowing, the organization is taking its first step toward learning more. When leaders dismantle the barriers of fear, they liberate their teams from the shackles of conformity. In doing so, they enable a depth of creative thinking and collaboration that drives groundbreaking solutions. Leaders who earnestly endeavor to build psychologically safe workplaces are constructing the very scaffoldings upon which the future of Platform Engineering will rise, innovate, and ultimately triumph.

A crucial aspect of building such a culture is how an organization approaches failure. Embracing and celebrating failures can become a powerful catalyst for innovation and growth. Let's explore how recognizing failure as an opportunity for learning and improvement can drive resilience and creativity within any organization.

Embracing and celebrating failures

Embracing failures is a powerful catalyst for innovation, learning, and resilience within any organization. A culture that recognizes failure as a stepping stone to success fosters an environment of growth and continuous improvement. By shifting our mindset from viewing failure as a setback to embracing it as validated learning, we encourage the organization to take calculated risks and explore new possibilities.

In engineering contexts, metrics such as MTTR, change failure rate, and error budget burn rate provide concrete ways to monitor and celebrate failure tolerance. For example, a low MTTR indicates that the team is effectively learning from failures and recovering quickly while tracking change failure rate highlights areas for improvement in deployment processes. Similarly, error budget burn rate ensures a balance between innovation and system stability, allowing teams to take calculated risks without compromising reliability. These metrics quantify resilience and help teams visualize progress in cultivating a failure-tolerant culture.

Leaders can further enhance this approach by implementing regular empathy and team dynamic assessments. Simple exercises, such as conducting postmortem retrospectives that emphasize blameless analysis or using team surveys to gauge psychological safety and trust levels, can provide valuable insights into the organization's readiness to embrace failure. Checklists to evaluate how frequently lessons from failures are shared and integrated into processes help leaders consistently focus on growth and innovation.

Leaders who embrace the notion that one team's failure is a learning opportunity for the entire organization encourage a culture of collective growth and knowledge-sharing. This approach aligns with DevOps and Platform Engineering principles, where the iterative process of build, measure, and learn is fundamental. Businesses can build resilient, innovative teams that drive success by emphasizing learning from mistakes and focusing on team growth.

In hypothesis-driven development, only some experiments will succeed—the team factors the probability of failure into the cost of innovation. When a hypothesis doesn't yield the expected outcome, the organization should use it as a learning opportunity to improve future projects. Penalizing the team is counterproductive. Insights gained from dissecting the failure can inform future projects.

Perfection is like the horizon – unattainable, yet continuously pursued. The pursuit of excellence is an ongoing journey, not a final destination. Organizations must embrace this concept to create a safe space for employees to express their creativity, propose new ideas, and challenge the status quo without fear of negative repercussions. Doing so leads to a culture of innovation and growth.

In this journey toward excellence, it's essential to recognize that progress often stems from embracing imperfection. Organizations often struggle with the misconception that every process must be perfect before automation can be implemented. However, perfection is not a prerequisite for progress. For example, some companies delay automating workflows because certain steps remain too complex for current tools. A more effective approach is automating straightforward, repetitive tasks first, allowing humans to handle the nuanced or complex steps. This hybrid approach accelerates operational efficiency and frees employees to focus on higher-value activities, fostering creativity and innovation. Organizations can unlock significant value by embracing incremental improvements without waiting for unattainable perfection.

Leaders must safeguard their teams from the negative consequences of failure and create a culture of trust that encourages innovation. When employees feel supported, they are more likely to engage in behaviors that drive the organization forward rather than retreating into self-preservation modes that can stagnate growth. Leaders who prioritize protecting their teams from failure foster a sense of security that enables their employees to take calculated risks and achieve success.

However, leaders who wish to embrace failure must also be cognizant of the impact of their decisions on psychological safety. Abrupt decisions such as layoffs can undermine trust and safety, which are critical for encouraging people to take risks. Such actions can create a culture of fear, leading to lower morale, productivity, and innovation. Furthermore, it can alter a generative culture into a pathological one, which is antithetical to Platform Engineering and DevOps goals.

Effective leaders must lead with empathy to turn failures into opportunities for growth. Creating an environment where employees feel safe to share their failures will enable an organization to harness the full potential of its people and pivot failures into powerful learnings that drive success.

Embracing failure is essential in Platform Engineering. Agile and DevOps methodologies are built on it. Failure is the bedrock of rapid iteration and continuous feedback. It's what drives sustained innovation and competitive advantage for forward-thinking organizations.

Let's inspire teams to appreciate the learning that comes from failures. Every team member should feel safe and valued and contribute to collective success.

> **Dispel the myth that "Failure is not an option"**
>
> In a world of lean experimentation, what some call failure, empathic leaders see as unintended outcomes. Challenge the unrealistic desire for infallibility—100% uptime, zero defects—are these realistic, or do they hinder innovation? If each result teaches us something new, isn't that a form of success? Ask yourself, when is the pursuit of perfection actually a barrier to progress?

The role of an empathic leader is crucial in fostering this environment. Empathetic leadership goes beyond understanding; it involves creating a nurturing atmosphere where everyone feels valued and safe to express their ideas and learn from failures. Let's examine how empathic leaders can drive innovation through their unique approach.

The empathic leader's role in fostering innovation

Empathetic leadership is more than understanding your team; it is about creating a nurturing environment where everyone feels valued. Leaders who prioritize empathy foster psychological safety, essential for promoting creativity and innovation. They encourage team members to communicate their ideas, concerns, and questions without fear of negative consequences. Embracing failure is seen as an opportunity for collective learning and growth. Empathetic leaders create a culture that values feedback and uses it to improve together.

Empathic leaders start by being self-aware and emotionally intelligent. They manage their emotions and recognize the importance of the human element in the workplace, creating a positive, open, and collaborative atmosphere. They acknowledge that each person's unique experiences and insights contribute to a diverse, rich, and innovative organization.

Empathetic leaders are beacons for their teams during uncertain times. They build trust by showing genuine interest in their team's aspirations, being vulnerable, and cultivating an environment where ideas can be shared freely without criticism. This trust is the cornerstone of a culture that values innovation. Team members are motivated to venture beyond their comfort zones when they know their voices matter and they are supported.

In a world where technology and Platform Engineering are swiftly reshaping the business landscape, empathic leadership stands as a powerful ally. It ensures that technological advancement does not overshadow the human aspect of transformation. Through empathy, leaders can harness the full potential of their teams, guiding Platform Engineering endeavors with a humane and insightful approach that not only meets but exceeds expectations.

Empathic leadership is just the beginning. Organizations need robust strategic frameworks to truly transform and thrive in the digital era. Enter the POWER framework, a transformative strategy that combines innovation with operational excellence to convert vision into reality. Let's explore how this framework can empower your organization to lead with agility and foresight.

Orchestrating cultural transformation – The power of strategic frameworks

Navigating the digital era requires a strategic framework that can transform a vision into reality. Such frameworks empower organizations to direct change rather than react to it. Platform Engineering is a prime example, combining innovation with flawless operation to drive growth and deliver value. It's within this paradigm that operational excellence becomes versatile.

In this section, we will discuss the critical aspects of the POWER framework for cultural transformation. We will explore how to drive innovation with Platform Engineering by speeding up time to market, seamlessly scaling, and embracing rapid change. We'll also focus on creating a positive culture by fostering trust and empathy, ensuring psychological safety, and establishing quick feedback loops. Additionally, we will cover the measurement and optimization of operations, emphasizing continuous feedback and improvement while integrating security into the development life cycle. Finally, we will examine the significance of empowering teams by enabling, educating, engaging, and removing obstacles to innovation. Understanding these elements will help you grasp how the POWER framework can steer your organization toward sustained innovation and operational excellence.

Unleashing innovation with Platform Engineering

Platform Engineering is not just about building and operating systems—it is about creating an ecosystem where innovation is as natural as breathing. The endeavor begins with accelerating time to market—delivering swiftly with precision and relevance. This acceleration is not merely a rush to release but a calculated enhancement of pace, ensuring solutions are timely, customer-centric, and of superior quality.

Next, we must scale with agility seamlessly and automatically. Scaling seamlessly and automatically isn't just about growth; it's about scaling smart, where systems adapt in real time, effortlessly responding to user demands and market shifts. It is where the elegance of automation meets the robustness of design. Technology must be robust, resilient, and flexible, allowing businesses to grow without the growing pains of overhauling foundational systems.

Rapid change is the lifeblood of innovation. In the Platform Engineering ethos, we embrace and welcome change, allowing teams to pivot precisely and ensuring adaptability is an integral part of the organization's operations. Enabling quick and confident adjustments, whether in response to new insights, shifting trends, or unexpected challenges, ensures the organization remains proactive and reactive—resilient in the face of fluctuation.

What underpins these steps is cultivating a positive culture. Trust, empathy, psychological safety, and fast feedback loops are the elements that cultivate an innovative mindset, converting ideas into action. This is how a positive culture is engineered into every team interaction, every project, every initiative—making it part of the organization's DNA.

Measuring and optimizing operations is an ongoing commitment to excellence. It's a continuous loop of feedback and enhancement, ensuring systems don't just run but evolve, driven by data and honed by experience.

Minimizing security vulnerabilities is critical in a world where threats are as constant as they are elusive. By embedding security into the development life cycle, we ensure that robustness is a default, not an afterthought.

Finally, we must enable, educate, engage, and eliminate—a clarion call to empower teams, enlighten with knowledge, engage with purpose, and eliminate obstacles to innovation. It's where leaders catalyze action, and teams own their transformation journey.

The following figure illustrates the core processes that drive innovation in Platform Engineering: accelerating time to market, scaling seamlessly, enabling rapid change, fostering a positive culture, measuring and optimizing operations, minimizing security vulnerabilities, and empowering teams.

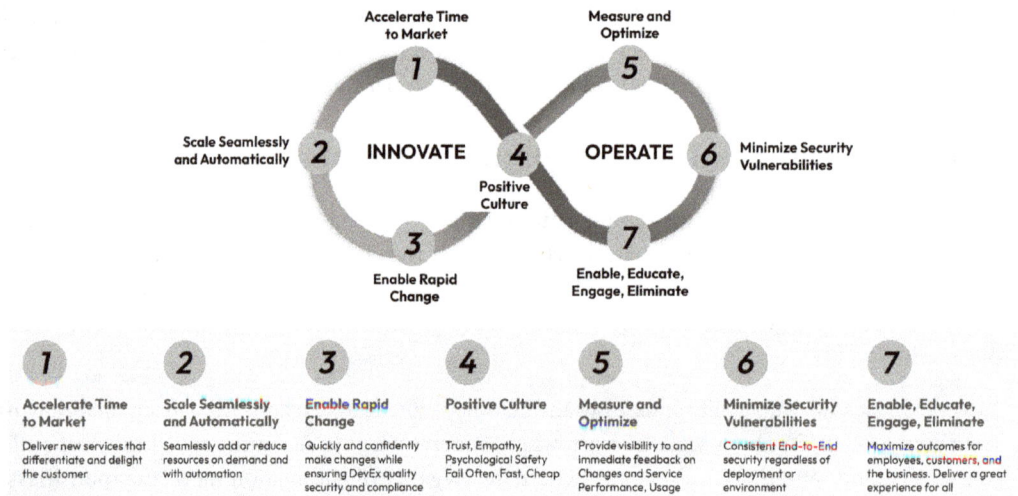

Figure 3.5: Unleashing innovation with Platform Engineering

This systemic thinking embodies a continuous, dynamic process reminiscent of the familiar DevOps loop but expanded in scope. **Innovate** and **Operate** replace the traditional **Dev** and **Ops**, reflecting a more inclusive approach. Innovation is no longer the sole province of developers; it is the remit of every individual within the organization. Similarly, operation is a collective endeavor, ensuring the sustainability and quality of service delivery.

Platform Engineering advocates a shared responsibility for innovation and operational excellence. The *Innovate-Operate loop* is a subtle nod to the DevOps methodology, echoing its principles but expanding them to foster a broader, organization-wide commitment to continuous improvement and excellence. The POWER framework serves as a strategic compass to accelerate the delivery of business value. It crystallizes Platform Engineering into a transformative strategy, molding technology, processes, and people into a cohesive force that delivers unequivocal value.

The POWER framework

In a rapidly transforming organization, strategic direction is crucial to accelerate the delivery of business value. The **POWER framework** is the answer to this call. It is a compass in the complexity of modern enterprise, crystallizing Platform Engineering into a transformative strategy. It's a mindset that molds technology, processes, and people into a cohesive force geared toward delivering unequivocal value. The POWER framework consists of the following:

- **Purpose**: The genesis of any transformative journey begins with *Why*. The purpose is the compass that navigates Platform Engineering endeavors, ensuring that every technological pursuit or process innovation aligns with the organization's overarching mission. It's about delivering value that resonates not just with market trends but with the intrinsic objectives that define the company's existence. By embedding purpose into workflows, teams can ensure their efforts contribute meaningfully to business objectives. For example, aligning platform goals with customer satisfaction metrics ensures that engineering outputs directly impact user value.

- **Outcomes**: The endgame of Platform Engineering is not to deploy technology for its own sake but to achieve meaningful outcomes that propel the business forward. Outcomes are the tangible manifestations of purpose, the benchmarks against which success is measured. They transform abstract goals into concrete targets, forging a path that's clear, quantifiable, and relentlessly pursued. In practice, these include measurable improvements such as reduced system downtime, increased deployment frequency, or enhanced developer productivity. Using tools such as DORA metrics (deployment frequency, lead time for changes) helps teams focus on outcomes that matter most to the business.

- **Workflow optimization**: Efficiency is paramount, but not at the cost of efficacy. Workflow optimization in Platform Engineering means streamlining processes to deliver value quicker, reducing friction in the value stream, and optimizing the flow of value from conception to customer. It's a meticulous orchestration of tasks, ensuring that each step is refined for maximum impact with minimum waste. Techniques such as value stream mapping and tools such as Planview help identify and address bottlenecks. For example, automating repetitive tasks such as CI/CD deployments enables teams to deliver faster while maintaining quality.

- **Empower**: The true potential of a team is unleashed when each member is empowered. In Platform Engineering, empowerment involves equipping teams with tools such as self-service developer portals and providing autonomy to make decisions. Empowerment ensures that developers can innovate without being hindered by dependencies or bottlenecks, fostering a culture of ownership and accountability. For instance, introducing a provisioning dashboard allows developers to deploy resources independently, accelerating development cycles.

- **Reduce manual toil**: Automation is the backbone of modern Platform Engineering, but its real aim is to reduce manual toil. This is not merely a pursuit of convenience but a strategic move to liberate human intellect for higher-order thinking. This principle is exemplified by tools such as Terraform for infrastructure as code or automated testing pipelines. Reducing manual toil enables teams to focus on creativity, innovation, and strategic problem-solving while eliminating repetitive, error-prone tasks. By eliminating repetitive tasks, we allow creativity and strategy to flourish, paving the way for innovation and growth.

Each of these components of the POWER framework is a cog in the business value machine to create an ecosystem where Platform Engineering is not just a function but a strategic advantage. It's a mindset that permeates through every layer of the organization, empowering teams, optimizing workflows, and delivering on the promise of technology with purpose and precision.

Figure 3.6 highlights the POWER framework, detailing its essential pillars: Purpose, Outcomes, Workflow Optimization, Empowerment, and Reducing Manual Toil, as drivers of organizational excellence.

Purpose
Clearly articulate the Why
What value are we providing?

Outcomes
What do we want to achieve?
What is the definition of success?

Workflow Optimization
How can we deliver value quicker?
How can we reduce friction in the value stream?

Empower
How can we empathize, enable, entrust, and equip our teams for success?

Reduce Manual Toil
Improve automation footprint
Lean experimentation. Agile methods

Figure 3.6: The POWER framework

Case study – POWER in action

A FinTech company adopted the POWER framework to overcome challenges in scaling their infrastructure and improving developer productivity. Here's how they applied each component:

- **Purpose**: The team aligned their Platform Engineering efforts with the company's mission to provide seamless, reliable financial transactions. They prioritized projects that improved transaction uptime and developer experience, ensuring their work resonated with the broader organizational goals.

- **Outcomes**: To measure success, they defined clear objectives, including a 20% increase in deployment frequency and a 30% reduction in lead time for changes. They used DORA metrics to track progress, ensuring their efforts were directly tied to quantifiable improvements.

- **Workflow Optimization**: The team identified bottlenecks in their CI/CD pipeline by conducting value stream mapping. They implemented Argo Workflows to automate deployment processes, reducing friction and enabling faster, more reliable releases.

- **Empower**: The team developed a self-service developer portal using Backstage, allowing the developers to provision resources and manage deployments independently. This eliminated dependencies on the operations team, increasing autonomy and reducing wait times.

- **Reduce Manual Toil**: The team adopted Terraform for infrastructure as code, automating the provisioning and management of cloud resources. This reduced the time spent on repetitive infrastructure tasks, freeing engineers to focus on strategic initiatives.

Measurable outcomes and continuous feedback

Implementing the POWER framework led to a 25% increase in deployment frequency and a 40% reduction in MTTR. Monthly feedback loops with developers ensured continuous improvement and alignment with evolving needs. By embracing the POWER framework, the FinTech company created a scalable, resilient, and efficient platform that empowered developers and aligned with organizational goals.

The POWER framework is a revolutionary tool that positions Platform Engineering as a beacon of strategic thought. It urges leaders to recognize the integration of technology and human ingenuity as keystones to a future where innovation is systemic, leadership is enlightened, and success results from a deliberate, empathic strategy. By embracing the POWER framework, leaders can find a blueprint for excellence, creating an environment where Platform Engineering becomes the driving force behind sustainable innovation and competitive edge.

Incorporating other transformation frameworks

Integrating the POWER framework with venerable change models such as **Kotter's 8-Step Change Model** and the **McKinsey 7-S Framework** creates a multidimensional strategy for organizational transformation that aligns seamlessly with Platform Engineering and DevOps initiatives. This integration ensures that the pursuit of transformation is not merely sequential but holistic, recognizing the multifaceted nature of change.

Purpose becomes the guiding principle, akin to Kotter's creation of urgency and McKinsey's shared values, underscoring the mission that mobilizes and unites teams toward a common goal. The POWER framework ensures that the organization's heartbeat is synchronized with the rhythm of change, driving every initiative forward with clarity and conviction.

Outcomes are the tangible benchmarks, reflecting Kotter's vision and strategies and McKinsey's system, where strategic goals and tangible results define the success of Platform Engineering projects. By delineating clear objectives, the POWER framework operationalizes the vision, setting ambitious yet achievable milestones and ensuring that every technological advancement contributes to the organization's overarching goals.

Workflow Optimization in the POWER framework leverages Lean principles to minimize waste and maximize value, mirroring the continuous enhancement ethos of Platform Engineering. This streamlining is further bolstered by Kotter's notion of enabling action and the structural alignment within McKinsey's framework, ensuring that every process is refined for peak performance.

In **Empower**, we amalgamate Kotter's empowerment for broad-based action and McKinsey's style and staff elements to create a culture of autonomy and decisive action. The POWER framework recognizes that for Platform Engineering to thrive, teams need the tools and the authority to innovate and make impactful decisions.

The focus on **Reducing Manual Toil** resonates with Lean's drive toward efficiency and the technical agility inherent in DevOps. It reflects a strategic pivot from rote tasks to cognitive, innovative work, enhancing job satisfaction and sparking creative problem-solving.

This strategy does not suggest merely adopting a new framework; it champions a transformative paradigm and calls on leaders to recalibrate their approach. Integrating the POWER framework with these established change models arms leaders with a dynamic array of tools for managing transformation. It affords a nuanced view of the organization, aligning operational aspects with the agility and innovation demanded by modern Platform Engineering.

Benefits of the POWER framework

The POWER framework, which focuses on purpose-driven action and outcome-oriented strategies, is pivotal in shaping organizational culture. It is a catalyst that inspires innovation and instills a generative culture—a fertile environment where ideas flourish and collaboration reigns.

In Platform Engineering, applying the POWER framework accelerates development cycles and enhances delivery speeds, ensuring that business value is delivered consistently and with a velocity that aligns with market demands. The framework builds a foundation for agility and adaptability by streamlining workflows and empowering teams—a necessary stance in today's ever-evolving technological landscape.

Moreover, the POWER framework is instrumental in cultivating psychological safety. It encourages an empathic leadership style focused on reducing manual toil, thereby creating happier workplaces where team members can engage without fear, innovate without restraint, and operate with the confidence that their well-being is a priority.

For leaders, the POWER framework is invaluable. It provides a clear, actionable blueprint for driving change beyond mere process adjustments. It transforms an organization's ethos, guiding it towards a generative culture where continuous improvement, employee satisfaction, and operational excellence become the norm.

Effectively, the POWER framework is not just about changing development or operations—it's about transforming lives. It redefines the leader's role from being a mere overseer of tasks to becoming a visionary architect of a workplace that is as human-centered as it is technologically advanced. Doing so ensures that organizations don't just survive in the competitive business arena—they thrive.

Summary

This chapter highlights the power of cultural transformation and empathic leadership, using strategic frameworks such as POWER to navigate modern enterprise complexities. The pillars of building a generative culture are purpose, outcomes, workflow optimization, empowerment, and reducing manual labor. These elements redefine leadership and create an organizational ethos that fosters innovation, nurtures psychological safety, and embraces failure as a pathway to learning and growth. Now, we will delve into the Platform Engineering ecosystem to put these principles into practice through technology.

This journey equips leaders with the tools and insights to create a transformative, generative culture within their organizations.

> **Call to action**
>
> **Cultivate empathic leadership**: Start by assessing your leadership approach through the lens of empathy. Conduct workshops and training sessions within your organization to foster empathic leadership qualities across all levels. Encourage leaders to practice active listening and vulnerability, and prioritize their teams' well-being, setting the tone for a culture of psychological safety and openness.
>
> **Adopt and adapt the POWER framework**: Evaluate your current organizational frameworks and processes in light of the POWER principles. Identify areas for integration and enhancement. Implement the framework step by step, ensuring that each aspect of POWER is aligned with your organizational goals. Thus, you will foster a culture conducive to innovation and operational excellence.
>
> **Embrace and learn from failure**: Create policies and practices that celebrate failures as essential learning opportunities. Establish forums or channels where teams can share their unintended outcomes and the insights gained, promoting a mindset shift across the organization to view failures as stepping stones to success and innovation.

Further reading

- Westrum, R. "A Typology of Organisational Cultures." *Quality and Safety in Health Care*, vol. 13, no. suppl_2, 1 Dec. 2004, pp. ii22–ii27, https://doi.org/10.1136/qshc.2003.009522.

- State of Agile Culture 2020-21 Report - https://www.agilebusiness.org/static/d33daf7d-d4ad-4fb1-80d9a2ff857ffb9d/State-of-Agile-Culture-Report-2020-21.pdf.

- Schaefer, Edward. "Agile Ideation." *Agile Ideation*, 10 July 2023, https://agile-ideation.com/blog/generative-culture-cornerstone-values.

- Leleux, Benoit F., et al. "Freitag: Designing the Agile Company (Video Case) - IMD Business School for Management and Leadership Courses." *IMD Business School for Management and Leadership Courses*, 18 Sept. 2024, www.imd.org/research-knowledge/agility/case-studies/freitag-designing-the-agile-company-video-case/.

- Gulati, Ranjay, Allison Ciechanover, and Jeff Huizinga. "Netflix: A Creative Approach to Culture and Agility." Harvard Business School Case 420-055, September 2019, https://hbsp.harvard.edu/product/420055-PDF-ENG.

- Edmondson, A. C., Higgins, M., Singer, S., & Weiner, J. (2016). Understanding Psychological Safety in Health Care and Education Organizations: A Comparative Perspective. *Research in Human Development*, 13(1), 65–83. https://doi.org/10.1080/15427609.2016.1141280.

Get This Book's PDF Version and Exclusive Extras

Scan the QR code (or go to packtpub.com/unlock). Search for this book by name, confirm the edition, and then follow the steps on the page.

Note: Keep your invoice handly. Purchase made directly from packt don't require one.

4

The Platform Engineering Ecosystem

Recently, Platform Engineering has become a staple for those interested in DevOps solutions to accelerate time to market. Just like DevOps engineers, platform engineers have become the up-and-coming roles to hire as a new skill set to potentially fix old problems. Platform Engineering is not just about installing a single software solution or implementing configuration as code but adjusting the entire delivery ecosystem. Ecosystems are systems of interacting parts, in this case, all the parts needed to create an operational environment. Good platforms incorporate numerous tools and capabilities to achieve success. Integrating those tools within different aspects of the platform is a key element of effective platforms. Further, those tools should be incorporated into **Continuous Integration/ Continuous Deployment (CI/CD)** pipelines through a DevOps methodology.

In this chapter, you'll gain insights into selecting and integrating the tools and practices that align with your platform strategy. We'll explore how to incorporate essential tools into various platform architectures and identify the technologies that most effectively support platform performance and scalability. You'll also learn how to implement Kubernetes-based solutions for building and managing containers across the platform. Finally, we'll cover how to integrate pipelines into the platform build, focusing on how platforms manage these pipelines to ensure reliability, scalability, and consistent delivery of new features.

We will be covering the following main topics:

- The essential platform ecosystem tools
- Orchestrating the platform ecosystem
- Platform software delivery ecosystems

The three sections in this chapter each address the key areas to understand to integrate platforms. The first section discusses legacy tools through building infrastructure, addressing baseline configurations, and integrating version control. The next section deals with orchestrating the system to ensure all pieces function correctly. Finally, the last section discusses converting the platform into a delivery engine, expediting the delivery of production applications to the user.

The essential Platform Engineering tools

Starting an ecosystem can be challenging. When we think about ecosystems, we typically think about how to integrate with an existing ecosystem rather than building one from scratch. You must consider not only the tools desired but also the conjunction of those tools in operating successfully. A platform with broad tool options that do not interact with each other can increase operation costs and provide only a small amount of value, if any. Integrating a platform ecosystem requires evaluating and comparing multiple interactions to find the best fit for your organization.

A number of years ago, one of us received a locked aquarium with a plant, a snail, and two African Dwarf frogs in about 350 milliliters of water as a holiday gift. The idea was that the ecosystem would be self-sustainable: the frogs would eat the plant and the snail would eat the waste. Every participant would be happy, and no external cleaning would be required other than the occasional feeding. The drawback was that the frogs required 7.5 liters of water each to be social. This meant the frogs first killed the snail and then fought each other to the death. At first, we thought that the snail and the frog had been sick, so we simply replaced them. The same thing happened several times before we realized what was happening. At that point, we decided to leave a single frog in the tank, with a plant, and we had to clean the tank regularly. The ecosystem was much different from what had been intended. The same thought applies to the platform ecosystem. Platforms that are too small consume local resources and prevent broad expansion. There must be an expert balance for the platform to function successfully.

Engineering an effective platform goes beyond just identifying different pieces that worked well in a different scenario. Many times, we have seen a presentation at a conference or an online demonstration that offers multiple different, and apparently integrated, capabilities. In some cases, the integration was the result of significant manual work, and in others, those translations happened behind the scenes within a proprietary software black box. Combining those elements within the platform you build requires identifying those linkages and finding the best way to make them work consistently. The goal is a single platform that offers integrated success for anyone involved, moving beyond the individual developer to a broad scope of activities.

Beyond simple integration, two other elements should be considered within a platform ecosystem: compute and storage. Remember, using the cloud means using someone else's servers. **Compute** describes the resources available to conduct computing actions and manage threads through the virtual CPUs available. **Storage** relates to the persistent disk space available on those instances. AWS offers EC2 instances with set numbers, while Azure tends to separate by function, as does Google. A sample of the top-level options for the various functions is shown as follows:

Amazon EC2			
Instance	**vCPU**	**Mem (GiB)**	**Store**
t3a.nano	2	.5	EBS
t3a.micro	2	1	EBS
t3a.small	2	2	EBS
3a.med	2	4	EBS

Azure	
Compute Service – capacity and scale on demand	
App Service	Create cloud apps for web & mobile
Azure CycleCloud	Create, manage, operate, and optimize HPC & clusters
Azure Quantum	Explore quantum hardware, software, solutions
Azure Spot VM	Provision space for interruptible workloads

Google	
Compute	
App Engine	Managed App platform
Bare Metal Soluton	Specialized workload hardware
Cloud Run	Serverless for containerized workloads
Compute Engine	VMs, GPUs. TPUs. Disks
GKE	Managed Kubernetes/containers
VMware Engineer	VMware as a service

Figure 4.1: Sample environments

As AWS was the first to implement this, their cloud offerings provide detail to a more technical specification as the first purchasers wanted to know exactly what they received. The later entrants in selling cloud space offer a more packaged format, to integrate with the functions the customer desires. Each of these providers offers multiple offerings beyond basic compute, some of which may be beneficial in engineering your platform.

Functionally derived options tend to use autoscaling, which can create challenges in assessing pricing early. Techniques can be used to automatically adjust compute and store resources based on demand, meaning you never miss a customer. But this can also lead to excessive charges if a developer leaves an instance running. Another detail is whether you require basic CPUs to host apps or are diving into a machine learning application that requires GPU access from the cloud provider. A third key element for the cloud provider is bandwidth for how fast cloud machines communicate with external users. Any type of platform will require some detailed research on best-fit cloud options, which, unfortunately, is beyond the scope of this chapter.

There are many different elements to consider when developing a unique platform ecosystem. We will dive further into some of the technical and process elements required to bring those various tools to life in the platform. As with the frog scenario, you want to be sure that the included elements have sufficient space and then interact together. Some tools require cloud connections, a larger amount of compute, or more storage available to conduct multiple activities. Each of those interactions must be addressed when building an effective ecosystem.

The next section breaks down the pieces in order to discuss the constraints and challenges associated with each element. In *Chapter 1*, these additions were considered from a generic standpoint of what was possible in engineering. *Chapter 2* then added where these pieces fit into the overall architecture. This section addresses the **Infrastructure as Code (IaC)**, **Configuration Management (CM)**, version control, and monitoring solution elements. The next section addresses specific demands for Kubernetes and service mesh options, while the last considers CI/CD. This allows us to explore the required elements in greater depth.

Infrastructure as code

When starting with a platform, we should think about everything that follows as IaC. This means that all the basic parts of the environment are unpacked and connected to the initial installation. This allows for the unpacking of all the material all at once. You can think about this as having movers who leave all the boxes in the living room versus movers who unpack all the boxes to place items in the same configuration as in the previous house. This provides advantages in rapidly being able to update new versions and automating those unpacking elements, as well as reducing the need to manually configure items when unpacking.

The previous chapter mentioned using Terraform as a declarative language. **Declarative IaC** means only the end requirements are specified, while the platform, in this case, Terraform, handles the steps. The other option is **imperative code**, where the exact elements are defined and the interpreting system does not deviate from those steps. Chef is an example of an imperative tool. Examples of declarative IaC with Terraform are shown here:

```
terraform {
  required_providers {
    aws = {
       source = "PlatformOps/aws"
       version = "~> 3.15"
      }
  }
required_version = ">= 1.2.0"
}
 provider "aws" {
   region = "us-west-2"
}
resource "aws_instance" "ops_server" {
   ami = "ami-830c94e3"
   instance_type = "t3.large"
tags = {
  Name = "ExampleOpServer"
  }
}
```

You can see how various high-level categories are called through the script. In using an imperative language, each call relates to a lower-level script to call forward. When Terraform calls a resource or a version that has backend information, it allows the code to create the required elements. As an example, this would create a t3.large EC2 instance that sets an IP address, allows user access, manages security, and coordinates interactions without specifying those elements directly in the code.

Instead of listing the provider and resources within the code, the language in Chef would call a script that had those items listed as a distinct file. Chef's features help align all the different code elements but can still pose challenges over time. Writing and developing in Chef are completely different areas of study. As a quick reference, Chef uses cookbooks that contain resources, or recipes as a collection of resources. A resource is a Ruby block stating a type, a name, properties associated with values, and a set of actions. However, within the Chef community, many recipes and cookbooks already exist that can be quickly modified to apply to your use case. Here is a sample of the format, and then what a resource line might look like to install an open source Java development kit, or OpenJDK:

```
Type 'name' do attribute 'value' action :type_of_actionend
Package 'java-1.8.0-openjdk do action :installend
```

These lines then use a similar approach to generate recipes that are composed of a number of resources. The functions can be linked together into the overall cookbook to execute the infrastructure across the desired platform. You can easily see the increased control allowed with the imperative approach but also the increased time required to build and deliver. The Chef exception is when a community element already provides sufficient services.

In implementing a platform infrastructure, imperative code would build a unique tool set based on local instructions every time, while with declarative code, high-level modifications could be made to alter instances, clusters, and additional tools. Many third-party tools that you may want to use in infrastructure already have their portion of IaC developed. The challenge becomes integrating those declarative and imperative elements into an overall element that creates the platform. That initial IaC should set code versions, potential linkages, and cloud structures. Obviously, the full IaC for your platform will likely be much longer. Implementing IaC provides some significant security benefits, such as traceability, version control, and reducing manual intervention for routine fixes. Part of a successful IaC integration depends on how it implements CM tools to configurations beyond the initial environment variables.

Configuration management tools

The primary goal for our CM tools is to structure hardware and software usage. An initial interpretation may be that good CM practice means only authorized changes are allowed within a system. When examining our DevOps practices, the goal becomes to automate those configurations, allowing easy deployment. Implementing these goals moves system administration from a manual approach to an automated solution. For example, when setting up an EC2 cloud on Amazon, you can choose the size, the Linux distribution desired, security features, and a variety of other options. These selections allow the management of resources on demand, with each user selecting the desired options, rather than depending on a third party. The traditional practice was submitting a ticket to a help desk, waiting for resolution, and hoping all the parameters were correct. Automation removes the bottleneck and enables a faster flow.

One challenge with CM from the platform context is that each element requires some configuration elements. While the initial IaC provides some options, further configuration requires additional changes. Adds in version control, CI/CD pipelines, and Kubernetes implementation also require managed configuration approaches. The challenge is in separating the various CM elements into manageable and integrated pieces. Returning to the definition of approving only authorized pieces, our platform CM tools should be the ones that are in between the initial system launch and the ongoing development work. Going back to our woodshop analogy from previous chapters, think about CM as how the different tools are placed on the workbench for different users. Good CM can be applied at multiple levels, but this definition has some limits for effective learning.

The best practices for our CM mean we can assign an identification, baseline, version control and audit practices against a regular process. The previous chapter discussed using Ansible, Chef, and Puppet to deploy and control CM. With IaC creating the framework and interactions between all the tools, CM should then approach how those tools are structured within the process. As an example, our IaC deploys an IDE, a workflow tool, a chat function, and a CI/CD process. What we want to do with configuration is create one place where a new user can access those applications and virtual devices.

One example would be using a Terraform instance to create accounts within all those different tools when an overall CM tool is utilized. When starting, this splash page would provide a basic introductory view. The user would then create some workflow structure likely based on an organization, team, and individual user. The organization level would create properties to allow a certain set of tools to be used. For example, one user group on the platform might want exclusively Go-based tools, while another might need Jupyter Notebook and Anaconda. The CM tool links those tools, allowing teams to be created with those same tools, and then moving to users. *Figure 4.2* demonstrates how these links might be constructed:

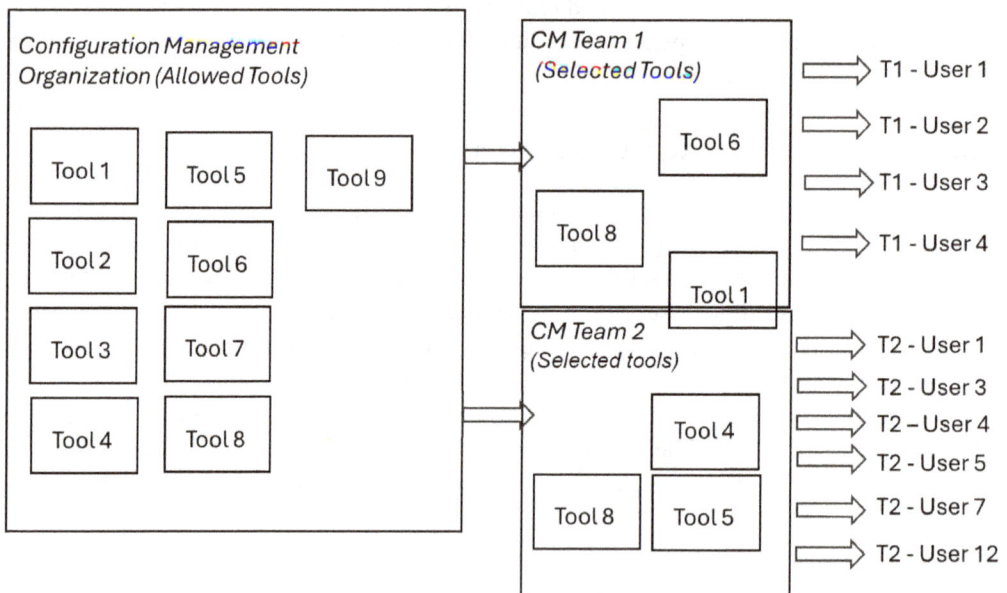

Figure 4.2: Configuration management example

You can see the wide selection of possible tools at the organization level, which are whittled down to only the tools needed for the team. This helps to manage license control and reduce costs. In the example, if **Tool 1** was an asynchronous chat tool such as Mattermost, it might be shared between teams, while **Tool 8** might be a GitHub application that allows each team to manage their own version control. Then, the teams differ on which other applications might be used. These selections can be expanded to allow for one toolset within the collaboration environment and another in the deployment targets, allowing shared pipelines and CI/CD spaces as well.

In looking at the links between tools, some of the important elements are the specification for which features are allowed, specified endpoints, and connections to secret services that hold passwords and encryption keys. These systems might be shared but proper CM ensures only the right person accesses them at the right time. The next aspects of CM tie into version control by only allowing the right software to reach production. This is because an effective version control tool can manage configuration settings as well as software settings.

Software version control systems

Software **Version Control Systems** (**VCSs**), sometimes referred to as source control, are the functions that allow tracking and implementing software code changes. Their primary purpose is to deliver consistent quality across a process, ensuring all users are submitting through the same function. The most widely known tool for VCS is GitHub. GitLab expands its capabilities, and both offer additional paid options. Some alternative VCSs, are Bitbucket, **Subversion** (**SVN**), and Mercurial, which offer a different perspective. The most important element is tracking the original code and then managing forks and branches to this code, as well as integrating those changes into new baselines. Each of these comes with multiple options to display and demonstrate integration. GitKraken, in their web documentation (`https://www.gitkraken.com/`), shows how different versions can be visually displayed.

When visiting the page, one can see samples of various GitKraken implementations. The different colors and branching lines on a GitKraken model show how different changes link to the main source code. Blue lines show the baseline code while the green, purple, and indigo branches show when the code has been split. This allows determining exactly where a change was made and what was included.

To understand the VCS options, we must briefly review what might be included. The basic approach remains relatively simple: you establish a repository and then allow users to duplicate it to make corrections. The most common options integrate distributed version control, allowing multiple users to work at the same time. Repositories can include a single set that must be replicated or multiple file branches allowing users to work on an entire element or a smaller set. Examine the following figure to see how those options might be integrated:

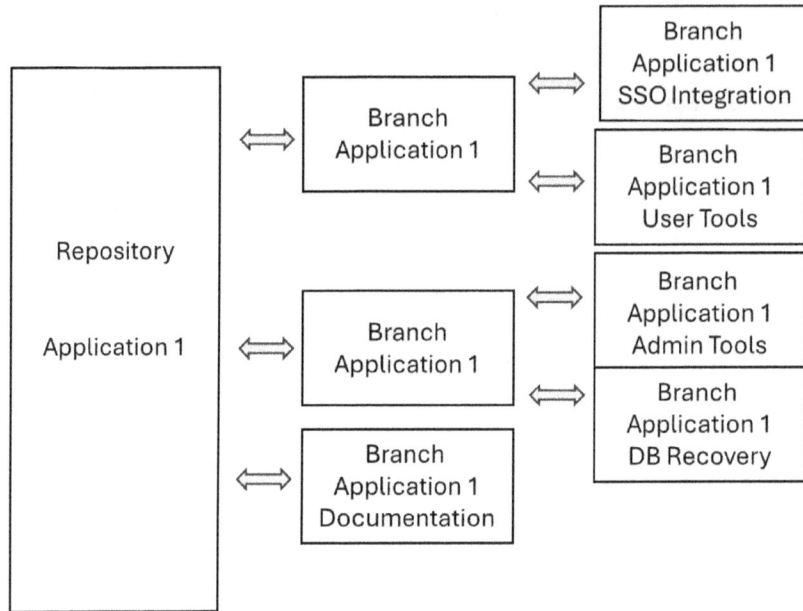

Figure 4.3: Version control illustration

Similar to the GitKraken illustration, but without the pretty colors, the preceding figure shows how different teams can branch different versions to work. The diagram indicates that one set of teams can work on an isolated application to build SSO integration and user tools, another can work on system admin tools and database recovery, while a third team can work on documentation. If these branches do not overlap, then each can be fully tested and reintroduced without affecting other teams. If they do overlap, good VCSs allow approving specific changes. When the two branches are merged back to the repository and then deployed, all the changes would be visible to the user. Each merge is accompanied by pipeline results, merge requests, and approvals, showing exactly where each change became a part of the baseline.

Legacy tool observability

Merely deploying the different tools is not sufficient. You must be able to observe that all elements are functioning correctly and establish metrics. As an easy reference, three basic metrics can be used for each of the preceding elements to create observability. These categories with the associated metrics are listed here:

- **Infrastructure as code**: Deployed version, **Lead Time to Change (LTC)**, system operations.
- **Configuration as code**: Deployed version, time to restore, bug reports.
- **Version control systems**: Deployment frequency, LTC, value stream flow.

When deploying IaC, there are three key observability elements. The first element is the deployed version. Since each IaC element deploys a complete package, it is important to know the version. This allows for changes in security controls, operational items, and other features. If you establish the platform as a core element within the DevOps process, then measuring the LTC shows the difference between each new version. All metrics should be correlated and measured at multiple levels, including individual, team, project, and organization. This allows an organization to measure how long it takes to adapt or change the overall platform. Also important is the influence of various events on the overall value stream. IaC should also create initial dashboards showing elements for storage and compute usage at a minimum. These operational metrics create the ability to plan resource usage and manage system operability.

Monitoring configuration as code enables some key metrics across the platform. When deploying configurations, similar to managing infrastructure, you must always know which configurations customers are executing and in which clusters. This allows quick analysis when problems occur to determine whether they are user errors or system problems. This leads to the next metric, understanding the time to restore. When a platform supports rapid development for multiple teams, any bugs must be addressed quickly. The common understanding is that bugs are things the system should do but does not, compared to new features, which are things you want the system to do but do not appear in the current baseline. The last critical metric is understanding those bug reports and being able to compile an overall perspective of how configuration as code functions within the platform.

The last section, and most clearly tied to the **DevOps Research Association (DORA)** metrics, is understanding the VCS. The DORA metrics are deployment frequency, mean time to change, change failure rate, mean time to recover. The distinction between baseline code, forks, branches, and integration allows you to analyze deployment frequency, that is, how often new code deploys. This integrates with the LTC in showing how long an organization takes to submit a new idea, develop new code, and then push that code into production. The first two metrics then support the broader value stream flow analysis for how the deployed code directly supports profit. One of the main goals of having efficient platforms is rapid profitability, so understanding how much each new version costs and the revenue generated is key to enabling the high-level adoption of platform models within the organization.

We will now take those initial concepts and bring them together. This section has outlined all the pieces required before you even start creating a platform. The next section details the path to start creating a production application.

Orchestrating the platform ecosystem

At this point in the DevOps journey, in moving forward from initial DevOps implementations in 2011, most companies understand that containers and microservices are the primary tools for success. Not all successful models require microservices; some can still use monolith-type approaches to gain success, but those instances are few. The following is an explanation of the two approaches:

- **Microservices**: Architectural model using loosely coupled, focused services with logical operations based on reusable capability in using lightweight protocols to maximize cloud compute and store functions.

- **Monolith**: Single, unified software application, entirely self-contained and independent. Tends to lack flexibility for revision and reversion especially when developers are working in parallel.

Delivering cutting-edge software, maintaining constant updates, and eliminating bugs requires teams of developers to make rapid changes without worrying about infrastructure. Container-based systems work based on efficient container orchestration systems and integrated monitoring across multiple clusters.

Container orchestration systems

The standard for most container orchestration remains **Kubernetes**. Kubernetes functions as a portable, extensible model for managing containerized workloads with a wide range of services available. Alternatives are systems such as **Docker Swarm** and **Apache Mesos**, which present simpler, albeit less feature-rich, options. In a traditional deployment model, one operating system runs all the applications. This has moved to virtualized services where a shared hypervisor creates different virtual machines, each with its own operating system. Container models, such as Kubernetes, share the system kernel between multiple containers to better manage the efficiency of individual containers.

The primary advantage of running containers is a distinction between the build and release cycles compared to deployed functions. Containers have three primary attributes: they should be distributed, ephemeral, and immutable. Distributed means containers can operate in multiple machines, clusters, zones, or regions with the same effects. Multiple instantiations can support similar functions and report back to a common database while maintaining operational integrity. Ephemeral means you never depend on a single running container but on the base code supporting instantiating the same container across multiple clusters to generate similar effects. This allows the creation of temporary and replaceable effects. Containers do not get fixed; you build a new image and destroy the old container when the new one deploys. Finally, good container programming is immutable, meaning once deployed, while the data through those containers can be modified, the baseline code never changes. Maximizing these three characteristics is one of the reasons Kubernetes approaches have been so successful from among the orchestration choices. The following figure (*Figure 4.4*) demonstrates a high-level architecture for each of these orchestration concepts:

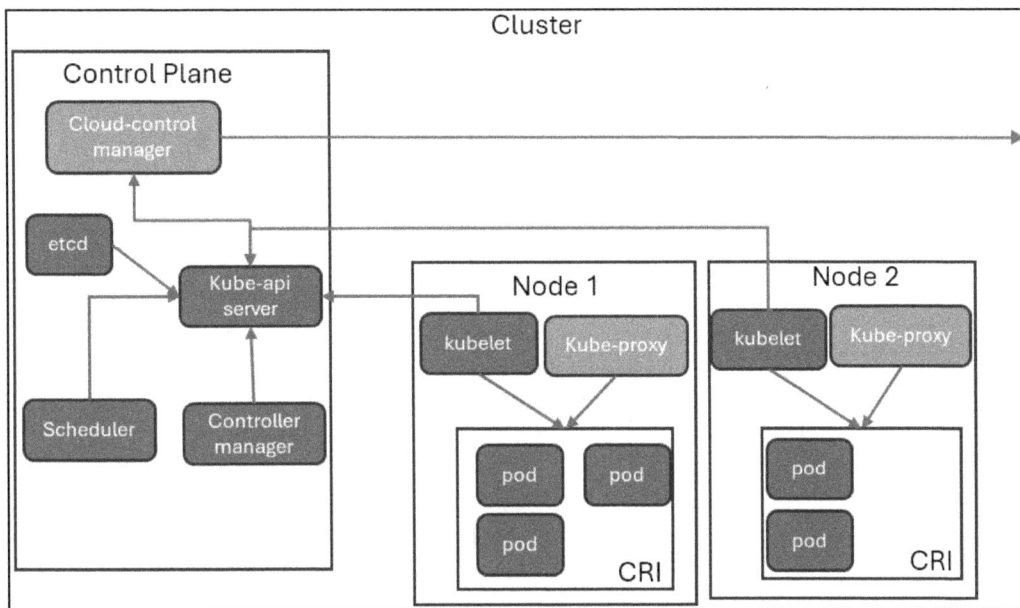

Figure 4.4: Kubernetes architecture

Kubernetes offers several advantages over traditional hosting approaches. These advantages include service discovery, load balancing, automated rollout, self-healing approaches, and secrets management. When implementing Kubernetes, other benefits often appear but the aforementioned advantages are the primary benefits to successful Platform Engineering. Service discovery enables you to use embedded commands to discover which containers are currently running, while load balancing distributes compute and store needs across multiple containers. Service discovery can expand to allow containers to find and communicate with each other as well, a critical function when dealing with microservices. Automated rollout refers to linking deployments to the CI/CD process, ensuring only current versions are available to the user. The self-healing approach integrates load balancing and good security practices by ensuring that whenever a container fails, the system can kill the process and launch another container with minimal user impact. Finally, secrets management allows secrets such as passwords and program keys to be centrally stored and encrypted while still being accessible to multiple container deployments.

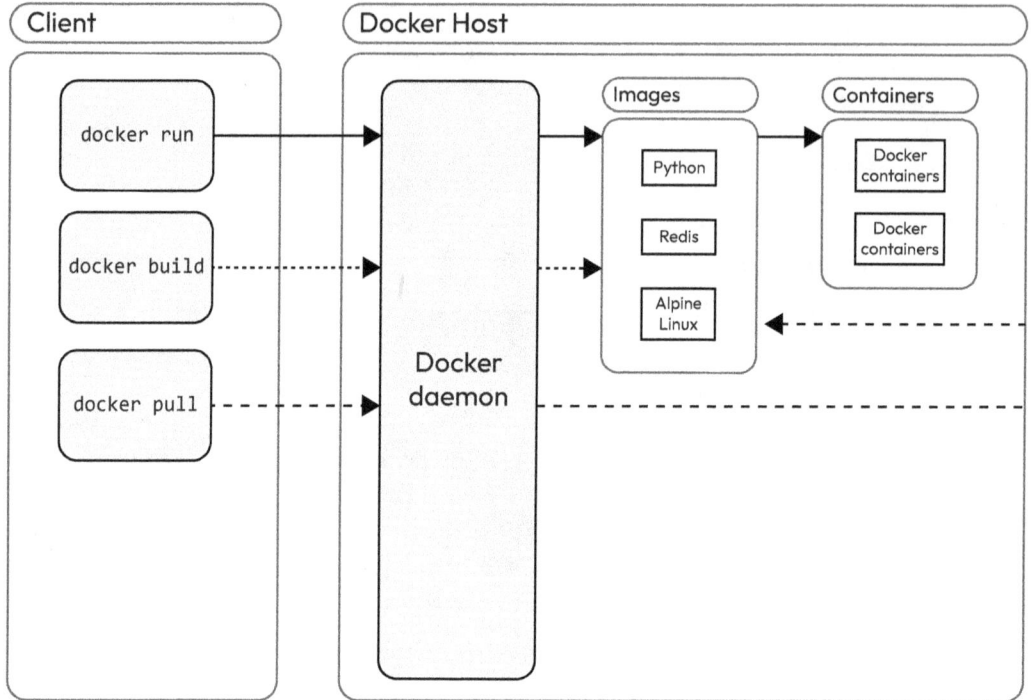

Figure 4.5: Docker architecture

Docker offers a different approach through an open platform that distinguishes applications from infrastructure. This system creates images and containers while using namespaces to preserve the isolated workspace within the container. Docker Swarm varies from Kubernetes in that it is tied to the Docker API, rather than being an independent solution. You still use nodes, services, and load balancers to manage actions, but the connection to the Docker API makes it more linear than Kubernetes. While being potentially easier to install at first, the functionality and automation are limited compared to the Kubernetes toolbase. A clear example is that Docker only uses **Transport-Level Security (TLS)**, while Kubernetes can use multiple security options through RBAC, SSL, TLS, and various secrets management tools. Another example is that Docker Swarm only monitors through third-party integrations, while Kubernetes has both internal monitoring and third-party options.

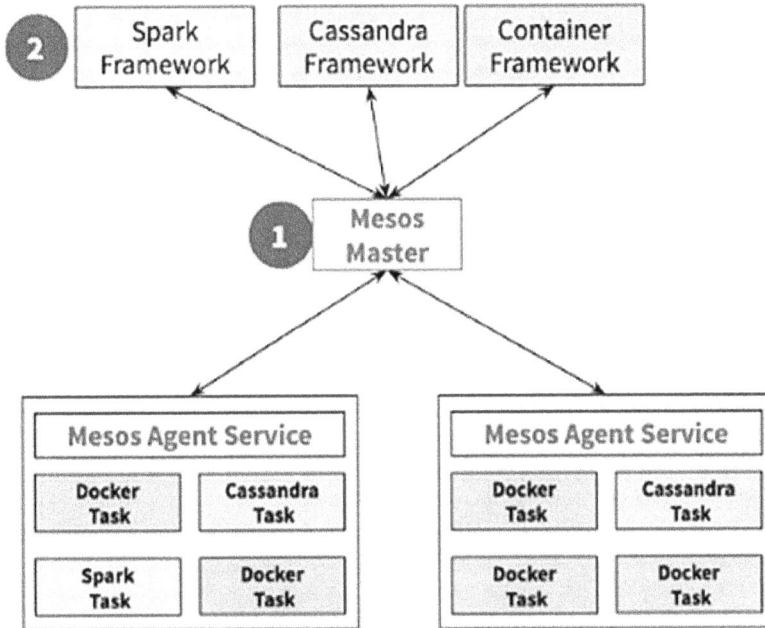

Figure 4.6: Mesos architecture

The third orchestration system, Apache Mesos, takes another design approach to address more advanced containers and data distribution. This leads Mesos to be primarily a resource management tool, ensuring containers can reach the right databases, make appropriate requests and changes, and maintain high availability. This approach enables supporting tens of thousands of nodes, which can be difficult for other applications. Mesos is not technically a container orchestration tool but a higher-level function that can support tools running container orchestration. Within Mesos, the Marathon tool is the one that provides those functions. Like Docker, Mesos does not have an integrated monitoring solution but can manage containers to report on those solutions. The core goal of Mesos is executing diverse workloads on a common platform.

You should remember that no container orchestration system solves all problems, which is why it is merely part of the overall platform solution. Each of these tools could play a part within Platform Engineering, but the first step is choosing the development community supported. Docker offers quick options for application developers to move into microservices and run something. Kubernetes uses Docker containers but also integrates with the underlying infrastructure. Mesos specializes in running organization-critical workloads on thousands of machines and across multiple data centers. This comparison helps with picking the right platform. For most platforms, Kubernetes will be the easy choice. For start-ups focused on reaching market, Docker Swarm likely becomes the best option. For a mature business running thousands of containers and globally integrated databases, Mesos will likely be the best option. Our targeted community is that middle ground, building a stable platform, integrating infrastructure, allowing observability, and managing resources, which is why most examples in this book will suggest Kubernetes.

Kubernetes interfaces

There are two substantial Kubernetes interfaces that are critical to mention in building a platform. The first is Crossplane (`https://www.crossplane.io/`), which connects Kubernetes within the cluster to external, non-Kubernetes resources. This uses a **Custom Resource Definition (CRD)** to represent external functions as native Kubernetes objects so each responds to standard Kubernetes commands (*Figure 4.5*).

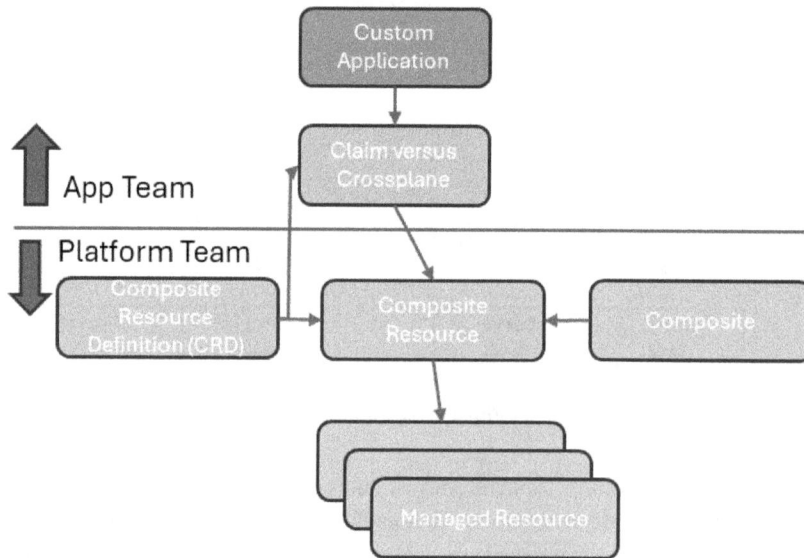

Figure 4.7: Crossplane integration

This overwrites some of the advantages of Docker Swarm in using a common API by making a Kubernetes API that treats all external functions similarly. You can then implement a Kubernetes solution without having the end-state resource or container written in Kubernetes, limiting the burden on the developer. Crossplane can be a key advantage in controlling Platform Engineering within your platform design. Investigating emerging tools such as Crossplane can help with finding missing pieces in your platform orchestration.

Another type of common tool associated with Kubernetes involves sidecar security, such as Istio (`https://istio.io/`) or Linkerd (`https://linkerd.io/`). Both tools provide an open source service mesh to enhance orchestration capabilities. These service mesh tools add functions such as traffic management and security, and can increase observability without having to refactor the company's own code. These functions operate using a transparent process linked to service instances. A comparison can be made to how OTel operates within the containers; these tools operate next to the container at the service mesh level. Each takes advantage of Kubernetes interactions to establish a control plane to integrate data. When previously discussing architectural patterns, challenges in maintaining observability were discussed. These tools can integrate observability and management into common functions without disrupting application development.

Monitoring and logging

Prometheus offers powerful monitoring capabilities and works particularly well with Kubernetes, while the Elastic stack (Elasticsearch, Logstash, and Kibana) offers comprehensive logging solutions that excel in data visualization and analysis. These tools are first integrated at the collaboration point of the platform and then extend through webhooks into the deployment targets. Building these tools into the overall platform provides the ability to store data within a stable framework and monitor ongoing activities.

Orchestration observability

Orchestration observability comprises four key pillars: metrics, logs, traces, and measurements. You should remember that orchestration denotes an action while observability denotes a measurement. When discussing orchestration observability, we are talking about using orchestration actions to create a foundation for useful metrics. Useful to remember here is that observability is the final step of the observation process. The first element is deciding on points to observe, making the desired data observable, and then creating observability to report that data through the appropriate metrics.

Kubernetes observation can be based on several key areas: cluster and Pod monitoring, Deployment and Ingress metrics, persistent storage, and control plane metrics. Platform architecture establishes a Kubernetes baseline within the collaboration and deployment targets, so cluster monitoring ensures those nodes are functioning effectively. This helps determine how the applications are running within the node and the resources used overall. Cluster monitoring ties into Pod monitoring, ensuring not only that the entire cluster functions but also that each application functions.

The next element of Kubernetes observation to consider is a tool such as Prometheus, which can be used to monitor active Kubernetes Deployments. Common metrics are compute utilization through the CPU and the overall Kubernetes state and memory. Establishing a Prometheus server creates a data model based on key-value pairs to enable query language, scrape targets for service discovery, and integrate modular components.

In establishing a Prometheus architecture, there are several basic steps.

The first steps are to pull data from the Kubernetes API (**1**), microservice autodiscovery (**2a**), or directly from Kubernetes nodes into the Prometheus server (**2b**). The Prometheus server then forwards information to an alert manager and visualization dashboard (**3** and **4**). The alert manager can then individually notify users (**5**) through asynchronous messages. The following architecture shows how different data can be incorporated (*Figure 4.8*):

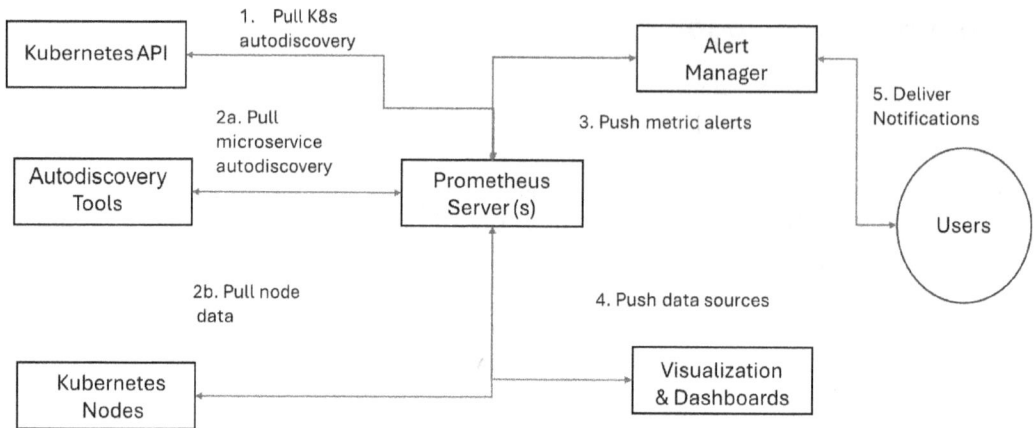

Figure 4.8: Sample Prometheus architecture

This diagram shows how an effective tool can convert data from existing linked discovery into the Kubernetes orchestration, incorporate autodiscovery such as Fluentd, and push alerts and visualization. Another common tool for autodiscovery is OTel. Grafana is often used to display metrics. The visualization of metrics creates the desired observability for the overall architecture and applications. Further reading on Prometheus and specific implementations is available at `https://prometheus.io/`.

These tools are just part of the solution as full capability depends on having effective CI/CD processes aligned with your DevOps culture.

Platform software delivery ecosystems

The last step in our essential ecosystem for Platform Engineering incorporates pipelines to deliver software. Delivering software involves moving from a coded idea to where customers can interact with delivered software. Pipelines are the step-by-step directions to build code and then allow deployment. The standard approach involves creating tasks, which are grouped into jobs, which are then grouped into stages within the pipeline. Passing each stage of the pipeline allows the code to progress to the next stage and then deploy. Each task produces artifacts that are observable to quickly detect any bugs or defects within those pipelines. This helps clarify when a merge has been successful and when additional coding may be required. Incorporating effective tools into the platform ecosystem focuses on three knowledge areas: establishing CI/CD tools, integrating DevOps practices, and observing pipelines.

CI/CD tools

The first step in understanding a CI/CD tool ecosystem is understanding that all vendors aim to make sticky options. These sticky options ensure that once development begins, user options are limited to remaining on the current tool, enabling continuing revenue for these tools. Despite tools ranging from open source to premium options, the more connected options a CI/CD solution can offer, the better chance for return usage. Even with that understanding, there are some exceptional tools that enable delivering CI/CD solutions. The top candidates within the ecosystem are Jenkins, GitLab, and CircleCI. These tools are followed by less comprehensive but still manageable tools, such as Bitbucket, Spinnaker, Argo CD, and Harness. The most common distinction between these tools is how much CI/CD each offers as a part of an integrated platform. You can see this distinction in that GitLab offers a full DevOps platform, while Jenkins creates a dedicated automation server. Then, there are extended options, such as Azure Pipelines, which is capable of using AWS CI/CD elements to supplement the internal pipelines.

A 2023 CI tool survey (`https://www.jetbrains.com/lp/devecosystem-2022/team-tools/#do-you-use-any-of-the-following-tools-in-the-cloud-`) shows that most organizations use Jenkins (47%), GitHub Actions (27%), GitLab CI (27%), and Azure DevOps (13%). While the survey focused on tool usage, factors for selecting the right tool included development workflows, usability, pipeline configuration and feedback, scalability, and security. Factors associated with but external to the tool included selecting for cost efficiency and hosting model. Some of these elements (development workflow, usability, scalability, security, and cost) were previously discussed as part of the platform ecosystem, and handling those issues concurrently provides a benefit to the core platform. This leaves the core element as selecting an appropriate tool within the platform as the configuration.

The first part of a pipeline addresses how the initial pipeline is configured. Some code uses direct code as YAML files, which could include a variety of approaches from Terraform or Helm charts. YAML has become one of the most common approaches. Even tools that offer **Graphical User Interfaces (GUIs)** to create pipelines then translate into some form of YAML. Working directly from coding languages can offer options to rewrite pipelines quicker, but again, many processes are shortened through the GUIs. For instance, GitLab separates pipelines into jobs as individual instructions, runners that execute jobs, and stages that combine different jobs (*Figure 4.9*).

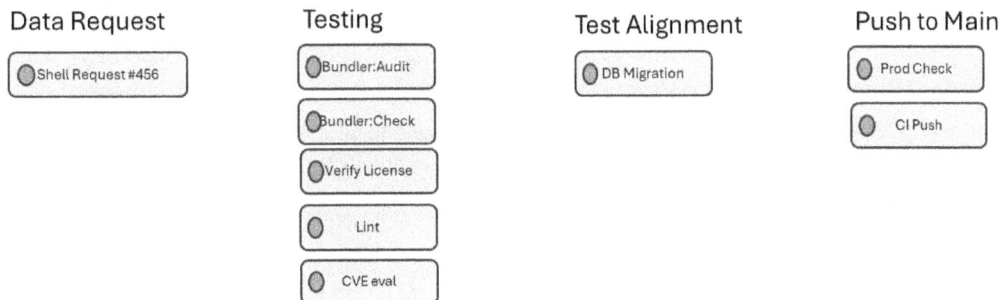

Figure 4.9: Sample pipeline for GitLab

Jenkins offers stages along the top of its display but presents jobs on a different window. The Jenkins visualization compares the number of times each stage was run and the time it took for each stage. Both GitLab and Jenkins applications call jobs from the individual elements within the pipeline stages. Executing jobs leads to the next element of workflow configuration. Many of the differences in the various ecosystem tools are more about style than substance. The best way to get familiar with them is to try the different options. The underlying functionality remains similar. The challenge then becomes how you align different teams if they are each using different tools. Platforms provide opinionated decisions and allow tailored training to ensure all employees meet the same standards. Some of these initial standards are addressed by how the DevOps culture handles the delivery process.

DevOps integration

DevOps involves flow, feedback, and improvement, and these are strongly reflected within the CI/CD environment and the chosen pipelines. Using known DevOps best practices shows all pipelines should be structured into the following four areas:

- **Develop**: Initial code push. Moves code from the source repository into the pipeline and conducts static tests to ensure basic formatting and language errors are removed. Potential artifacts include code files and review logs.

- **Build**: Uses the code file to build into integrated source code, making changes to the baseline and again verifying through static testing that new code elements continue to work and variables remain consistent. Potential artifacts include integrated code files, review logs, and version control.

- **Test**: Runs integrated code against a number of tests, such as functional, system, or unit, to reveal any errors in execution. This can include security tests. Moves the code from a static element into a completed application. Potential artifacts include test reports, vulnerability analysis, **Software Bill of Materials** (**SBOM**), and code files.

- **Deploy**: Deploys the final version to production. Ensures completed software matches the selected environments. Potential artifacts include working applications and production logs.

Each stage has a specific role that is characterized by the defined artifacts. When matching the desired CI/CD strategy to a DevOps framework, the goal should be identifying the tasks and jobs needed to complete each stage. Identifying those elements helps you select the artifacts needed. As an example, the level of security artifacts needed can vary greatly between different use cases. A retail store might only run vulnerabilities after deploying code for real-time changes, while a financial institution might be more concerned with underlying gaps. The artifacts allow you to make detailed decisions about pipeline stages.

One common DevOps concern is whether all code items need to pass all pipeline stages. In some instances, the code is deployed to a test instance for user acceptance or other factors. That test instance may not require the fully detailed tests desired if an application is moving directly to a production environment. Selecting tasks and jobs within stages allows you to comment out, or turn off, pipeline tasks at any stage. The final artifacts should reflect the unsupported areas. If you make the assumption that any pipeline passes all implemented functions, it can still lead to errors later. The platform's strength is in delegating those decisions about pipeline task requirement to the admin level, rather than allowing the user to graduate poor applications. This helps to improve the overall quality.

Another benefit of platform DevOps is the ability to create multiple pipelines within set repositories. This means that while the user may not be able to turn off pipeline elements, they can start by selecting a pipeline with fewer elements. This allows code to be built to different completion levels. It also aids in upskilling individuals by gradually using more advanced pipelines. An example might be a coding element passed between one dev team and another to execute a specific function. Security, functional, and smoke tests might be a step too far for those early stages, leading to a specific dev pipeline for that one team. Having a centralized template allows the organization to more thoroughly understand how, and why, which code passes which pipelines.

While emphasizing artifacts, you can sometimes lose track of why those artifacts are important. The artifacts within the pipeline allow for comparison between different pipelines, and different results from the same pipeline. If the security scanner or SBOM tool is always the same, reverting to the platform standard, the different results can be compared through a diff tool (a difference checker) to quickly spot the changes between items. In security results, some vulnerabilities might be just manual, such as having a backup power supply, so elements within the pipeline can be grayed out or turned off so those vulnerabilities do not appear. Making these changes at a platform pipeline level then automatically adjusts the artifacts and prevents users from chasing errors that cannot be fixed with code. This leads then to the final element of being able to observe the pipeline effectively.

Pipeline observability

In our opinion, pipelines are one of the most overused and least understood concepts within modern software development. Pipelines depict the processing element chain, with each output contributing to the following input. Pipelines begin with the previous CI/CD elements, but a well-built software pipeline adds factors for monitoring and operations. The challenge becomes ensuring you differentiate between the software pipeline as a conceptual tool and aspects of those pipelines as software tools. In managing observability within the platform ecosystem, the pipeline should be treated like the software approaches to create functional code.

Pipeline observability depends on being able to collect, process, and route logs from the pipeline process to any other location that is owned and managed. Here, the observability comes from compiling the artifacts associated with the pipeline stages. Where the artifacts arrive depends on the early choices you make about the pipeline. One of the primary goals here is using a diff tool to distinguish between various elements. **Diff** tools come in different formats and languages but compare the output from one section to another. Comparing changes between different builds allows feedback and continuous improvement to be key DevOps parts of the essential platform ecosystem.

As we close this section, one of our favorite stories about pipelines comes to mind. A development team we were working with had recently been introduced to DevSecOps. They called us and informed us that all their security issues had been solved, the new feature was integrated into the pipeline, and the product was secure. We asked to see the security log results and received a blank look. Rather than creating security logs, the security tool within the pipeline was set to "true," meaning the only requirement was for the security scanner to run. This, obviously, is not the goal for secure software development. Platforms help create opinionated pipelines, so the needed artifacts are always created, rather than leaving those decisions to developers. With the team, we adjusted the pipeline, set up a diff tool, and were clearly able to demonstrate the risk changes between one version and the next. Consolidating these issues and knowing the needed parts helps bring the platform ecosystem from an initial design to a workable infrastructure.

Summary

This chapter started by introducing the concept of a platform ecosystem, with a platform being more than a single tool but rather the interaction of multiple tools working together. We discussed establishing IaC for the basic platform tools and then using configuration as code to establish working areas. Choosing options early may cause an initial training burden but this is made up for by the time gained in delivering working applications.

We next focused on those working applications by looking at how you orchestrate the platform environment. This section built an understanding of how different systems can be configured for different elements as you move from the core platform cluster to the deployment targets, and containers within those targets. Multiple options were considered but the preferred approach for this book remains working in Kubernetes to deliver efficient tools. While Kubernetes is not always the most effective as an out-of-the-box solution, it offers sufficient power at the platform level to make the needed changes.

Lastly, we discussed the importance of CI/CD systems as the end element of the platform ecosystem. All applications must pass through pipelines, so having the right tool is important. Tools such as GitLab, Circle CI, and Jenkins were all considered, but the best solution will be the one that is right for your team. The next chapter moves beyond these initial solutions to discuss how AI-generated solutions can help expedite the build and deploy phases associated with your platform.

> **Call to action**
> - Determine the right IaC/configuration as code integration to support the platform's architecture and requirements.
> - Implement monitoring solutions and confirm data arrives at the right elements for action.
> - Confirm the CI/CD tools generate the right artifacts for continuous observability.

Get This Book's PDF Version and Exclusive Extras

UNLOCK NOW

Scan the QR code (or go to `packtpub.com/unlock`). Search for this book by name, confirm the edition, and then follow the steps on the page.

Note: Keep your invoice handly. Purchase made directly from packt don't require one.

Part 2: Execute
Run Enterprise Platforms with Precision

This part equips us to operate modern platforms securely, intelligently, and efficiently. We will integrate AI, observability, security, performance tuning, and platform team design to manage platforms in production environments. Each chapter focuses on execution with clarity, so we can deliver stability, scale, and speed under real-world conditions.

This part has the following chapters:

- *Chapter 5, Incorporating Artificial Intelligence into Platform Engineering*
- *Chapter 6, Engineering Platform Data Management*
- *Chapter 7, Security, Compliance, and Risk Management*
- *Chapter 8, Real-World Applications and Case Studies*
- *Chapter 9, Testing, Quality Assurance, and Operations*

5

Incorporating Artificial Intelligence into Platform Engineering

Incorporating **artificial intelligence (AI)** into Platform Engineering represents a seismic shift in how we approach technological ecosystems and operational efficiency. This chapter is dedicated to unraveling the multifaceted roles that generative AI plays in refining, optimizing, and revolutionizing Platform Engineering strategies.

By integrating AI, organizations can transcend traditional boundaries, enabling more dynamic, responsive, and intelligent systems that move businesses toward higher levels of innovation and operational dexterity.

We will delve into how AI is not merely a tool but a pivotal element in the evolution of Platform Engineering, offering actionable insights and strategic advantages that reshape the landscape of technology and business.

In this chapter, we'll explore how Platform Engineering is evolving in response to the AI revolution, with a focus on embracing the transformative potential of generative AI. We'll examine practical, real-world use cases where AI is being integrated into Platform Engineering workflows, highlighting the tangible benefits and efficiencies it can deliver. Finally, we'll address the common challenges organizations face when incorporating AI into platform ecosystems and offer strategies for overcoming these obstacles to unlock AI's full value.

We're going to cover the following main topics:

- Embracing the AI revolution in Platform Engineering
- Strategic implementation of generative AI systems
- Practical applications and use cases of generative AI
- Navigating the complexities of AI integration

Technical requirements

While specific technical skills are not required for this chapter, a basic understanding of AI, including generative AI, is beneficial. The ability to distinguish between AI, machine learning, artificial neural networks, deep learning, generative AI, and **large language models (LLMs)** from a business application perspective will enhance comprehension of the content. Additionally, familiarity with the topics covered in *Chapters 1–4* is vital to fully appreciate the discussions in this chapter.

Embracing the AI revolution in Platform Engineering

Platform Engineering is radically transforming with the advent of generative AI technologies. This change is not just a progression but a complete shift that redefines how platforms are developed, maintained, and scaled. Generative AI brings speed, precision, and adaptability to engineering processes, pushing the boundaries of digital infrastructure. It is a revolution that promises to drive innovation and unlock new possibilities. This paradigm shift can be best understood by comparing traditional Platform Engineering practices with those empowered by AI, highlighting the revolutionary impact AI brings to the table.

Feature	Traditional Platform Engineering	AI-Driven Platform Engineering
Development speed	Relies on manual coding and processes, often leading to longer development cycles.	Accelerates development through automation and AI-assisted code generation, significantly reducing time to market.
Operational efficiency	Dependent on manual monitoring and maintenance, which can be resource-intensive and prone to human error.	Utilizes AI for predictive maintenance and automated monitoring, enhancing efficiency and reducing downtime.
Scalability	Scaling requires manual intervention and planning, potentially leading to bottlenecks.	AI enables dynamic scaling by predicting demand and automatically adjusting resources, ensuring seamless scalability.
Error detection and quality	Relies on manual testing and reviews, which may miss subtle bugs or inefficiencies.	Employs AI-driven tools for real-time error detection and code quality analysis, improving reliability.
Innovation capability	Innovation is limited by manual processes and the speed at which human teams can operate.	AI facilitates rapid prototyping and experimentation, fostering a culture of innovation and continuous improvement.

Table 5.1: Feature comparison of traditional and AI-driven Platform Engineering

Businesses can anticipate and overcome challenges in real time by integrating deep learning and machine learning capabilities into platform operations. This improves efficiency, as well as ensuring resilience and future-oriented solutions. Organizations that leverage generative AI gain a competitive edge, accelerating strategic objectives in a constantly evolving digital landscape.

AI as the vanguard of Platform Engineering

AI is transforming and redefining Platform Engineering by enabling platforms to operate more efficiently and proactively. It has a multifaceted impact on Platform Engineering and is pivotal in leading the industry to a future where adaptability and foresight are essential for platform success.

Here are some ways by which AI enhances Platform Engineering:

- **Automation of development processes**: AI, including generative AI, assists in automating specific aspects of development processes, such as code suggestions, test case generation, and deployment configurations, significantly enhancing productivity. While AI tools such as GitHub Copilot, Amazon Q Developer, and Tabnine expedite tasks by providing contextual code suggestions and automating repetitive coding steps, human oversight remains essential to refine outputs, address errors, and optimize performance. These tools act as accelerators rather than replacements, enabling engineers to focus on higher-value tasks such as strategy and innovation. Additionally, frameworks such as TensorFlow and PyTorch facilitate machine learning model integration, while CI/CD platforms such as Jenkins and GitLab integrate AI-driven testing and deployment, making development cycles more efficient and reliable. This collaborative method promotes quicker development and superior quality while emphasizing the essential contribution of human expertise.

- **Predictive maintenance and real-time optimization**: AI technologies, particularly machine learning models, excel in predictive maintenance by analyzing vast volumes of operational data to detect anomalies and anticipate potential issues before they escalate into system failures. This proactive approach enhances platform reliability and minimizes downtime, which is critical for businesses reliant on continuous operations. Tools such as Azure Machine Learning, AWS SageMaker, and Splunk facilitate anomaly detection and predictive analytics, ensuring system resilience. Additionally, AI-driven optimization systems dynamically adapt to workload changes and operational conditions in real time, improving efficiency and resource utilization. Frameworks such as TensorFlow and PyTorch enable real-time decision-making by powering advanced algorithms, while tools such as GitLab Duo and Red Hat Ansible streamline AI integration into operational workflows. These capabilities ensure platforms remain robust, responsive, and aligned with business demands.

- **Enhanced security protocols**: AI is a critical asset in cybersecurity, leveraging machine learning and advanced algorithms to identify and respond to threats faster than traditional methods. Tools such as SentinelOne analyze vast datasets in real time to detect anomalies and mitigate risks. Deep learning models such as **Long Short-Term Memory** (**LSTM**) networks and Transformers predict malicious activity patterns, enabling proactive defense mechanisms.

Platforms such as Splunk and Datadog integrate these models to monitor behavior, flag unusual activity, and strengthen networks against attacks. In cloud environments, tools such as OpenTofu analyze access patterns to prevent breaches. By continually learning and adapting, AI-driven security systems ensure platform resilience and efficiency, protecting organizations from evolving cyber risks.

- **User experience customization**: AI enhances user experiences by analyzing interactions, preferences, and feedback to create personalized digital journeys. For example, Netflix uses AI algorithms to recommend content based on viewing history, increasing user engagement and retention. Similarly, Amazon employs machine learning to tailor product recommendations, driving customer satisfaction and sales. AI also powers dynamic user interface adjustments, such as YouTube's AI-driven recommendations that adapt to individual viewing habits. Tools such as Adobe Sensei enable real-time customization in e-commerce platforms by optimizing product displays based on user behavior. These applications improve platform usability and foster deeper customer relationships and loyalty by delivering experiences uniquely tailored to each individual.

- **Strategic decision-making**: AI empowers strategic decision-making by analyzing vast datasets to uncover actionable insights, ranging from market trends to customer preferences. Machine learning models such as those used in Tableau and Power BI enable real-time data visualization and trend analysis, helping organizations adapt quickly to market changes. For instance, Walmart employs AI to optimize inventory levels by predicting demand patterns, reducing waste, and ensuring stock availability. AI-driven forecasting tools, such as those integrated into Salesforce Einstein, assist leaders in identifying emerging opportunities and mitigating risks. Companies such as JPMorgan Chase use AI to analyze market movements and guide investment strategies in the financial sector. This data-driven approach ensures decisions are aligned with strategic goals, improving agility and fostering long-term business growth.

- **Driving sustainability**: AI, particularly machine learning algorithms, drives environmental sustainability by optimizing resource utilization and minimizing waste. Tools such as AWS Auto Scaling and Google Cloud's Active Assist use AI to dynamically allocate cloud resources based on demand, reducing energy consumption and operational costs. Additionally, AI-powered systems analyze energy usage patterns in data centers, enabling more innovative cooling and power management to lower carbon footprints. Companies such as Microsoft employ AI-driven insights to achieve carbon-negative goals by optimizing supply chain logistics and resource allocation. By embracing these AI solutions, organizations can align their operations with global sustainability initiatives while enhancing efficiency and reducing costs.

As AI technologies advance, they integrate with Platform Engineering to create autonomous and adaptive ecosystems. The future of platforms is set to drive innovation, create new business opportunities, and automate tasks. This will redefine industry standards, making it essential for organizations to embrace these technological advancements. AI promises a new era where platforms are engineered to lead and transform industries. Organizations that embrace this change can stay at the forefront of technological evolution and leverage the vast opportunities of AI, especially generative AI, for enhanced Platform Engineering.

To fully appreciate the practical applications and real-world use cases that demonstrate the transformative impact of generative AI across various industries, it's essential to understand the core components of generative AI systems and their strategic implementations.

Strategic implementation of generative AI systems

Organizations need a robust understanding of the key elements of generative AI systems and a strategic approach to their implementation in Platform Engineering. These components are the building blocks of AI-driven systems, enabling intelligent functionalities and transformative capabilities within digital platforms. By implementing these elements strategically, organizations can harness the full potential of generative AI to revolutionize their operational frameworks, ensuring efficiency and adaptability to the evolving technological landscape.

Key elements of generative AI systems

To fully leverage AI's transformative potential, organizations must integrate generative AI into their Platform Engineering. Here are the key elements of generative AI systems that are essential for this integration:

*   **Data management and quality**: Data is the foundation of generative AI. The quality, granularity, and timeliness of data directly impact outcomes. Robust data management frameworks ensure accuracy and integrity. Advanced techniques for data collection maintain high-quality standards. Data anonymization processes are crucial for privacy and regulatory compliance. Organizations employing structured data pipelines see up to a 30% improvement in model performance, while regular audits of data quality reduce errors by 90%.

*   **Machine learning models**: Generative AI systems rely on machine learning models to make sense of massive amounts of data. These models require appropriate algorithm selection, continuous training, and re-training to adapt to changing conditions. Advanced techniques, such as deep learning and reinforcement learning, enhance the models' ability to make complex decisions and improve autonomously. It's crucial to rigorously test these models for accuracy and effectiveness under various operational scenarios. For instance, reinforcement learning models reduce error rates by 25–35% in decision-making processes, while organizations employing regular re-training cycles achieve up to 40% improved accuracy over static models.

*   **Integration architecture**: A robust architecture is necessary to integrate AI effectively. It should be flexible and scalable to facilitate easy updates and real-time adjustments. Seamless integration with legacy systems is also essential, requiring custom adapters or middleware solutions that can translate between different technologies and protocols. It's crucial to get this right for successful AI implementation. Flexible integration reduces deployment times by 50–70%, while middleware solutions that bridge legacy and modern systems minimize downtime by 40%.

- **Automation frameworks**: AI-powered automation significantly enhances operational workflows by reducing the need for manual intervention. AI is leveraged to handle routine tasks across various domains, such as network management, user support, and application deployment. The frameworks perform tasks and learn from each iteration to continuously refine processes and increase efficiency. This adaptive automation speeds up operations, identifies and resolves inefficiencies within the system, and enables organizations to transform their operations for the better. Automation frameworks reduce manual intervention by up to 70%, resulting in 30–50% faster task execution times and improved workflow efficiency.

- **Scalability and maintenance**: AI systems must scale efficiently to handle changing demands and market fluctuations. This means scaling up for larger workloads and down during off-peak times to save resources. Regular updates to software and hardware components are necessary to keep these systems secure and efficient. Continuous monitoring and predictive maintenance techniques detect and resolve potential issues before they impact system performance. Organizations employing predictive maintenance report a 50% reduction in downtime, while scalable systems reduce resource waste by 20–30% through dynamic workload adjustments.

- **Security considerations**: AI integration presents unique security challenges, particularly for generative AI, which is vulnerable to attacks such as adversarial manipulation. Attackers can subtly alter input data to deceive models, resulting in harmful outputs. Unlike traditional IT systems, generative AI's reliance on complex data models creates specific vulnerabilities. To mitigate these risks, adversarial training helps improve model resilience, while homomorphic encryption allows computations on encrypted data to protect sensitive information. Anomaly detection algorithms, such as those in Splunk, can identify unusual behaviors almost in real time, enhancing response times. Generative AI also faces model inversion attacks, where sensitive data can be inferred. Strategies such as differential privacy obscure individual contributions to maintain model utility. Regular audits, role-based access controls, and strong encryption further safeguard systems against threats. By implementing these measures, organizations can effectively tackle the security risks of generative AI, building resilient and trustworthy platforms while protecting sensitive operations.

These core components are strategic assets that, when implemented and managed effectively, can improve the operational efficiency and innovation capacity of platforms. Next, we will explore the strategic implementation of AI in Platform Engineering to optimize performance further.

Strategically implementing AI in Platform Engineering

Implementing generative AI within Platform Engineering is a strategic endeavor that requires meticulous planning and phased execution. Here are the detailed steps organizations should undertake to successfully incorporate generative AI technologies into their platform operations.

Assessment and planning

Organizations must begin by comprehensively assessing their technological infrastructure, data systems, and staff capabilities. This evaluation identifies areas for AI improvement and potential integration challenges. During the planning phase, organizations must establish measurable goals, such as reducing operational costs or enhancing customer satisfaction, and develop a strategic roadmap outlining key milestones, resource allocation, and timelines. Integrating observability tools such as Grafana, Prometheus, and the Elastic stack can enhance this assessment by providing real-time insights into system performance, resource utilization, and potential bottlenecks. These tools ensure the continuous monitoring of AI-powered Platform Engineering systems, helping organizations maintain alignment with strategic objectives.

Incremental integration

Teams should integrate generative AI gradually to reduce risks and manage complexity. Start with pilot projects for specific processes or business areas, operating as a controlled test environment for refining AI functionalities. Gradually expand successful pilots, applying lessons learned to broader implementations to demonstrate the technology's effectiveness and build confidence among users and stakeholders.

Training and support

Effective AI training programs are crucial to maximizing productivity. They should cover both the technical aspects and operational changes brought by AI tools. Comprehensive support, including technical teams and detailed documentation, should be provided to foster a positive attitude toward the new technology. Empower users through education and support to ensure smoother adoption.

Evaluation and scaling

Continuous evaluation of AI systems is crucial to measure their impact against initial goals. Establish key performance indicators to track effectiveness, user engagement, and **Return on Investment** (**ROI**). Use assessments to identify successes and areas for improvement. Insights gained from evaluations guide the scaling of AI functionalities for broader impact. Optimize AI operations to ensure cost-effectiveness and alignment with business objectives during scaling.

Adaptation and evolution

AI is constantly evolving, so it's essential to keep AI solutions up to date to stay competitive. Organizations must proactively learn and innovate by updating AI models and algorithms, adopting new AI technologies, and revising integration strategies to respond quickly to market changes. By staying adaptable, businesses can ensure that their AI systems remain effective and provide ongoing value to the organization.

Sustainability and ethical governance

As AI becomes integral to platform operations, organizations must prioritize ethical governance and sustainability. Implementing ethical AI frameworks is crucial to ensure fairness, transparency, and accountability in AI operations. Additionally, organizational leaders must consider sustainability practices to minimize the environmental impact of AI systems, such as optimizing energy usage and selecting eco-friendly infrastructure options.

Integrating generative AI into Platform Engineering requires clear implementation steps that optimize maximum impact. Embracing these practices unlocks a new era of operational excellence and innovation. This foundation lays the groundwork for a more thorough examination of practical applications and use cases of generative AI in various industries. We will explore how generative AI can transform platform operations by improving efficiency, security, and strategic agility.

Practical applications and use cases of generative AI

Generative AI is not just a technological advancement; it's the key to unlocking unparalleled innovation and efficiency in Platform Engineering. In this section, we will explore how generative AI is transforming Platform Engineering by driving technological advancements and creating unprecedented opportunities.

We will discover how to integrate generative AI to streamline operations, enhance capabilities, and foster innovation within organizations. By understanding these applications, we will gain the skills to automate tasks, optimize deployments, and push the boundaries of what's possible in DevOps and Platform Engineering.

Automating development workflows

The adoption of generative AI marks a new era where human intellect and AI merge to significantly boost productivity and creativity in development workflows. This convergence enhances efficiency and transforms how developers create and maintain software. Here are some ways to speed up development and improve code quality and collaboration.

Augmenting developers

Generative AI extends developers' skills, enabling rapid ideation. These tools offer on-demand expertise as coding assistants, making complex coding accessible to all skill levels. Collaborative AI assistants such as **GitHub Copilot** and **Amazon Q Developer** (previously called CodeWhisperer) help teams with everyday development tasks using natural language interactions. These tools utilize **Natural Language Processing** (NLP) models, which analyze developer input by breaking it into tokens, understanding syntax and semantics, and matching it with extensive training datasets of code examples. Based on the context and input, the AI generates relevant code snippets or suggestions that align with the developer's intent. For example, when prompted with "create a REST API endpoint in Python," the NLP model recognizes the task, retrieves relevant patterns, and generates a functional code block. This capability allows developers to prototype new features quickly, avoid roadblocks in manual coding processes, translate code between programming languages, and guide cloud resource configurations. These tools significantly boost productivity by leveraging AI and free up time for innovation and high-value work.

Improving code quality

AI integration in platforms such as **Google's Gemini** and Amazon's Q Developer has redefined code quality, automating clean, efficient code generation, refactoring, and robustness testing pre-deployment. Such tools analyze code bases to optimize them by identifying performance bottlenecks, security vulnerabilities, and outdated dependencies. For example, these platforms can detect vulnerabilities such as SQL injection risks by analyzing database queries embedded in code and recommending parameterized queries or input sanitization techniques. They also measure code quality through metrics such as cyclomatic complexity, ensuring code is more straightforward to test and debug, and the maintainability index, quantifying how easily a code base can be understood, modified, or extended. By providing actionable insights, such as suggesting ways to reduce redundant loops or flagging deprecated libraries, these tools help developers save time, enhance security, and ensure code maintainability. This approach transforms software development, enabling organizations to remain secure, current, and efficient while producing lean, robust systems.

Brainstorming and problem-solving

AI-driven tools contribute significantly to problem-solving by proposing a plethora of solutions and approaches. This capability is invaluable during brainstorming sessions, where the breadth of AI-generated ideas can inspire innovative solutions. Google Gemini and **AskCodi** are excellent tools for brainstorming and problem-solving. They provide insights and suggestions that developers might not have thought of, helping them come up with innovative solutions.

Code suggestions and autocompletion

The likes of Tabnine and AskCodi redefine the realm of code suggestions and autocompletion. These tools learn from vast code repositories, providing insightful recommendations that streamline the coding process and elevate the developer experience to new heights.

Transforming the developer workflow

Generative AI can revolutionize the developer workflow from ideation to production. AI-powered assistants such as GitHub Copilot, Amazon Q Developer, Google Gemini, and GitLab Duo integrate into the development process, providing an interactive environment for generating code, explanations, documentation, and unit tests. This streamlines the process, reduces context switching, and centralizes development.

AI at the speed of thought

To evaluate the profound impact of generative AI on developer workflows, we prompted ChatGPT, Microsoft Copilot, Google Gemini, and Perplexity AI to create a comparison table of the most popular tools enhancing code quality and productivity. Our motivation was to quantify the efficiency and precision of AI tools in automating and significantly reducing time to value for tasks such as technology research, comparative analysis, suggestions, and brainstorming.

To this end, we conducted an experiment using the following prompt:

```
Create a table that compares the features of the most popular tools
that use generative AI for automating developer workflows, augmenting
developers, improving code quality, code suggestions, and auto-
completion. The columns should list the tools, and the rows should
list the features
```

Each of the generative AI models generated results within seconds. On the other hand, it took us several days to research, analyze, and collate the required information for this section. We then focused on the accuracy of these AI models and assessed their capacity to interact and adapt to developer-specific needs.

ChatGPT 4

Here is the table that was generated by ChatGPT-4o:

Feature/Tool	GitHub Copilot	Amazon CodeWhisperer	Tabnine	Kite
AI Technology	OpenAI Codex	Custom AWS models	GPT-3 & Custom Models	Deep learning models
Code Suggestions	Yes	Yes	Yes	Yes
Autocompletion	Extensive	Extensive	Extensive	Extensive
Integration	VS Code, Neovim, etc.	Eclipse, VS Code, IntelliJ	All major IDEs	VS Code, IntelliJ, others
Supported Languages	Broad (50+ languages)	Java, Python, JS	JavaScript, Python, Java, etc.	Python, JavaScript
Code Refactoring	Limited	Yes	Yes	Yes
Inline Documentation	Yes	Yes	Yes	Yes
Security Features	Security advices	Security scans	Basic	None reported
Learning from User Code	Yes	Limited	Yes	Limited
Pricing	Part of GitHub subscription	Free during preview	Free and paid plans	Free and paid plans

Feature/Tool	GitHub Copilot	Amazon CodeWhisperer	Tabnine	Kite
Real-time Collaboration	No	No	No	No
Usage Insights & Analytics	No	Yes	No	Yes

Table 5.2: Comparative feature list of leading generative AI tools
for developer workflows created by ChatGPT-4o

The table presents a comprehensive overview, demonstrating a broad understanding of various tools, their integration capacities, and features such as AI technology usage and language support. This output illustrates ChatGPT's strength in delivering detailed, expansive insights across multiple aspects of developer tools.

Microsoft Copilot

Here is the table that was generated by Microsoft Copilot:

Features/Capabilities	GitHub Copilot	Google Gemini	Amazon CodeWhisperer	AskCodi	Tabnine
Code Generation and Completion	Yes	Yes	Yes	Yes	Yes
Optimization and Refactoring	Yes	Yes	Yes	No	No
Test Generation	Yes	Yes	Yes	Yes	No
Documentation and Knowledge Lookup	Yes	Yes	Yes	Yes	No
Collaborative Assistance	Yes	Yes	Yes	Yes	Yes
Cloud Integration and Guidance	Yes	Yes	Yes	No	No
Bug Detection	No	No	Yes	No	No
Code Reviews	No	No	Yes	No	No
Code Optimization	No	No	Yes	No	No
Refactoring	No	No	Yes	No	No
Natural Language Queries	Yes	Yes	Yes	Yes	Yes

Table 5.3: Comparative feature list of leading generative AI tools for
developer workflows created by Microsoft Copilot

Microsoft Copilot's output focuses on seamless integration with diverse IDEs and languages, emphasizing its analysis of a wide range of features and capabilities required for development environments. This table reflects the tool's adaptability and role in facilitating developer tasks across different platforms.

Google Gemini

Google Gemini's table was limited to a high-level feature comparison of the technologies, but it responded the fastest.

Feature	Amazon CodeWhisperer	GitHub Copilot	Tabnine	Bardeen
Code Generation	Yes	Yes	Yes	Yes
Code Completion	Yes	Yes	Yes	Yes
Context-aware Suggestions	Yes	Yes	Yes	Yes
Multi-language Support	Limited	Yes	Yes	Limited
Integration with IDEs	Visual Studio Code, AWS IDEs	Various IDEs	Various IDEs	Various Integrations
Focus	Code generation and optimization	General code completion and suggestions	AI-powered code completion	Workflow automation with generative AI
Learning Curve	Requires familiarity with AWS services	Requires GitHub account	Requires familiarity with IDE integration	Minimal setup required

Table 5.4: Comparative feature list of leading generative AI tools
for developer workflows created by Google Gemini

Perplexity AI

Perplexity AI's Pro version distinguished itself by requesting additional clarification, underscoring its capability to understand and adapt to specific user inputs, as shown in *Figure 5.1*.

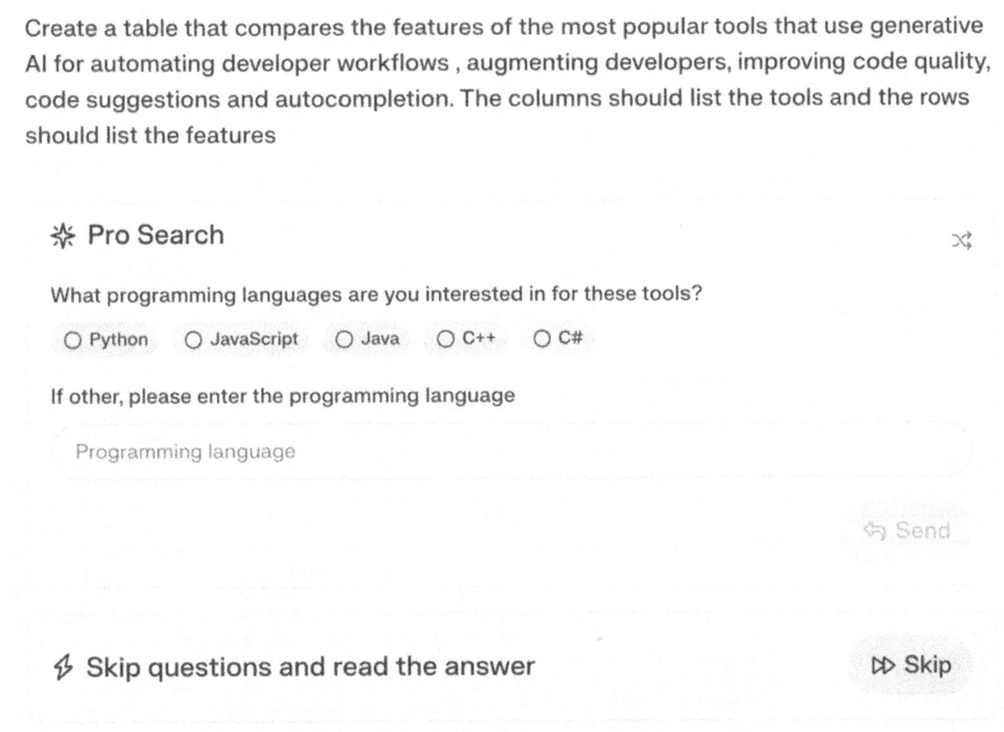

> Create a table that compares the features of the most popular tools that use generative AI for automating developer workflows , augmenting developers, improving code quality, code suggestions and autocompletion. The columns should list the tools and the rows should list the features

❋ Pro Search

What programming languages are you interested in for these tools?

○ Python   ○ JavaScript   ○ Java   ○ C++   ○ C#

If other, please enter the programming language

Programming language

↩ Send

⚡ Skip questions and read the answer   ⏩ Skip

Figure 5.1 – Perplexity AI Pro asked for clarification to improve the quality of the response

This interactivity ensures that the outputs are rapid and precisely aligned with the user's needs, illustrating a more sophisticated application of AI in software development environments. For consistency across the various models, we selected the option to skip the question and go directly to the answer.

Feature	GitHub Copilot	Visual Studio IntelliCode	Tabnine	OpenAI GPT-3
AI Model Used	OpenAI's Codex	Proprietary AI models	GPT-3	GPT-3
Programming Languages Supported	Python, JavaScript, TypeScript, Ruby, etc.	Multiple languages	Python, JavaScript, C++, etc.	Multiple languages
Integration	IDEs like Visual Studio Code	Visual Studio	Various IDEs	Custom integration via API
Code Suggestions	Real-time code analysis and suggestions	Predictive code completions	Contextual code completions	Contextual code suggestions
Code Autocompletion	Yes	Yes	Yes	Yes, through API calls
Functionality	Code generation, translation, rapid prototyping	Personalized suggestions, code quality improvement	Deep contextual understanding, error detection	Code autocompletion, natural language understanding
Learning Capability	Learns from project database	Learns from user code patterns	-	-
Security and Privacy	Potential security risks mentioned	-	-	-
Cost	Free for certain users, otherwise $10/month	-	-	Requires API key, pricing varies
Additional Features	Collaboration tools, version history tracking	Flags potential issues in code	Code generation, code translation	Customizable integration

Table 5.5: Comparative feature list of leading generative AI tools
for developer workflows created by Perplexity AI

Perplexity AI's output demonstrates not only the tool's precision but also its potential for customization, catering to specific user needs and enhancing the relevance of its assistance.

Analysis

Our experiment revealed that while generative AI models such as ChatGPT, Microsoft Copilot, Google Gemini, and Perplexity AI all deliver rapid responses, their outputs vary significantly in detail and focus. For instance, none of these models recognized that Amazon CodeWhisperer is now called Amazon Q Developer, and none of the models could agree on the most popular tools. Additionally, Perplexity AI had some empty cells, which indicates gaps in its comparative analysis, and Microsoft Copilot's responses were limited to Yes/No cells, lacking the nuanced details provided by the others. This variance underscores the necessity of selecting the right tool for specific tasks, as each AI model has its strengths and limitations. It also highlights the importance of thorough evaluation and cross-referencing to ensure comprehensive and accurate insights.

To evaluate the capabilities of generative AI models such as ChatGPT, Microsoft Copilot, Google Gemini, and Perplexity AI, we used a set of controlled tests based on three primary criteria: accuracy (precision and correctness of generated outputs), processing time (speed in generating responses), and ease of integration (how seamlessly the tool fits into Platform Engineering workflows). These benchmarks enabled a comparative analysis to assess the strengths and weaknesses of each model in practical scenarios.

Criteria	ChatGPT	Microsoft Copilot	Google Gemini	Perplexity AI
Accuracy	85% – High detail in responses	70% – Limited to Yes/No answers	80% – Balanced but generic	65% – Inconsistent with gaps
Processing time	~3 seconds per query	~2 seconds per query	~4 seconds per query	~2.5 seconds per query
Ease of integration	Moderate – Requires customization	High – Seamless in Microsoft ecosystem	Moderate – Early-stage tools	Low – Limited integration tools
Strengths	Detailed explanations	Fast response speed	Broad feature support	Multi-source aggregation
Weaknesses	Occasional inaccuracies	Lacks nuanced detail	Longer response times	Missing data in certain tasks

Table 5.6: Comparison of leading AI assistants across key performance criteria

This analysis emphasizes the importance of selecting the right tool for the task, as no single model excels in all areas. However, it's crucial to note that these tools continuously improve and evolve. Refinements and enhancements are regularly being made, meaning their capabilities today may already surpass what we observed during our experiments.

We may require multiple AI assistants for comprehensive research in selecting tools or augmenting workflows for Platform Engineering. Yet, a singular, well-integrated tool is optimal for aiding developers directly. Leveraging more than one AI tool in the development process could paradoxically increase friction and reduce efficiency, as developers might end up having to navigate excessive information rather than engaging in productive coding. Hence, strategic selection is crucial to harness AI effectively without adding overhead.

AI in infrastructure management

Integrating AI with infrastructure management significantly shifts IT operations, enabling more intelligent, efficient, and adaptive systems. While not all existing tools natively include AI capabilities, there are emerging technologies and integrations that bring AI-driven features to the infrastructure management landscape. The following are examples of accurate tools and frameworks facilitating this transformation:

- **GitLab Duo**: GitLab Duo, particularly Duo Workflows, exemplifies proactive AI use in infrastructure management. Duo combines AI-assisted code generation and integration across the **Software Development Life Cycle** (**SDLC**). It enhances automation by recommending infrastructure-as-code snippets and enabling seamless collaboration between development and operations teams. Duo Workflows further incorporate AI-driven orchestration, empowering organizations to address system demands and streamline CI/CD pipelines proactively.

- **Red Hat Ansible Lightspeed with IBM watsonx Code Assistant**: While Ansible doesn't inherently include AI capabilities, Lightspeed with IBM watsonx adds generative AI features for creating playbooks. This integration simplifies playbook creation by leveraging AI to generate and refine automation scripts. Organizations can use this to reduce the time required to develop robust automation workflows, making infrastructure management more efficient and less error-prone.

- **Terraform (via AI integration)**: While Terraform lacks native AI capabilities, AI tools such as GitHub Copilot or GitLab Duo can assist in writing and optimizing Terraform configurations. By using AI-generated infrastructure as code, organizations can automate resource provisioning with greater accuracy and efficiency. Third-party integrations with monitoring and predictive analytics tools can also enable proactive infrastructure scaling and optimization.

- **GitHub Advanced Security and Actions (with external AI)**: GitHub Advanced Security provides code scanning powered by CodeQL, which enhances security in infrastructure management workflows. While not AI-driven, GitHub Actions workflows can integrate with external AI-powered monitoring, alerting, and automation tools. These integrations bring intelligence to processes such as deployment orchestration and incident response.

- **Frameworks and APIs enabling AI in infrastructure**: Frameworks such as **Kubeflow** for Kubernetes and **MLflow** for managing machine learning workflows help bridge AI with infrastructure management. APIs such as AWS SageMaker and Google AI Platform can be integrated into DevOps pipelines to introduce predictive analytics, anomaly detection, and optimization, enhancing operational efficiency.

While still evolving, AI's role in infrastructure management demonstrates its potential to streamline workflows, improve security, and optimize resource utilization. By leveraging tools with accurate AI capabilities and integrating frameworks into existing workflows, organizations can prepare for the next generation of intelligent IT operations.

Security enhancement through AI

AI has transformed digital security, creating a robust and resilient ecosystem. It helps secure software supply chains, proactively combat cyber threats, and implement comprehensive security solutions. AI anticipates vulnerabilities, mitigates risks, and safeguards digital assets, fostering a trustworthy ecosystem. This shift is redefining security paradigms and catalyzing organizational transformation. Every step in this journey adds value and significantly impacts our digital world.

Secure software supply chains

Secure software supply chains are essential for businesses to protect their digital assets and maintain the integrity of their software products. While not all tools natively incorporate AI capabilities, advancements in AI-powered integrations have enhanced software development and deployment processes. Next, we discuss accurate examples of AI's contributions to secure supply chains and highlight actionable practices:

- **AI in static code analysis**: AI-powered static code analysis tools, such as GitLab Duo, enable a "shift-left" approach by identifying vulnerabilities and suggesting code improvements during the early stages of development. Duo integrates generative AI into IDEs and CI/CD pipelines, empowering developers to address security issues, code quality concerns, and compliance violations before they escalate. This reduces the risk of introducing vulnerabilities into production environments and accelerates delivery timelines.

- **AI-driven compliance management**: GitLab includes compliance features that scan software licenses and evaluate the number of **Common Vulnerabilities and Exposures** (**CVEs**) against compliance baselines. Although these capabilities don't inherently use AI, AI integrations such as GitLab Duo enhance compliance management by providing intelligent recommendations to ensure regulatory alignment and reduce manual oversight.

- **Container security with third-party tools**: Platforms such as **Red Hat OpenShift** and **VMware Tanzu** can integrate with tools such as Clair, an open source container security scanner. While Clair itself doesn't use AI, organizations can combine these platforms with AI-driven monitoring solutions such as **Sysdig Secure** or **Deep Instinct** to automate the detection and mitigation of vulnerabilities in containerized applications.

- **GitHub Advanced Security integrations**: GitHub's Advanced Security uses CodeQL to scan for vulnerabilities and allows third-party integrations with AI-enabled tools for enhanced scanning. While GitHub Copilot is a generative AI solution for coding assistance, it complements Advanced Security by guiding developers with AI-based recommendations to resolve detected issues efficiently.

- **AI in CI/CD pipelines**: AI is critical in optimizing CI/CD workflows by integrating predictive analytics and anomaly detection into the pipeline. Tools such as **Harness** leverage AI to monitor deployments, analyze patterns, and prevent risky updates, ensuring secure and stable rollouts.

- **Shift-left practices enhanced by AI**: The shift-left approach in secure SDLCs is driven by embedding AI tools directly into developer environments. Examples include real-time code analysis, AI-assisted test case generation, and vulnerability management integrated into CI/CD workflows. These practices empower developers to proactively resolve issues, enhancing software quality and security.

AI's role in secure software supply chains extends beyond detection to include proactive prevention and real-time monitoring. By integrating AI into the SDLC, businesses can create resilient, compliant, and secure systems, safeguarding their digital assets while accelerating time to market.

Proactive cybersecurity

The complexity of today's cybersecurity threat landscape demands advanced, proactive solutions. While some platforms such as Splunk, Elastic, and Datadog integrate AI features, their roles in cybersecurity are limited to generating insights and assisting with log analysis, rather than direct network security capabilities. To effectively address sophisticated threats, AI-powered tools take a proactive stance, focusing on analyzing network traffic patterns and correlating data to identify and mitigate risks. The following examples highlight how AI-powered tools and techniques are being applied across various layers of cybersecurity to enhance threat detection, prevention, and response in today's complex digital environments:

- **AI-driven network traffic analysis**: Advanced algorithms analyze traffic patterns by establishing baselines of normal behavior using historical data. AI models detect deviations such as unusual access patterns, high data transfer rates, or anomalous device interactions that could indicate potential attacks. For example, **Intrusion Detection Systems** (**IDSs**) such as **Darktrace** and **Vectra AI** employ machine learning models to analyze data from log files, device telemetry, and packet captures. These tools can flag deviations that signify **Advanced Persistent Threats** (**APTs**) or insider risks.

- **Endpoint protection tools**: Tools such as **SentinelOne** and **CrowdStrike** leverage AI to protect endpoints by monitoring device telemetry and user behavior. These solutions apply anomaly detection algorithms to identify unusual activity, such as unauthorized file access or lateral movement within a network. By correlating data sources, such as endpoint logs and system activity, AI-driven endpoint protection proactively detects malware, ransomware, and phishing attempts before significant damage occurs.

- **AI techniques in cybersecurity**: AI techniques such as supervised learning identify known attack patterns, while unsupervised learning detects novel threats without prior signatures. Reinforcement learning models, known for their adaptability, refine their real-time detection capabilities to handle evolving threats. These techniques enhance threat detection accuracy and minimize false positives, improving incident response efficiency.

- **Predictive analytics for cybersecurity resilience**: AI also powers predictive analytics, allowing businesses to anticipate potential threats by analyzing trends across vast datasets. For instance, tools such as **Cortex XSOAR**, **PhishEr Plus**, and **FortiSOAR** integrate predictive insights into security orchestration workflows, enabling faster mitigation of risks. Businesses can allocate resources effectively and bolster their defenses by identifying vulnerable points and potential attack vectors.

- **Visualizing detection workflows**: AI-enhanced workflows typically begin with data ingestion from diverse sources (e.g., logs, telemetry, and network packets). Tools such as Darktrace establish behavioral baselines from network telemetry to detect anomalies, Vectra AI identifies unusual communication patterns indicating lateral movement, and Cortex XSOAR integrates diverse data sources to prioritize alerts and automate response workflows. Data is preprocessed, filtered, and fed into machine learning models to establish behavioral baselines. Anomalies trigger alerts, prompting human analysts or automated systems to investigate and respond. These steps create a feedback loop, continuously refining the AI's accuracy and adaptability.

Integrating AI into cybersecurity strategies empowers organizations to stay ahead of evolving threats, shifting from reactive to proactive security measures. By leveraging AI-driven tools and workflows, businesses can enhance their cybersecurity resilience and protect their digital assets in an ever-changing threat environment.

Comprehensive security solutions

AI is transforming critical security areas beyond network monitoring, intrusion detection, and cybersecurity. It is being integrated into various technologies to protect platforms and assets.

AI-enabled **Video Management Systems (VMSs)** are revolutionizing physical security. Solutions such as **Avigilon** and **Milestone Systems** use computer vision and deep learning algorithms to identify and flag suspicious activities in real time. This provides valuable insights and early warnings, allowing security teams to proactively address potential security breaches before they escalate. These AI-powered VMSs continuously learn and adapt to the environment, making them an essential tool for organizations to monitor and respond to potential threats.

AI is also revolutionizing access control and identity management. Biometric authentication systems, such as facial recognition and fingerprint scanners, now incorporate AI-driven capabilities for enhanced security and convenience. These solutions accurately and quickly verify individual identity, reducing the risk of unauthorized access while streamlining entry for authorized personnel.

Moreover, AI is playing a crucial role in securing **Internet of Things (IoT)** devices. As the number of connected devices continues to grow, the attack surface for cybercriminals has expanded exponentially. AI-powered IoT security platforms analyze network traffic, device behavior, and contextual data to detect and mitigate threats in real time, identifying anomalies and vulnerabilities. This helps organizations maintain IoT ecosystem integrity and protect against emerging threats.

Organizations should adopt solutions that enable real-time device authentication using machine learning models trained on device behavior patterns and contextual data to implement AI in IoT security effectively. For example, anomaly detection algorithms can instantly monitor deviations in device activity, such as unexpected communication patterns or unauthorized access attempts, flagging potential breaches. Leveraging AI-enabled identity and access management tools ensures that only verified devices and users can access IoT networks, enhancing security while minimizing false positives. Combining these approaches with continuous learning models ensures adaptive protection against evolving threats in IoT ecosystems.

Integrating AI into physical and IoT security is more comprehensive than detection and response capabilities. AI-driven predictive analytics transform risk assessment and management by analyzing historical data, environmental factors, and other relevant information. AI systems provide valuable insights into potential vulnerabilities and their impact, enabling proactive risk management.

The threat landscape is constantly evolving, making it crucial for organizations to adopt comprehensive and adaptable security solutions. AI-powered technologies can help organizations stay ahead of physical and cyber threats by proactively identifying and mitigating risks before they can cause significant harm.

Integrating AI-driven solutions should be a top priority for businesses looking to modernize their security strategies. It gives a significant advantage in safeguarding their platforms, assets, and digital infrastructure. However, implementing AI in Platform Engineering can be challenging and comes with its own set of risks, requiring careful planning and robust execution to manage and mitigate them accordingly.

> **Explore further: Generative AI in action**
>
> We invite you to extend our experiment outlined in the *AI at the speed of thought* section and apply the same methodology to other critical areas listed in the *AI in infrastructure management* and *Security enhancement through AI* sections. Adjust the original prompt to fit these contexts and discover how generative AI can transform these domains. This exploration will deepen your understanding of AI's capabilities and empower you to leverage cutting-edge technology to streamline and secure your operations, enhancing your strategic initiatives with AI-driven insights.

Navigating the complexities of AI integration

Integrating generative AI into Platform Engineering offers substantial benefits but brings significant challenges. The primary concerns are data privacy and security, as AI systems handle sensitive and proprietary information. Organizations must also navigate a complex and evolving regulatory landscape, ensuring compliance across jurisdictions. Ethical considerations are critical to avoid unintended consequences such as bias and lack of transparency. This section addresses these challenges and presents strategies to mitigate risks, empowering leaders to harness AI responsibly and effectively.

Data privacy and security concerns

As generative AI technologies become increasingly integrated into Platform Engineering, the data privacy and security implications are significant, especially the vulnerabilities that may arise. Strategies must be implemented to safeguard sensitive information effectively. To address these concerns, organizations should focus on several critical aspects of data privacy and security when implementing generative AI, as outlined in the following key areas:

- **Vulnerability to data breaches**: Generative AI systems process and store vast amounts of data, some highly sensitive or proprietary. Their complexity can introduce vulnerabilities, making them potential targets for cyberattacks. Organizations must implement robust cybersecurity measures, such as encryption, secure access protocols, and IDSs, to protect against unauthorized access and data breaches.

- **Privacy compliance**: With the global landscape of data privacy regulations continually evolving, compliance becomes a critical challenge. Generative AI systems must be designed and operated to comply with laws such as the General Data Protection Regulation (GDPR) in Europe, CCPA in California, and other regional regulations. This involves implementing data protection by design, conducting regular privacy impact assessments, and ensuring that data-handling practices are transparent and accountable.

- **Data anonymization techniques**: Generative AI applications should employ advanced data anonymization techniques to remove individual identifiers from datasets and mitigate privacy risks. However, maintaining the utility of data while ensuring anonymity can be challenging, as overly anonymized data may lose its effectiveness for training AI models.

- **AI and consent**: Using personal data in AI systems raises questions about consent. Organizations must obtain explicit consent from individuals when their data is used for training or operating AI systems, particularly in applications that may impact personal rights or freedoms. Clear communication about how data is used, stored, and shared is essential to maintaining trust and compliance.

- **Security of AI models**: Beyond data security, the AI models themselves can be targets for attacks. Techniques such as model inversion or adversarial attacks can exploit weaknesses in AI algorithms to extract sensitive information or manipulate model behaviors. Protecting AI models involves securing both the data they use and the models themselves, including implementing measures to detect and respond to attacks on AI systems.

- **Ongoing monitoring and audits**: Given the dynamic nature of generative AI systems, continuous monitoring and regular security audits are essential to ensure that privacy and security measures remain effective. This includes reviewing access controls, evaluating data protection strategies, and updating security protocols in response to new threats. AI-powered tools are critical in monitoring data flow and access control across multi-cloud environments by analyzing user behavior, detecting unauthorized access attempts, and providing real-time insights to ensure comprehensive data security.

Addressing these data privacy and security concerns requires a multifaceted approach that includes technological solutions, organizational policies, and compliance with legal standards. By prioritizing data protection and ethical considerations, organizations can build trust and ensure that their use of generative AI in Platform Engineering enhances capabilities without compromising security or privacy.

Regulatory and compliance issues

The rapid advancement and integration of generative AI into Platform Engineering introduce a complex web of regulatory and compliance challenges. As governments and international bodies strive to keep pace with technological innovations, organizations must navigate an ever-evolving regulatory landscape. To navigate these challenges effectively, organizations must consider several key areas of compliance and regulatory responsibility:

- **Understanding diverse regulatory environments**: Generative AI applications often span multiple jurisdictions, each with its own set of rules and standards regarding data privacy, AI usage, and cybersecurity. Companies need to be well versed in the regulations specific to the regions they operate in, such as the GDPR in the European Union, which imposes strict guidelines on data usage and individual privacy. Staying compliant requires a thorough understanding of these regulations and adapting quickly to regulatory changes.

- **Industry-specific regulations**: Depending on the sector, additional layers of regulation may govern the deployment of AI technologies. For instance, the healthcare industry faces stringent regulations concerning patient data and medical devices, while the financial sector must comply with laws designed to prevent fraud and ensure transparency. Understanding and adhering to these industry-specific regulations is crucial for the successful and lawful use of generative AI in specialized fields.

- **Certification and standards compliance**: AI systems often need to meet specific standards and obtain certifications to build trust and ensure quality. These might include standards for AI safety, ethics, and interoperability. Compliance with international standards such as ISO and IEEE can demonstrate a commitment to best practices and quality assurance in AI development and deployment.

- **Intellectual property concerns**: As AI systems become capable of creating content or inventing new products, Intellectual Property (IP) issues become increasingly complex. Organizations must navigate the legal implications of AI-generated output, determining ownership and ensuring that their use of AI does not infringe on existing IP rights.

- **Liability and accountability**: Determining liability in cases where AI systems cause harm or financial loss is a significant legal challenge. Organizations must establish clear accountability frameworks to address potential damages or legal actions resulting from the actions of their AI systems. This includes developing robust risk management strategies and liability insurance policies to cover AI-related risks.

- **Engagement with regulatory bodies**: Proactive engagement with regulators can help organizations influence the development of AI regulations and ensure that their interests and concerns are addressed. Participating in industry groups, policy discussions, and public consultations can also provide insights into upcoming regulatory changes, allowing companies to prepare and adapt.

Organizations must navigate regulatory and compliance issues in Platform Engineering to ensure the legal and ethical integrity of generative AI applications. Compliance frameworks, legal education, and active engagement with regulatory developments are necessary investments that align innovative AI use with legal requirements and ethical standards. Organizations can streamline compliance efforts by leveraging tools such as **OneTrust** for privacy compliance or **BigID** for data governance. These tools, along with AI-driven solutions, can automate compliance monitoring by analyzing data flows, identifying potential violations, and generating actionable reports to meet regulatory requirements efficiently.

By integrating these tools and practices, organizations mitigate legal risks and foster responsible AI adoption. This is not just about meeting legal requirements, but about ensuring societal trust and accountability. This proactive approach underscores the need for organizations to consider the broader ethical and societal implications of their AI-driven initiatives, balancing innovation with fairness and equity. It's a significant responsibility that should not be taken lightly.

Ethical and societal implications

Deploying generative AI in Platform Engineering brings with it not just technical and regulatory challenges but also profound ethical and societal implications. As these technologies can influence major decisions and operations within enterprises, the responsibility to deploy them conscientiously grows. Let us delve into generative AI's ethical considerations and societal impacts, highlighting the need for responsible innovation and deployment strategies:

- **Bias and fairness**: AI systems can perpetuate bias and lead to unfair outcomes, often caused by the data used to train AI models, which can reflect historical inequalities or prejudices. To ensure fairness, rigorous testing and continuous monitoring of AI systems are essential to identify and mitigate biases. Organizations must commit to developing inclusive and equitable AI to prevent discrimination against any group.

- **Transparency and explainability**: As AI systems become more involved in decision-making processes, stakeholders need transparency in making decisions. To maintain trust and accountability in AI, its developers must develop explainable AI that provides understandable reasons for its decisions. This is necessary for employees and customers to have confidence in and understand the basis for AI-generated decisions.

- **Privacy and surveillance**: Generative AI's ability to process vast amounts of data raises significant privacy concerns. AI systems with access to sensitive personal and corporate data pose a high risk of privacy breaches and surveillance. Organizations must adhere to strict data protection standards and prioritize privacy rights when using AI to prevent unauthorized access and misuse.

- **Impact on employment**: Generative AI's automation capabilities can significantly change the job market by making certain roles redundant while creating new ones. Ethical organizations must proactively address these changes by providing retraining and reskilling opportunities for affected employees. This approach mitigates the negative impact on employment while building a future-ready workforce.

- **Societal impact and responsibility**: Generative AI has the potential to impact broader societal structures and norms beyond individual organizations. The ethical deployment of AI should consider long-term societal outcomes, including the potential for increased inequality or shifts in social dynamics. Companies are responsible for evaluating these broader impacts and working toward solutions that benefit society overall.

- **Governance and ethical frameworks**: To address these ethical challenges, robust governance frameworks that include ethical guidelines, oversight mechanisms, and regular audits are necessary. These frameworks should be developed in collaboration with diverse stakeholders, including ethicists, sociologists, and representatives from affected communities, to ensure a well-rounded and just approach to AI governance.

By carefully considering these complexities—data privacy and security, evolving regulatory landscapes, and ethical implications—organizations can navigate the integration of generative AI in Platform Engineering with innovation, efficiency, and social responsibility. Implementing comprehensive strategies to address these challenges ensures that AI's deployment not only enhances operational capabilities but also aligns with ethical standards and societal expectations. Understanding these factors will significantly help in developing better AI policies for your organizations and promoting responsible AI. This proactive approach positions organizations at the forefront of technological advancement, ready to leverage AI's full potential while safeguarding against its risks.

Summary

This chapter has showcased the transformative potential of incorporating generative AI into Platform Engineering, demonstrating how AI can elevate platform strategies and streamline operations across multiple dimensions. From enhancing decision-making to fortifying security protocols, AI applications in Platform Engineering optimize current processes and open doors to innovative approaches to software development and infrastructure management. Integrating AI can help organizations achieve efficiency, agility, and responsiveness, setting a new standard in the technological landscape.

Call to action

- **Pilot AI-driven initiatives**: Identify opportunities within your current platform operations where your teams can integrate AI. Begin with pilot projects focusing on automating tasks, enhancing security measures, improving resilience, and continuously assessing their performance. These pilots will serve as a foundation to scale AI integration across the organization, fostering a culture of innovation and continuous improvement with your leadership at the forefront.

- **Invest in AI skills development**: As AI becomes a critical component of Platform Engineering, investing in upskilling your team becomes imperative. Provide training and resources to help your staff understand and implement AI technologies effectively, ensuring that your organization remains at the forefront of innovation.

- **Establish AI ethics and governance**: Develop and implement policies and guidelines to ensure the responsible use of AI within your organization. Focus on creating ethical AI frameworks that promote transparency, fairness, and accountability, as well as safeguarding against bias, and ensure that AI-driven solutions align with organizational values and legal standards.

In the next chapter, we will delve into advanced generative AI techniques that further expand on the capabilities discussed here. This exploration will deepen our understanding of AI's potential and equip us with sophisticated tools and methodologies to revolutionize Platform Engineering.

Get This Book's PDF Version and Exclusive Extras

UNLOCK NOW

Scan the QR code (or go to packtpub.com/unlock). Search for this book by name, confirm the edition, and then follow the steps on the page.

Note: Keep your invoice handly. Purchase made directly from packt don't require one.

6

Engineering Platform Data Management

Centering around successful platforms can be difficult. One way to make a successful transition easier is to consider data early in the process. No platform succeeds without data. Successful data management starts with considering effective strategies that lead to delivering business value. These strategies are best when one carefully plans for integrating data, managing the culture, considering generative AI solutions, and then driving to success with architecture and operations.

In this chapter, we'll explore key strategies for effective data management, focusing on best practices and proven techniques that drive efficiency and reliability. We'll examine how to optimize data strategies to deliver meaningful business value by coordinating data recovery, production, and delivery processes. Additionally, we'll look at how aligning platform data architecture with operational goals can maximize performance, enabling higher returns and supporting sustainable growth.

We will be covering the following main topics:

- The crucial role of data in Platform Engineering
- Data strategies in Platform Engineering
- Implementing data in Platform Engineering
- Achieving outcomes through data strategies
- The role of data in delivering business value
- Case studies and examples of successful data-driven businesses
- Data architecture in Platform Engineering
- DataOps – Streamlining data management and operations

The crucial role of data in Platform Engineering

In the modern digital landscape, data is the lifeblood of enterprises, driving innovation, efficiency, and strategic decision-making. After exploring AI in Platform Engineering, we now focus on data—a critical component that powers AI and underpins business success. Understanding the intimate relationship between data and Platform Engineering is essential for maximizing their potential to deliver substantial business value.

The fusion of data and Platform Engineering is a powerful concept that drives significant business value. Data, often called the new gold, powers modern enterprises by providing insights for informed decision-making and strategic planning. Integrating data into Platform Engineering is about transforming raw data into actionable intelligence. Data within **machine learning** (**ML**) requires training, test, and production elements to be successful, and managing those elements is the first step. Sound data practices help ensure success for AI and ML initiatives. With a robust data foundation, AI and ML models can function effectively and may lead to optimal outcomes.

The integral role of data in AI and business success

Data serves as the foundation of AI, supplying the raw material for AI algorithms to learn, adapt, and make predictions. High-quality, well-structured data is essential for training accurate and reliable AI models. A robust data infrastructure is vital for successful AI initiatives as it prevents subpar outcomes and missed opportunities.

Data is also vital for achieving business objectives. It provides insights into customer behavior, market trends, and operational efficiency, aiding strategic decision-making and process optimization. Ultimately, data becomes a strategic asset driving business success. Data-driven decision-making transforms organizations by replacing intuition with factual evidence, leading to more accurate forecasting, improved risk management, and optimized resource allocation. Predictive analytics can identify trends and issues early, enabling proactive measures that save time and resources. Integrating data analytics into Platform Engineering allows organizations to continually enhance operations, improve customer experiences, and drive business growth. This approach ensures that every decision is backed by reliable data, reducing uncertainty and improving overall business performance. Each step requires collecting data, analyzing it against a baseline, and applying it to ML algorithms.

The correlation between data and Platform Engineering

Platform Engineering creates the infrastructure and tools to manage and process large volumes of data efficiently. It involves designing and implementing scalable, resilient, and flexible platforms to support data-intensive applications. These platforms enable seamless data flow across different systems, ensuring readily available information for analysis and decision-making.

Organizations must prioritize Platform Engineering for robust data infrastructure to support complex AI applications. This involves designing scalable, resilient platforms that integrate diverse data sources, facilitate advanced analytics, and ensure data security and compliance. Platform Engineering enables advanced data strategies such as **DataOps**, a methodology that combines data engineering and operations to streamline data management. DataOps ensures consistent, high-quality, readily available data, empowering organizations to make faster, more reliable data-driven decisions.

Improving operational efficiency in Platform Engineering is crucial. Data analytics helps organizations understand their operations, pinpoint bottlenecks, and identify improvement areas. Real-time monitoring and analytics provide immediate feedback on system performance, allowing quick adjustments and minimizing downtime. Data-powered predictive maintenance anticipates equipment failures and scheduled maintenance and prevents costly disruptions, extending equipment lifespan and ensuring reliable service. Let's learn about a few strategies through which data can be integrated within Platform Engineering.

Data strategies in Platform Engineering

Due to AI, ML, and big data technologies, the role of data will expand in Platform Engineering. Increasing data volumes requires effective management and analysis, becoming a critical business differentiator. Organizations integrating robust data strategies into Platform Engineering will leverage their data assets for valuable insights, driving strategic decisions and business success. Adapting to the data-driven landscape is crucial for the future of Platform Engineering, requiring continual evolution to meet the demands of the digital age.

Having established the importance of data in AI and Platform Engineering, we must explore effective data strategies that we can integrate into Platform Engineering practices. These strategies encompass selecting appropriate tools and technologies, optimizing processes, driving innovation through data integration, and fostering a culture prioritizing data-driven decision-making. The following table outlines key data management strategies, comparing their complexity, cost, and typical use cases to help organizations choose the most effective approach for their needs.

Strategy	Complexity	Cost	Use Cases
Tools and Technology	Med	Low to high	Data lake, data warehouse, analytic platforms
Process Optimization	Medium for governance, high for automation	Low	Data governance frameworks, quality standards, automated workflows
Enhance Operational Efficiency	Low	Medium	Real-time monitoring, operations centers, transparency
Data Integration	High	Medium	Silo removal, unified views
Cultivate Culture	High	Low	Agile foundations, retrospective, innovation first, observability

Table 6.1: Comparison of Data Management Strategies by Complexity, Cost, and Use Cases

With that foundation in place, let's take a closer look at how to select the right tools and technologies to support effective data management within your platform ecosystem.

Tool and technology selection

The choice of tools and technologies is fundamental to effective data management. Organizations must select solutions that align with their specific needs and goals. This could include data lakes, data warehouses, **extract, transform, load** (**ETL**) tools, and advanced analytics platforms. Ensuring these tools are seamlessly integrated into the Platform Engineering ecosystem is essential for maintaining data integrity and accessibility.

How do you select the proper data management tools for your organization? The key is understanding your data requirements, scalability needs, and integration capabilities. Choosing the right tools ensures that your data infrastructure is solid and can support advanced analytics and AI applications.

Process optimization

Optimizing data processes involves implementing best practices for data collection, storage, and analysis. This includes adopting data governance frameworks, establishing data quality standards, and automating data workflows. Data governance frameworks set guidelines for data collection and usage, ensuring data quality and compliance. Establishing data quality standards involves defining and maintaining data accuracy, consistency, and reliability. Automating data workflows reduces manual intervention, minimizes errors, and accelerates the delivery of insights.

How can your organization streamline data processes to enhance efficiency and reduce errors? The answer lies in adopting automated workflows, implementing stringent data quality checks, and continuously monitoring data processes to identify and address inefficiency. Some key tools to help ensure workflow efficiency are Azure Data Factory, Luigi, and Google Cloud Composer, especially with data streaming. The key goals in orchestration are workflow automation, error handling, governance practices, data scalability, and overall observability for all data practices.

Enhancing operational efficiency

Data plays a crucial role in enhancing operational efficiency within Platform Engineering. By leveraging data analytics, organizations can comprehensively understand their operations, identifying bottlenecks and areas for improvement. This insight enables the optimization of workflows, reducing redundancy and improving productivity.

For example, real-time monitoring and analytics can provide immediate feedback on system performance, allowing for rapid adjustments and minimizing downtime. Predictive maintenance, powered by data, can foresee potential equipment failures and schedule maintenance before issues arise, thus preventing costly disruptions. This proactive approach to maintenance extends the equipment's lifespan and ensures continuous, reliable service.

Driving innovation through data integration

Integrating data strategies within Platform Engineering is a powerful driver of innovation. Access to high-quality data allows organizations to experiment with new ideas, validate hypotheses, and iterate quickly. This environment fosters a culture of innovation where teams are encouraged to explore and develop cutting-edge solutions.

Data integration also facilitates collaboration across different departments, breaking down silos and enabling a more holistic approach to problem-solving. Platform Engineering ensures all stakeholders can access the information they need to innovate effectively by providing a unified view of data. This collaborative atmosphere accelerates the development of new products and services, driving competitive advantage and market leadership.

Cultivating a data-driven culture

Integrating data with Platform Engineering provides the foundation for making well-informed, real-time decisions. This transformative approach enables leaders to base strategies on empirical evidence, leading to more accurate forecasting, improved risk management, and optimized resource allocation. Cultivating a culture that prizes data-driven decision-making is crucial for successful data strategy integration. This involves promoting data literacy, fostering collaboration between data and business teams, and supporting continuous learning and development. Leadership sets the tone for a data-centric culture, emphasizing data as a strategic asset and empowering everyone to contribute to its success.

For instance, predictive analytics can identify trends and potential issues before they become critical, enabling proactive measures that save time and resources. By embedding data analytics into the core of Platform Engineering, organizations can continuously refine their operations, enhance customer experiences, and drive business growth. This approach ensures that every decision is backed by solid data, reducing uncertainty and improving overall business performance.

How can your organization foster a culture that values data-driven decision-making? The answer lies in promoting data literacy, encouraging cross-functional collaboration, and supporting continuous learning and development. By emphasizing the importance of staying up-to-date with the latest data trends and technologies, you can keep your team engaged and committed to the success of your data strategies in Platform Engineering.

As we delve deeper into implementing data strategies in Platform Engineering, we will explore how these strategies drive business value, the essential components of data architecture, and the role of DataOps. Real-world examples and case studies will illustrate the transformative impact of integrating data with Platform Engineering, providing practical insights and actionable guidance. This exploration will inspire and motivate you to leverage data for the success of your Platform Engineering initiatives. Once one decides on a strategic approach, one critical element becomes how data drives that strategy through metrics-driven approaches.

Implementing data in Platform Engineering

How can your organization better harness the power of data to enhance AI capabilities and drive business success? The knowledge gained from the previous chapter on AI serves as a foundation for understanding the pivotal role of data in Platform Engineering. As we move forward, understanding and leveraging the critical role of data will be essential for any organization aiming to thrive in the competitive, data-centric world.

Data is an asset and a foundational element of successful Platform Engineering. Its integration into platform strategies enhances decision-making, drives innovation, and ensures operational efficiency. By reflecting on these insights and embracing a data-driven approach, organizations can unlock new levels of innovation, efficiency, and competitive advantage. We will continue building on this foundation in the following sections, providing insights into integrating data strategies, architecture, and operations within Platform Engineering. This journey will equip you with the knowledge and tools to harness data's full potential and transform it into a powerful driver of business success.

Implementing data strategies for optimal Platform Engineering

In the fast-paced digital landscape, integrating data strategies into Platform Engineering is not just a competitive edge but a strategic necessity. Data-driven platforms are fundamental for successfully deploying AI and ML models, relying on vast amounts of high-quality data. This section explores crucial data strategies for Platform Engineering, their impact on driving business value, and best practices for integration.

Critical data strategies in Platform Engineering

Effective data strategies are central to maximizing the potential of Platform Engineering. These strategies encompass various aspects of data management, from collection and storage to analysis and utilization. Here are some critical data strategies that organizations should consider.

Mastering data integration and interoperability

Seamless data integration and interoperability are crucial for organizations in data-siloed environments. Companies can create a unified view that supports real-time analytics and informed decision-making by combining data from different sources. Achieving seamless data flow enables a comprehensive understanding of business operations and customer behavior. Mastery in data integration and interoperability ensures that platforms remain Agile, scalable, and ready to leverage emerging data sources.

Excellence in data governance and quality management

Creating reliable AI models and insightful analytics relies on solid data governance and quality management. Rigorous data governance frameworks are essential for ensuring data accuracy, consistency, and security. Organizations must invest in stringent data quality management processes, which include cleansing, validation, and enrichment. High-quality data fuels AI with reliable inputs, leading to effective analytics and strategic decision-making. Upholding data integrity through disciplined governance practices builds stakeholder trust and ensures compliance with regulatory mandates.

Goals for checking data should include early error detection, improving overall quality, reducing the cost of gathering and analyzing data, increasing efficiency through speed, and building scalable processes. Determining initial steps relies on a needs assessment often leading to tool selection. Open source tools are Great Expectations, dbt, and Talend, while some paid tools are Informatica Cloud Data Quality, RightData, and Deepchecks.

Fortifying data security and privacy

In today's environment of increasing data breaches and stringent regulations such as the GDPR, fortifying data security and privacy is essential. Implementing advanced security measures such as encryption, access controls, and regular audits is crucial for protecting data from unauthorized access and breaches. Ensuring data privacy involves anonymizing sensitive data and maintaining transparency about data usage. Prioritizing data security and privacy not only safeguards against legal and financial repercussions but also fosters customer trust. A reliable data security and privacy approach establishes a resilient foundation for data-driven initiatives.

Integrating advanced analytics and AI for innovation

Harnessing advanced analytics and integrating AI within Platform Engineering provides deeper insights and fosters innovation. Deploying AI models for analyzing large datasets, identifying patterns, and making predictions transforms data into actionable intelligence. Advanced analytics tools empower organizations to conduct complex analyses, from predictive modeling to natural language processing.

AI integration enables automated decision-making, enhancing operational efficiency and reducing human error. For instance, AI-powered recommendation systems tailor customer experiences, while predictive maintenance models optimize asset management. Embedding advanced analytics and AI into Platform Engineering helps organizations drive continuous innovation and maintain a competitive edge.

Achieving outcomes through data strategies

Implementing effective data strategies within Platform Engineering can help organizations achieve success in their strategic outcomes in several ways:

- **Elevating decision-making:** Data-driven decision-making is transformative, enabling organizations to base strategies on empirical evidence rather than intuition. Leveraging real-time data analytics leads to more accurate forecasting, superior risk management, and optimized resource allocation. Predictive analytics can identify trends and potential issues before they become critical, enabling proactive measures that save time and resources.

  When organizations embed data analytics into their core operations, they continuously refine processes, enhance customer experiences, and drive business growth. Data-backed decisions reduce uncertainty and improve overall business performance.

- **Fueling innovation and competitive advantage**: Effective data strategies empower organizations to experiment, innovate, and iterate quickly. Access to high-quality data allows teams to test new ideas, validate hypotheses, and refine products and services. This culture of innovation is crucial for staying competitive in a rapidly changing market.

  For instance, financial institutions leveraging data analytics to develop new financial products, optimize pricing strategies, and improve risk management exemplify how data-driven experimentation can drive continuous improvement and market leadership.

- **Enhancing operational efficiency**: Data strategies streamline operations by providing insights into process efficiencies and inefficiencies. Real-time data analytics can identify bottlenecks, predict equipment failures, and optimize resource allocation. This proactive approach to operations management reduces costs, minimizes downtime, and enhances productivity.

  Implementing predictive analytics and real-time monitoring systems provides the insights needed to optimize workflows and prevent disruptions, significantly improving operational efficiency.

- **Transforming customer experience**: Data-driven platforms enable organizations to deliver personalized and seamless customer experiences. By analyzing customer data, businesses can tailor offerings to meet individual preferences and needs, improving customer satisfaction and loyalty. E-commerce platforms using data analytics to recommend products, optimize pricing, and personalize marketing messages exemplify this transformation.

  Integrating AI-powered recommendation systems and advanced analytics can provide the personalization modern customers expect, enhancing overall customer experiences.

Next, we will learn some best practices to achieve optimal outcomes.

Best practices for integrating data strategies with Platform Engineering

Integrating data strategies with Platform Engineering requires a comprehensive and systematic approach. Some strategies apply to Platform Engineering as well as the broader organization. For example, successful platforms require good data practices beyond the platform bounds to handle customer data, governance standards, and other elements. Here are five best practices to ensure successful integration across the platform:

- **Cultivating a data-driven culture**: Establishing a data-driven culture is essential for the successful implementation of data strategies. Promoting data literacy across the organization, encouraging collaboration between data and business teams, and supporting continuous learning and development are critical steps. Leadership must set the tone, ensuring data is viewed as a strategic asset.

  Encouraging cross-functional collaboration, providing data literacy training, and celebrating data-driven successes help embed this mindset throughout the organization.

- **Investing in scalable and flexible infrastructure**: Building scalable and flexible data infrastructure is crucial for supporting data-intensive applications and future growth. Investing in cloud-based solutions, data lakes, and data warehouses that can handle large volumes of data and support real-time analytics is essential.

  Modern, cloud-based infrastructure provides the scalability and flexibility needed to support advanced data strategies and AI integration, ensuring the organization can adapt to changing data needs.

- **Implementing robust data governance frameworks**: Robust data governance frameworks ensure data accuracy, consistency, and security. Establishing clear policies and procedures for data management, including data quality standards, data stewardship roles, and compliance requirements, is essential for maintaining data integrity.

  Regularly reviewing and updating data governance policies ensures they meet current regulatory requirements and support high-quality data management, which is critical for successful Platform Engineering. Specific frameworks and foundations can be found in *Chapter 2*, and *Chapter 9*.

- **Leveraging advanced analytics tools**: Advanced analytics tools are critical for deriving actionable insights from data. Investing in tools that support predictive analytics, ML, and real-time data processing enables organizations to perform complex analysis, identify patterns, and make data-driven decisions.

  Regularly evaluating and upgrading analytics capabilities ensures alignment with business needs and technological advancements, maximizing the potential of data-driven initiatives. For a broader evaluation, see *Chapter 4*.

- **Ensuring data security and privacy**: Maintaining robust data security and privacy is paramount in the digital age. Implementing advanced security measures, such as encryption, access controls, and regular audits, protects data from unauthorized access and breaches. Ensuring compliance with data privacy regulations builds trust with customers and can prevent legal repercussions.

  Regular assessments of security practices and staying updated with the latest security technologies and regulatory requirements protect data assets and support the integrity of data-driven strategies. For a broader discussion, see *Chapter 7*.

The integration of effective data strategies within Platform Engineering is essential for harnessing AI's full potential and driving business success. By focusing on crucial data strategies such as data integration, governance, security, and advanced analytics, organizations can transform data into a strategic asset that drives innovation, enhances decision-making, and improves operational efficiency.

As we continue to explore the role of data in Platform Engineering, we will delve deeper into data architecture and DataOps, providing practical insights and real-world examples that illustrate the transformative impact of these strategies. Mastering data in Platform Engineering begins with recognizing its importance and implementing best practices that align with organizational goals and technological advancements. The next step converts those strategies into business value through data.

The role of data in delivering business value

In the current business landscape, data is not just a tool but a strategic asset that drives significant business outcomes. The strategic impact of data on business operations, decision-making, and innovation cannot be overstated. When effectively harnessed, data can transform organizations, enabling them to operate more efficiently, respond to market changes swiftly, and deliver exceptional value to customers.

Strategic impact of data on business outcomes

The strategic impact of data on business outcomes is multifaceted. Fundamentally, data offers insights for making informed decisions, optimizing operations, and driving innovation. Utilizing data for decision-making allows businesses to spot opportunities and threats in real time, leading to a proactive approach to strategy and operations. Analyzing large volumes of data to extract actionable insights can significantly boost competitive advantage.

In a competitive market, businesses that use data to gain insights into customer behavior, market trends, and operational efficiency are better positioned to outperform their competitors. Data-driven organizations are Agile, responsive, and capable of making decisions based on empirical evidence rather than intuition. Data also plays a crucial role in risk management. By analyzing historical data, businesses can identify patterns and predict potential risks, enabling them to implement preventive measures. This proactive approach to risk management mitigates potential threats and ensures business continuity and resilience.

Aligning data initiatives with business goals

Organizations must align their data initiatives with their overall business objectives to utilize data fully. This alignment ensures that data efforts are focused on delivering tangible business results rather than operating independently from strategic goals. The first step in this process is clearly defining the business goals and identifying the **key performance indicators** (**KPIs**) to measure success.

Organizations should then create a data strategy that supports these goals. This involves identifying the necessary data sources, establishing data governance frameworks, and implementing appropriate tools and technologies. Data initiatives should be prioritized based on their potential impact on business outcomes, ensuring that resources are allocated to the most critical projects. Additionally, it's vital to foster a data-driven culture within the organization. This includes promoting data literacy, encouraging collaboration between data and business teams, and embedding data-driven decision-making in the organizational culture. Leadership plays a crucial role in championing data initiatives and setting the tone for a data-centric culture.

Using AI and data to deliver business value

AI and data are tightly linked, with data fueling AI models. Integrating AI and data can unlock substantial business value by automating processes, improving decision-making, and delivering personalized customer experiences. AI requires high-quality data to learn and make predictions. By leveraging AI, businesses can analyze complex datasets, identify patterns, and derive insights to optimize operations, reduce costs, and improve efficiency.

For instance, AI-powered predictive analytics can forecast customer demand, helping optimize inventory levels and reduce waste. AI-driven recommendation systems can personalize marketing efforts, increasing customer engagement and sales. Delivering tailored experiences based on customer data enhances satisfaction and loyalty. Learning the best AI practices involves reviewing case studies for feedback, finding those elements that succeeded, and viewing those that failed as paths to improvement.

Case studies and examples of successful data-driven businesses

Several leading companies have successfully harnessed the power of data and AI to drive business value. Let's explore four notable examples.

Netflix – Revolutionizing entertainment with data-driven insights

Netflix is a prime example of a company that has leveraged data to revolutionize the entertainment industry. By analyzing user data, Netflix provides highly personalized content recommendations, enhancing the user experience and increasing viewer engagement. The company uses data to inform content creation, ensuring that new shows and movies resonate with its audience. Data from various areas drives the platform strategy from development and marketing areas.

Netflix's data-driven approach extends to its marketing strategies. By analyzing viewing patterns and user preferences, Netflix can effectively tailor its marketing efforts to target specific segments. This data-centric strategy has contributed to Netflix's dominance in the streaming industry, demonstrating the profound impact of data on business success. Additionally, Netflix utilizes A/B testing to determine the most effective user interfaces, promotional strategies, and content delivery methods. This meticulous analysis ensures that every aspect of the platform is optimized for user engagement and satisfaction.

Moreover, Netflix leverages predictive analytics to anticipate viewing trends and manage content licensing agreements efficiently. This proactive approach allows Netflix to secure rights for potential hit shows and movies before competitors, ensuring a robust and appealing content library. Integrating advanced analytics and machine learning models enables Netflix to maintain a competitive edge in an increasingly crowded market.

Amazon – Redefining retail with data-driven strategies

Amazon's success in the retail sector is largely attributed to its data-driven approach. Again, similar to Netflix, having a successful data strategy becomes key to overall platform success. The company collects and analyzes vast amounts of data on customer behavior, purchasing patterns, and market trends. This data is used to optimize inventory management, personalize product recommendations, and enhance the overall shopping experience. Amazon's recommendation engine, powered by AI, analyzes customer data to suggest products that are likely to interest each shopper. This personalized approach not only boosts sales but also improves customer satisfaction. Additionally, data analytics helps Amazon streamline its supply chain, reducing costs and ensuring timely delivery of products.

Furthermore, Amazon employs predictive analytics to forecast demand and manage inventory levels more effectively. By anticipating customer needs, Amazon can reduce stockouts and overstock situations, optimize the supply chain, and minimize operational costs. This strategic use of data ensures that Amazon remains a leader in customer satisfaction and operational efficiency.

Amazon Web Services (**AWS**), another arm of the company, exemplifies how data-driven strategies can diversify business models and drive innovation. AWS provides cloud computing solutions that leverage data analytics, enabling businesses worldwide to harness the power of big data and AI. This contributes to Amazon's revenue and positions the company as a critical player in the global tech industry.

Databricks – Unifying data and AI for business innovation

Databricks is at the forefront of unifying data and AI to drive business innovation. The company's platform integrates data engineering, data science, and ML, enabling organizations to build and deploy AI models at scale. In this case, the delivered platform has become the product with the emphasis on allowing users to ingest and modify data. Databricks' unified approach simplifies data management, accelerates analytics, and enhances team collaboration.

By leveraging Databricks, organizations can unlock the full potential of their data, driving innovation and achieving significant business outcomes. The platform's ability to handle large-scale data processing and advanced analytics makes it a valuable asset for companies looking to harness the power of AI and data. Databricks also supports collaborative projects by providing a unified workspace where data engineers, scientists, and analysts can work together seamlessly. This collaborative environment fosters innovation and accelerates the development of AI-driven solutions.

Databricks has empowered numerous organizations to transform their operations through data and AI. For instance, global enterprises use Databricks to optimize supply chains, enhance customer insights, and streamline product development. By providing a robust and scalable platform, Databricks enables these companies to execute their data strategies effectively, resulting in measurable business value.

Uber – Data-driven transformation in transportation

Uber's use of data and AI has transformed the transportation industry. The company's platform collects vast amounts of data on ride patterns, driver behavior, and customer preferences. This data is used to optimize routes, predict demand, and set dynamic pricing. These effective data elements underpin a successful platform. Uber's AI-powered algorithms analyze real-time data to match riders with drivers efficiently, reducing wait times and improving service quality. Additionally, data analytics helps Uber identify areas for expansion, optimize driver incentives, and enhance overall operational efficiency. Uber's data-driven approach has enabled it to scale rapidly and maintain a competitive edge in the market.

Uber's commitment to leveraging data extends to its efforts in safety and compliance. By analyzing driver and rider behavior, Uber can identify potential safety risks and implement measures to mitigate them. This proactive approach enhances user trust and ensures regulatory compliance, which is crucial for sustainable growth.

Furthermore, Uber's advanced analytics capabilities enable the company to innovate continuously. For example, data insights drove the development of UberPOOL, a ride-sharing service that matches riders traveling in the same direction. By optimizing vehicle utilization and reducing riders' costs, UberPOOL demonstrates how data-driven strategies can lead to new business models and revenue streams.

Strategic insights from these case studies

Netflix, Amazon, Databricks, and Uber's success stories demonstrate the critical importance of data and AI in driving business value. A data-centric approach can provide significant competitive advantages, improve customer experiences, and enhance operational efficiency. Examples such as Netflix's personalized recommendations and Amazon's optimized supply chain showcase the transformative power of data-driven strategies. Organizations investing in data and AI are better equipped to navigate complexities, adapt to market changes, and deliver exceptional customer value.

Data as a strategic asset

Data is a strategic asset that drives business value when aligned with business goals, utilizing AI and fostering a data-driven culture. This strategic impact empowers companies to make informed decisions, innovate, and stay competitive. Exploring data architecture and DataOps within Platform Engineering provides practical insights and real-world examples of the transformative impact of effective data management and advanced analytics. Mastering data in Platform Engineering requires continuous learning, adaptation, and a commitment to excellence. In the following section, we will examine how a robust and carefully planned data architecture can improve Platform Engineering to expedite the delivery of business value.

Data architecture in Platform Engineering

Architecture should always design the form for distributing data within a platform. One should return to early evaluations of Conway's Law, ensuring the designed structure remains supportable by the broader organization. Data must flow through architecture in a manner the company can use and understand. The first step is designing a reliable, scalable architecture. This allows identifying key components and best practices for your platform data management. Once data is streaming, steps should ensure quality data, governance practices, and security. Finally, this section concludes with some examples of tools, especially in generative AI, that can assist in data solutions. For specific architectural patterns, reference *Chapter 2*.

Similar to any other aspect of the platform, data management requires a sound architecture to demonstrate a path. Data architectures consider data at rest and data in motion as well as transitions between those states. The more advanced architectures consider data not just as a single element but as a myriad of potential feeds and reports. Integrating all those elements in the modern IoT world requires careful planning.

Data architecture design

Designing a reliable and scalable architecture focuses on those two key components. Reliability is what ensures the platform soundness between data users, data providers, and platform teams. Those reliable discussions should focus on agreements between the different stakeholders, which are usually confirmed through the establishment of clear SLAs demonstrating a level of reliability. These measures can include technical specifications such as update rates, downtime, throughput, packet sizes, and encryption standards. Each agreement contributes to making the platform data more accessible at a higher rate than other alternatives. Contributing to reliability can address transmitted data accuracy, how closely data matches original sources, and at what point data changes or the extension of those data points occurs.

When examining reliable big data platforms with the 5 Vs (*velocity, volume, value, variety, and veracity*), you have to ensure not only transmission but that accurate data reaches the user. The following list highlights some characteristics of each of those big data components:

- **Velocity**: How quickly data is created within a system and how fast that created data moves to the next element. For example, traffic cameras record all events at a set location but may not instantly pass that data to a reporting element.

- **Volume**: The amount of data generated from multiple sources, including social media, commercial transactions, and user interfaces. Large data volumes allow high-level analysis to reveal patterns that may not be apparent in small data sets.

- **Value**: How much impact each element of data has on a company's business. Most big data value comes from the ability to achieve pattern recognition to generate insights to improve performance, operations, and other quantifiable benefits.

- **Variety**: How many different types of data are collected within a system. Modern systems collect text-based inputs, streaming video, and other factors. Data can be structured, semi-structured, or unstructured. Data management tools must be able to handle multiple types of data within common dashboards and visualizations.

- **Veracity**: Quality and accuracy of collected data. Data often contains errors, inconsistency, and other uncertainty from multiple sources. As an example, errors can occur in addresses, names, or other information tied to an individual. You might see an address with transposed street numbers, misspelled avenue names, or other bad inputs.

Data that meets these 5 Vs can be challenging to handle from a reliability standpoint. The impacts on collected data within the platform can impact velocity, volume, and veracity frequently. If a platform supports multiple users on the same application with teams deploying multiple times per day, the velocity is impacted. When you add the operational management of those systems, the user volume across development and operational aspects can drive challenging alignment. Finally, the data veracity might be challenged by having multiple versions running, different test measurements, and then the operational data. One way to manage big data consists of implementing scalable solutions.

Scalability forms the other data architecture component for platforms. Once you achieve initial reliability, measures should be introduced for scalability. Scalability enhances reliability by offering additional options. When the platform scales, options are introduced to manage data through other formats. One common example involves structuring data flows to have earlier stopping points before the data hits the full system. Testing scenarios on the platform can use captured data representative of the true data without streaming access. One example is a healthcare system that manages user requests, safeguards case management data, and provides clinical services, all subject to **personal identifiable information (PII)** and healthcare-restricted data. A scalable test solution could segment the data and prevent critical data from reaching other data stores.

Modeling data management

Modeling a reliable and scalable architecture might involve using a modeling language such as the **Unified Modeling Language (UML)**. UML serves as a general-purpose modeling tool published by the Object Management Group in 2005 and later published as an **International Organization for Standardization (ISO)** standard. These standards break every item into an object with attachments, associated by class and arranged into components. These groupings then represent functions within the architecture diagram. Items within UML are related by *association*, *inheritance*, and *aggregation*. As a simple example, all medical records for a particular clinic might be associated and inherited by the broader insurance, while all instances for a particular individual or medical case might be aggregated. The following image depicts an architecture for data entry within UML.

(Entry)   Data Entry   (Record)
           User enters data

              ↑ (Compare)

           Existing Data
           *Measures for
           duplicate data*

                            Initial Data Store
                            *Data entered in
                            initial model (SQL,
                            no SQL, Postgres,
                            Redis)*

                                    (Conversion)

                (Search)

           User Search   Final Data Store   (Transmit)   Data sent to Platform
           *User calls data with   *Data transitioned into   App
           manual or API search*   common format*   *Converted, de-dupped
                                                                     data received*

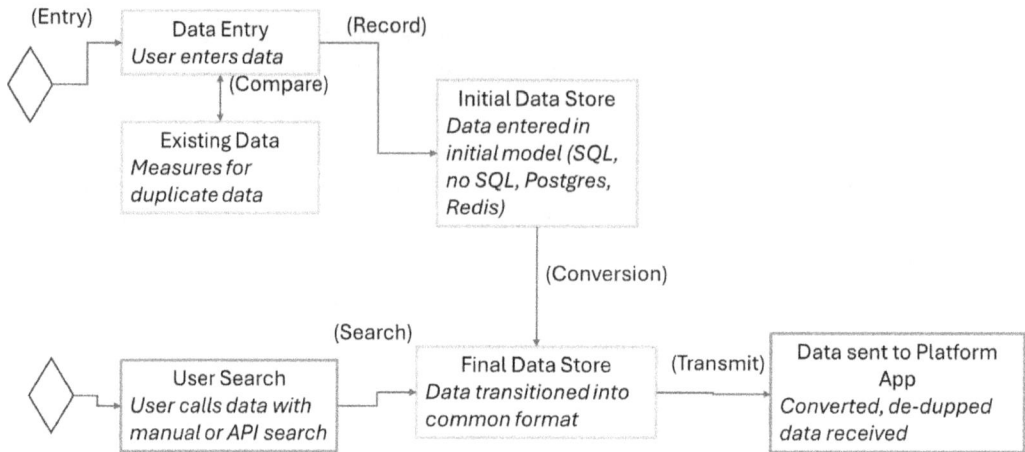

Figure 6.1: UML example of a data conversion architecture

The diagram displays how entry and search can be aligned into a common schema. Most tools provide an option to convert designed architecture into additional formats. The challenge can be ensuring the right key pairs are presented in the correct manner. As an example, Keycloak allows bringing user groups from one database to another, updating users from previous SSO solutions to a new one. However, during the conversion, Keycloak frequently adds a backslash to the user group's name. This prevents them from reaching the same areas although transferred users may still use Keycloak. This type of conversion error reinforces the name for a clear schema and conversion in data management.

Another modeling option involves **The Open Group Architecture Framework (TOGAF)**. TOGAF was first introduced in 1995 as part of a US Department of Defense project. The language was intended to address four goals:

- Improving return on investment
- Using more cost-effective resources
- Avoiding vendor lock-in
- Establishing a common language

Like UML, the language is relatively simple to use but additional certifications are possible. TOGAF uses three pillars of continuum tracking, an architectural development model, and enterprise architecture domains. The following figure demonstrates how TOGAF might show interactions within a data format:

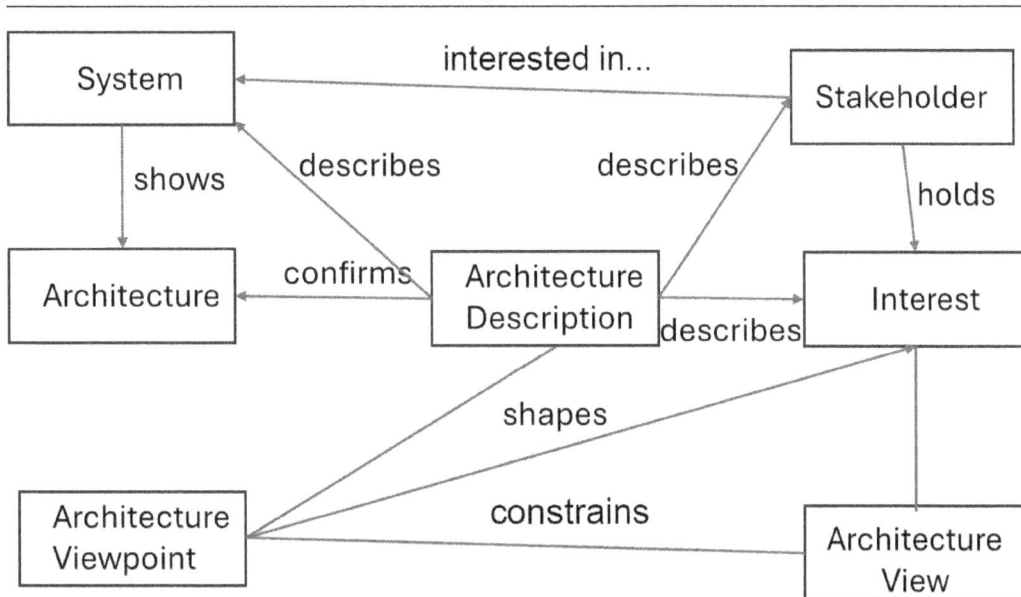

Figure 6.2: TOGAF architecture model

You can see how the system of interest, the platform, shows the architecture while linking with stakeholders at multiple points. These connections demonstrate which areas exhibit control over which factors in moving the design forward. The most important thing in Platform Engineering is the capacity to use the domains of business, data, applications, and technical architecture to diagram needs. TOGAF excels at modeling flow between the domains, making it a natural fit for some data concerns.

One other key to TOGAF is that every element within the architecture has four aspects:

- **Active**: Every time the data is received, an action must occur.
- **Passive**: Data is collected and held until an outside call to action is received.
- **Behavior**: The data, when collected, moves to a certain store point or repository.
- **Motivation**: Data objects are assigned a motivation for when they must shift from active to passive or exhibit a motivation.

The weakness of using TOGAF is that it requires much more depth than UML to develop a comprehensive architecture. This can work well if you have a lot of time, but it can be challenging with rapid projects. One suggestion is to begin with UML modeling structures and expand into the more complete TOGAF model as more data is collected.

Data architecture best practices

When considering some best practices, you should return to Conway, ensuring modeling mirrors business practices, and the proposed structure does not run counter to existing pathways. If the pathways diverge too much, even excellent data may be unavailable to individuals within the platform. Data architecture should strive to identify key areas for documentation and quality, performance monitoring, testing, and scalability.

Best practices start with how one documents the data architecture. The previous sections mentioned using formats such as UML or TOGAF, but this extends into clear terminology with visual representations. For example, if there is a date or time format, all entries should be in a common standard. If one set of data uses the MM/DD/YYYY (02/10/2012) structure and another uses the DD, Mon, Year (10 Feb 2012) structure, there may be difficulty in aligning records. Each format selected within the schema should be built on a clear rationale for why a particular scheme has been collected. This can range from a declared status, such as a date, to ingestion from other components that have set sales standards and inventory numbers.

The next area builds from initial documentation to creating quality data. Just as the standards for the initial data are set, those quality standards should live in the same documentation. The quick list to ensure quality data is that all data is complete, unique, timely, valid, accurate, and consistent. Quality in the platform might be verified users, links to testing structure, or comparison against the existing database to prevent duplication. When using the platform, you can allow guest users but not want those users to submit merge tickets during applications. At the same time, guest users might be allowed to develop without limits, but not move data into a testing environment. Qualifying data originators and verification during quality validation can help prevent erroneous data from reaching production.

Data versioning occurs in multiple areas. Data can be restricted to specific collection sets, evaluated as a time series in multiple sets, or distinguished by sensors. Multiple paths are usually assessed to determine the best data versioning for a specific implementation. Most platform data implementations prefer using a streaming approach with a constant data flow, so new data, once quality-checked, will become part of the overall stream. Using separate data versions is most appropriate during the initial stages of determining an initial dataset, test set, and then the production data for ML. Different sets can be used to periodically check the ML model for errors in quality, regression, or bias.

Our third best practice area involves performance monitoring. Effective monitoring follows best practices for observability in establishing clear objectives, automating data collection, creating scalability, and using alerting to notify exceptions. Clear objectives require clear metrics, such as the amount of data in throughput, required fields, and verified users. Required fields might be only the key ID field, or extend to other items such as prices, inventory numbers, and stocking rates. The required fields should always be inputted and allow for the extension of submitted data but not the alteration of existing elements. These first fields allow scalability because data can be either the lowest compute drain or one of the highest depending on the required validity. For example, if the primary data source archives video clips and every clip must be run to verify if an AI submission occurs, those checks can be difficult. Verifying data against an existing inventory for duplicate entries is much easier.

Moving on from monitoring should address how you test data during the initial ingestion and when data is stored in the platform. Not all data remains consistent all the time, and the system should test to ensure data meets new specifications. An easy check for data testing within platforms is to call only the latest data. The following example shows some initial code that may address calling only data within a specific timeframe from a SQL database:

```
with data
        as (select *,row_number() over(partition by subject order by
    createddatetime) as rnk from t
                )
        ,cte
        as(select id,subject,createddatetime as begin_date,
    createddatetime,cast(1 as int) as grp from data
            where rnk=1
            union all
        select b.id
                ,b.subject
                ,b.createddatetime
                ,case when datediff(minute,a.createddatetime,b.
    createddatetime) > 5 then b.createddatetime
                else
                a.createddatetime
                end as createddatetime
            ,case when datediff(minute,a.createddatetime,b.
    createddatetime) > 5 then a.grp+1
                else
            A.grp
                end as grp
        from cte a
        join t b
            on a.id+1=b.id
            and a.subject=b.subject
                )
    select * from cte order by 1
```

This code looks at all data in the platform and creates groups for each subject where the data is published within 5 minutes. Different groups are created by subject, so A entries are grouped in one set, and B entries in another. These differentiators can be easily integrated and extended into a variety of coding tools and APIs.

More testing formats are covered extensively in *Chapter 9*. There are some unique areas for testing that are specific to data. Data testing typically involves three separate types within a production instance. These tests are designed to measure whether the desired data inputs through an application correctly and are described as follows:

- **Standard test**: An expected input gives an expected output. If you enter a username and password, you expect to either enter the application or be informed the username does not exist.

- **Boundary test**: These tests form edge cases for multiple events. An example from the previous paragraphs is entering data in a non-standard format and the application rejecting the data.

- **Erroneous test**: The opposite of the standard test, these tests require the application to notify when bad data has been entered. One example is putting in inventory numbers in a non-standard format, or an inventory number that does not exist.

Data testing should look for some very specific database items. A shortlist includes data schema, table structure, columns, key IDs, stored macros within the elements, server validation, and data duplication. One frequent need for evaluating macros is a format called SQL injection, where code can be entered within the database, and when the form runs, the code is executed. These malicious code items can delete other data elements, ruin formats, and make it a very difficult day for developers. A suggestion when using data in tests is to employ software to generate fake tables from a known schema. This ensures testing processes are validated but do not break actual data. Many AI/ML processes are fairly efficient at generating large, alternative databases for testing. Similar to the versioning approach, metadata catalogs can be used to compare various sets. The metadata ensures the data catalogs measure similar features and provide comparison elements. Effective catalogs also allow scalability and comparison between elements.

The final best practice for data architecture is to ensure scalability. This seems an easy approach: ensuring enough compute and storage exist to manage the database. Other issues might address the number of users, consecutive use, and the SOLID principles addressed in *Chapter 2*. One example of scalability might be limiting an order number, or inventory number to a set number of characters. When the business expands past that initial limit or additional features are required, adjusting those factors to scale might require a full database revision. For example, if an inventory number is set for nine numbers, with a dash between characters four and five, the later addition of a three-digit code to the end might be difficult. You can always add additional columns, but that again causes a full database revision. These best practices in architecture are linked to being able to conduct effective DataOps within your platform.

DataOps – Streamlining data management and operations

DataOps integrates DevOps best practices with flow, feedback, and improvements to data engineering practices. As DevOps primarily focuses on delivering products, DataOps can often be a subset of overall business strategies, required in production but falling behind during development and test phases. Incorporating data management to test functions early ensures the best data becomes available to support analytics, ML, and continuous improvement models. Much like other areas, building effective DataOps concentrates on key areas such as collaboration, automation, and observability.

The importance of DataOps

When starting a DataOps journey, many of the best practices are common with the best practices in areas such as MLOps, DevOps, AIOps, FinOps, or any other construction of the operational mindset. Every operational journey should start with defined objectives, cross-functional teams, a commitment to automation, and observability. These factors are supplemented with data-focused language such as automating data pipelines, controlling data versions, emphasizing quality, and maintaining data security, especially with more sensitive data volumes.

You can define objectives for DataOps similar to any other operational factor. In *Chapter 9*, we take a detailed look at constructing metrics and service-level agreements to support various operations. For data, the best look measures those items against testing for standard, boundary, and erroneous use cases. You should ensure that users can reach the data, that the data meets quality standards, and that applications continue to function. Cross-functional teams then use the data to ensure success. In this case, cross-functional means including developers, database engineers, and analysts within the same spectrum. In the interest of maintaining small teams, these database specialists are often considered a support team, available for questions and support applications but not development team members. As platforms expand, the associated databases often expand.

One element to consider when launching a platform is whether you intend to manage the data or allow users to manage data as needed for applications. Some constructions manage every development aspect, while others use third-party software. There are some standard database tools that add options for better operations and management such as Oracle Database, MongoDB, Amazon RDS or Dynamo DB, SAP SE, or Snowflake. Each has different strengths and weaknesses depending on your database needs. One frequent requirement is automation in operations.

Database pipelines

Database pipelines should be constructed in a DevOps manner to ingest new data. Depending on your platform use case, you might need to handle streaming data, automated entries from a retail web service, or some other format. Just as application pipelines have stages, so too do automated data pipelines, and they are as follows:

- **Data ingestion**: Initial gathering from databases, microservice, APIs, and applications.

- **Data processing**: Cleaning, verifying, converting, and enriching data while ensuring it meets quality standards.

- **Data storage**: The process of storing data within a database, data warehouse, data lake, or other schema to make it readily accessible at the needed time.

- **Data analysis**: Evaluating data to determine trends across large ingestion elements, especially when considering big data input.

- **Data visualization**: Converting ingested data into easily visualized formats to allow users to observe activity, activate alert notifications, and address emerging needs.

Data pipelines handle data in either batch or real-time processes. In batch processes, data is stored until a certain point, either time or size, and then processed. In real-time processes, all data is immediately ingested into the database. In either case, two formats are typically used, **extract-transform-load (ETL)** or **extract-load-transform (ELT)**. The difference between the two is whether the transformation occurs in the primary database, or before it gets there. If there are multiple developers on a platform, it may be easier to use ETL format.

You can use pipeline elements to continuously monitor data drift and distribution changes. These changes can impact downstream ML models or analytics dashboards. For example, if you are monitoring power usage in an urban environment, unusual weather patterns can influence data. If you are using a time regression model comparing baselines from one seasonal average to the next, the influence of an event can alternate baselines. This may result in changes for preventative maintenance, or scalability within the platform. When dealing with a cold front, the analytics dashboard might show a significant increase in power usage but not one that would be repeated in previous seasons or years. Once you ingest data, it is time to consider security and observability for that data.

Data security and observability

Data security and observability mirror solutions that have been presented in later chapters to maximize platform performance. Security is a must for data but should be considered within the overall platform format. Implementing encryption and SSO techniques ensures that data remains protected within the platform security architecture. The biggest challenge emerges when you input data from external sources. The previous section briefly mentioned this with the ETL approach, ensuring that data meets quality standards before bringing those elements into your system. Addressing quality early stops the easiest failures, such as preventing SQL injection, and then allows delivering quality solutions.

The next step for security should be considering what happens if corrupted data does enter the system. You should always maintain an ability to recover previous data models from hot, warm, or cold storage. This can be challenging for businesses that depend on real-time communication. For example, in the e-retail industry, losing 30 minutes of customer data after launching a sale can be devastating. In addition to losing sales, customers can be unhappy at having to resubmit data, and inventory stocks might prevent order fulfillment.

Observability for DataOps occurs in two ways. Just like security is designed to signal and guard, observability for data should be the same. The signal standard notifies when new data is ingested, or data does not meet quality standards. The guard element prevents and notifies when bad data attempts to enter the platform. Most database management tools provide a path to observe data. These tools can be combined with the observability standards introduced in *Chapter 9*.

Summary

This chapter launched from the previous usage of generative AI tools to expand into using that data once it hits the platform. This begins by recognizing the importance of data within the platform. While the platform's basics solve many issues, these issues are frequently impotent until data has been added. Adding data means constructing an effective strategy to consume and manage data within various formats. Effective strategies demonstrated how to maximize value for the business, and we presented several case studies where businesses converted sound practices into actual dollars.

Once a strategy is in place, you must develop an architecture supporting those practices. The chapter demonstrated building an architecture, introduced several modeling languages, and suggested management techniques. Implementing sound data practices at the platform's early stages support DataOps management, working with data at rest and data in motion throughout the platform. The next chapter takes these initial platform stages and begins applying security, compliance, and risk management techniques to make your platform secure and reliable.

> **Call to action**
> - Understand the data needed for platform success and implement a strategy.
> - Design an architecture supporting your organization and platform.
> - Apply sound operational techniques to ingest and manage data during daily operations.

Get This Book's PDF Version and Exclusive Extras

UNLOCK NOW

Scan the QR code (or go to `packtpub.com/unlock`). Search for this book by name, confirm the edition, and then follow the steps on the page.

Note: Keep your invoice handly. Purchase made directly from packt don't require one.

7

Security, Compliance, and Risk Management

DevOps often appears as **DevSecOps** to emphasize security, but any operational solution requires security. Building a platform focuses on delivering value, allowing others to develop, and securing from end to end. Platforms provide the opportunity to provide secure by default solutions with details like vulnerability tracking, software bill of materials, and patching solutions before software ever reaches the customer. Comprehensive security and risk management solutions also manage those who connect to platforms, especially in PaaS and SaaS solutions. To further expedite delivery, AI tools can influence security outcomes, prevent inevitable manual failures, and support full-spectrum risk solutions.

The question regarding computers and software development frequently requires providing a secure offering. The most secure systems are those with no connections. However, while hardware in a vault may be virtually inaccessible, it also serves no purpose. Having functional and valuable software means having connections, and those links create risk. This chapter is not about pipelines or CI/CD but about making the platform to support those eventual actions.

In this chapter, we return to security basics to create the basics for platforms as secure by default and manage any extraneous risk. The following topics are covered:

- Designing a secure-by-default platform
- Network management and security practices
- Leveraging AI for security enhancements

Technical requirements

There are no specific technical requirements for this section. A basic understanding of architectural concepts, security scanners, and **identity and access management (IDAM)** will be helpful.

Designing a secure-by-default platform

Designing a secure platform starts with the idea that securing the platform considers internal and external threats. Security starts with two basic ideas, all security tools exist to either signal an alert that something is happening or guard against an event. Sometimes, one combines guarding and signaling in that there is an alert, and then the protection goes into place. The idea is similar to a bank vault receiving an alert and the big bars slamming across the vault area.

This thought then becomes the platform ideation. Ideation, as a concept, considers further formulating a thought or idea. Everyone today seeks secure software development with DevSecOps and Agile practices all shifting left. Despite shifting left, security remains bolted on to processes rather than integral to delivery, and no exchange exists to moderate values between functional and secure within application development.

Platforms integrate the idea that individuals experience security practices, move on to define guidelines for creating secure work, and then mix the two concepts to establish a platform as secure by default. When developing platform security, needed security functions are not bolted on but instead form initial core design. Program managers distinguish between *security* and *functionality* . Security are aspects adding to compliance, access, authorization, or regulatory requirements while function criteria are more tightly tied to what a program does. From the developer's perspective, all functions are functions; they merely accomplish different ends. Shifting left as a security function appears in *Chapter 1* as a basic concept of Platform Engineering

The platform security model relies on functions featuring external observability, internal integration, and end-user implementation perspectives. Security scans and dashboards should be integral to executed processes without thinking about the task. The question should never be if the scan ran, but which scan was run and how the results were displayed. Just like with early architecture requirements, security begins with questions about *what to secure*, *how to secure it*, and then *is there security* (i.e., demonstrating that security exists). Asking these questions begins the meta-approach to integrate the platform's multiple tasks into a common security framework. This common integration supports the software value chain. It is not enough to secure the initial login, one file within a framework, or a single vulnerability. Comprehensive platform security addresses all issues by creating the fence, adding a gate, and then putting bells on the swinging door.

All security practices should start as part of Agile software development. Above, we referenced developers see no difference between development, operational, and security functions. All items are simply a function with a specific set of results. When building a secure-by-default platform, part of the question should be how much security will be needed. Security experts will expound that more security is always needed, but sometimes the security resides in the basics or the Layer 8 humans rather than integrating another tool. *Layer 8 humans* refers to the seven-layer OSI model with the humorous approach that humans interacting with the system are level 8.The first step in any value chain is to assess how value affects overall objectives to create profitable products and services. Security perspectives can shift radically depending on an individual's perceptions about objectives. These shifts require a broad introduction to understand how thinking about security experiences clarifies understanding of platforms.

Too much security can be as harmful as too little security, posing a risk to the number of users rather than active users. The wrong types of security, and adding dynamic tools to an internal database can add cost and slow performance. The inability to create observability within security tools might catch an issue but prevent resolution. The ideas behind security are as important as the actual implementation. These initial areas decompose into people, processes, and technology across the team, organization, and enterprise levels. Each offers solutions that affect platform outcomes.

Basics of security ideation

Thinking about thinking is a meta-concept best understood by applying a phenomenological outlook. The concept of modern phenomenology, as a philosophical practice, originated with Descartes as a follow-on from the Socratic method. Phenomenology suggests that all aspects center on the thing itself. Things, in this case, security, are influenced by creation, observation, and experience to create a layered understanding. Creation for the platform occurs through shared development, observation from internal and external users, and the security experience as the platform combines functions.

Phenomenological thought suggests all experiences, and one's experience of those things, including concepts, begins with the process observer. Only by understanding the observer's perspective can one build understanding. The three core aspects of understanding are *the presence and absence of the thing, identity as manifold through the expression and expressed artifacts*, and *clarifying parts versus wholes during the experience*. Phenomenology does not create new understanding, rather it attempts to clarify the existing experience as understanding.

While esoteric, these terms readily apply to platform security. In presence and absence, one assesses how security relates between different elements within the collaboration or deployment targets. The root cause for identity in the experience reflects the need for **Single Sign On** (**SSO**), identity management tools, and the roles expressed as part of the **Role-based Access Controls** (**RBAC**) or **Attribute-based Access Controls** (**ABAC**) controls. The last element, parts versus wholes, is crucial in platform security. One can secure a single tool or multiple tools, to change platform levels within various applications. Think about a net of overlapping circles, each protecting a particular area, and requiring control elements when one passes across a line. *Figure 7.1* shows how confusing those security perspectives might be when looking from a top level.

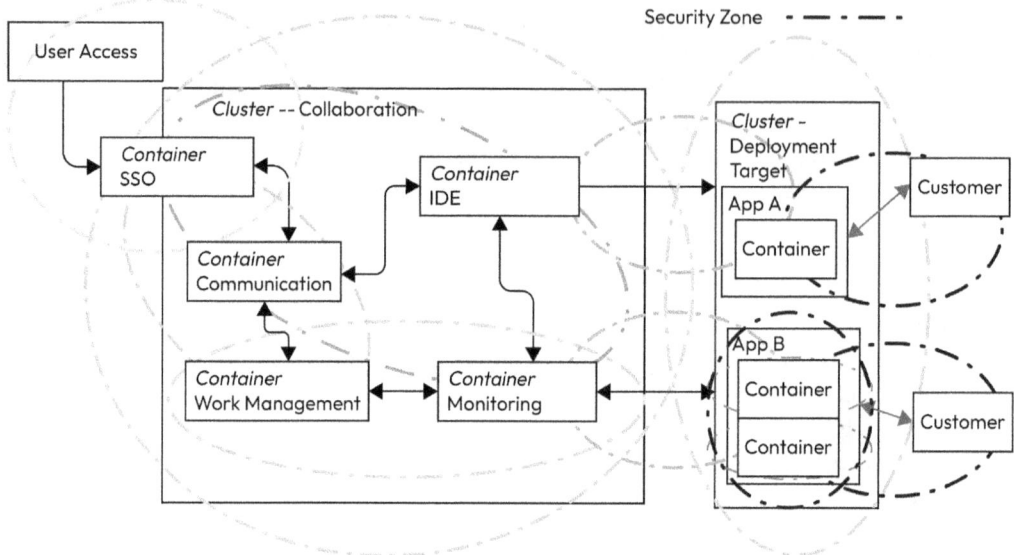

Figure 7.1 – Security control zones: Theoretical

Each circle represents a potentially different security consideration for a different area. Users tend to start with external access and move to internal, lateral accesses as moving across the environment. At the far end, customers also have external access to production elements. Starting from the left, the initial access zones need user and password security, the cluster needs identity and internal data protection, monitoring tools might need to be separated from the average developer, applications in deployment targets need container-level protection, and then monitoring and protection from the customers who use applications on the net. One common attack method, **SQL injection**, uses the capability to put certain characters into program inputs to affect program execution. One must block these areas while still allowing creation freedom across the platform. Understanding these areas requires knowing the conceptual security pattern for your platform.

Expanding to conceptual security looks differently at true facts versus assumptions. Conceptual security relates to the experience of "the thing itself" by removing the outside observer's perspective. Descartes used meditations on the thing to connect his faith to the physical. Another philosopher, Edmund Husserl, distinguished between material content and logical generality within the analyzed observations. It does not matter if the outside observer sees a fence or a moat as long as no castle access exists without using the approved gate. These distinctions carry over into building platform security by identifying what is known to be true, what should be true, and actions taken if the overall elements are false.

Coding allows a much clearer distinction to define experienced artifacts than philosophy. We suggest these distinctions are valid when assessing security as few distinguish between security concepts and the material representation delivered by development. At a high level, one can quickly think about three common security distinctions: *compliance*, *technical guardrails*, and *vulnerabilities*. Each offers different construction, but the user experiences all as a secure by default platform.

A common example starts with observing the physical rather than the more challenging conceptual understanding. Husserl used the term "eidetic" as essential, so eidetic reduction expands our understanding of the core concept. When one observes a table, it holds multiple physical and conceptual eidetic layers depending on observation. Depending on where one physically observes the table, it may be a rectangle, a rhombus, or even a triangle. Conceptually, a table can be a place to eat, meet, or hold things for later use. Some tables support gaming, puzzles or other purposes. The eidetic understanding might then be that the essence of a table is something to do with the capacity, whether intellectually or physically, that a table holds. The same applies to the security concept: every security artifact must guard or signal, and the challenge remains in creating effective, interlocking artifacts.

Security for people, process, and technology

For security, the eidetic ideation would be moving from the essential concrete object or idea to the pure essence derived by reducing the ideas to core components. This ideation applies when looking at security: does it appear as a comfort blanket to reduce risk, a process involving different individuals at different stages, or a technical solution to vulnerabilities and challenges? In a DevOps perspective, one adds observation layers, pipeline artifacts, and external interaction with customers, managers, and product owner. Each area functions as an individual part and an integrated whole through, describing outcomes with eidetic reduction, and demonstrating functionality.

Security ideation begins with people. One cannot experience, leaving out potential future AI options, without a person to describe the experience. Organizations all acquire people with roles, skills, and talents from multiple areas. An individual's background creates their experiential lens, and those lenses influence security outcomes. Each individual creates value and an understanding of value through judging security based on an individual perspective.

To return from the esoteric to the physical, companies often use **red-team assessments** to gauge security levels. A red team is a designated group of individuals who attempt to penetrate the security surrounding a platform, a system, or even a building. Many of these red teams start by requiring software implanted within the platform. Then, security areas that might prevent that item from working are disabled. However, this fundamentally changes the experience as that root item would not exist in the initial construct. This thought equates to testing only the front door while ignoring the yard's fence, guard dog, and land mines.

A developer might bring previous security experience with no development, work at a company that experienced multiple breaches, or endless hours chasing vulnerabilities. An Ops person might want to use security to reduce time on call, ease fixes, and minimize downtime. A product owner might want to sell more products and build a public image. The customer might want to know if their public data is protected. Each brings ideation, and an area is eidetically reduced to consider part and wholes, identity, and presence or absence before addressing other layers.

Ideation can be a singular event or the sum of the entire process. The process integrates individual pieces to accomplish end goals. The process takes multiple tasks, creates artifacts representing each, and constructs an understanding about how guarding and signaling must occur. The presence or absence of those artifacts defines how they experience the overall task. The expressed identity reflects whether a security scan happened, did the scan was complete, and how patching contributes to the experience.

Further, one must consider whether the security process constitutes a whole experience or merely the parts of the process creating the whole element. In the platform, the security experience should be an integrated part of the whole. Processes can be accelerated or derailed due to the presence of people and technology within the individual elements.

The final assessed element, in today's cybersecurity environment, must be the technology to either develop processes or augment people. Technology contains material elements but remains vital to the platform experience. Specific security requirements across on-premise, cloud, or mobile systems can change an individual's interaction with those elements. Later elements within this chapter focus on the technical pieces implemented with the understanding that people and processes can all change the technology. For example, if one leaves their keys hanging in the lock, how secure the door may be never matters.

We often blame technological failures without fully comprehending the interaction through people and processes. In many ways, *DevSecOps*, or *PaaS, IaaS, CI/CD, Infrastructure as Code*, and *Configuration as Code* are all previously ideated in a way to shape user interaction. The platform expands this by creating specific ideated platforms with defined experiences required to achieve secure outcomes. The variables remain to see whether those defining terms communicate the experience one has with various tools. In some cases, with some of the more advanced tools and metrics, it may be possible to examine how the technology experiences the user as much as the user experiences the technology. Understanding those experiences guides the next two sections in what must be secured and how to secure those elements.

What to secure

After understanding the conceptual approach, the question for designing our secure by default platform should be: *what do I secure within the workspace*? The first area to secure should be **external access**. Defining external access describes the process that allows transit to the platform and from circle to circle across the security architecture. Each circle appears as a **trust circle**, those within a circle can make changes, and communicating with other circles requires consensus through technical handshakes. These accesses are balanced against **internal vulnerabilities** within the different elements, preventing vulnerabilities from releasing in deployed software. Finally, one must secure **data at rest** and **data in motion**. The ways operational tools conduct business and users manage data all matter to the security outcomes.

External access

External access lies in two spots: accessing the platform initially and traversing across different elements. This access can also extend to dependencies within the programs, later referenced as a Software Bill of Materials. Initial security determines who can log in to see the platform and decides which areas they can attend. Think of external security as buying a ticket to a carnival; the initial access allows one into the carnival, but the rides and games require different tickets. One can purchase properties at the front gate or as one reaches the required segments.

In implementing the overall architecture, the initial security should be to the primary collaboration platform, creating a user account that can view all potential items but with limited edit properties. Different user roles within RBAC as developer, manager, or admin can limit the ability to reach unique tools or properties within those tools. One should subdivide roles into different elements depending on the type of tool. An initial example often occurs from the IDE. One might want a developer to be able to create branches, fork repositories, and write code but restrict merge permissions to approved individuals. The same individual may be approved to work within a project but not create new projects. This security creates logging for what has happened and prevents potential errors.

Traversing across different elements requires exchanging artifacts. The token between one element should empower the second element and allow the exchange of trusted data. Some of these become more of an internal vulnerability, but initial structuring requires architecting which elements each element requires. A typical example is the **Software Bill of Materials** (**SBOM**) that many production elements use. This artifact compiles all the dependencies used by software, usually in a textual format, but details the specific links used by the software. These artifacts include library versions, recent updates, and sometimes the elements required for the software to be successful. Understanding external vulnerabilities allows conversion to addressing internal vulnerabilities within tools.

Internal vulnerabilities: Common Vulnerabilities and Exposures and patching

Internal vulnerabilities are those inherent within any element of software. They are not part of the external dependency but elements within the desired software. These can be the properties within the software, such as allowing the creation of other artifacts, the presence of embedded secrets, or errors allowing malicious or misguided conversion. As mentioned above, SQL injection presents a typical example of an internal error with tools, even those integrated into a platform. SQL injection is when some software treats entries within the program as code, executes commands or allows unintended functions.

One advantage of a platform is that integrating various tools can reduce the potential scope of internal errors. Efficiently setting up the RBAC from the previous element can prevent escalation of privilege between different tools. For example, an error that allows escalation on one tool, from user permissions to administrative permissions within the IDE, would require a different access point to allow similar access within a deployment or management stack. These internal controls are a best practice between different tools on the platform.

To ensure the best performance, one should keep up with current **Common Vulnerabilities and Exposures** (CVEs) and required patches. The U.S. government sponsors the CVE library (`cve.mitre.org`) and uses the Mitre Company to proliferate errors within tools. Anyone can submit a CVE, and most companies respond reasonably quickly to mitigate any identified threats. The recent Solar Winds hack (2023) against the U.S. government was only possible because some customers failed to make required patches to systems (`https://www.techtarget.com/whatis/feature/SolarWinds-hack-explained-Everything-you-need-to-know`). The SBOM is the initial guide but platform maintainers should strive to ensure all systems possess the latest updates and patches. From a security perspective, one reason for continuous development is to ensure potential hackers do not have enough time to find and exploit holes within the software. None of the best patches can help if the data supporting those applications is not secured.

Data

Securing data falls into two major categories: data at rest and data in motion. Data within the platform should be considered *at rest* when contained in a deployment target or within a cluster and *in motion* when moving between clusters or across the network. Despite being in motion between containers, data can be secured within the cluster at rest by establishing shared repositories and databases. Sharing permissions occurs through tokens and RBAC controls, as discussed above. The rationale for sharing the tokens within the cluster is to maximize ease of use for each user and when working with teams between users.

Constructing shared data within clusters does not preclude creating individual data sites. It may be advantageous not to share data between teams or individuals at specific points, even when on shared resources. Implementing RBAC continues to work at those solutions. Implementing effective data security allows the creation of encryption keys associated with the data shared between individuals.

This pattern does open possibilities for malicious insiders, those with permissions on the cluster that take inappropriate actions. Some actions are technical, in locking down different areas and some are policy-based. Technical solutions amount to tighter RBAC controls that can prevent the platform from operating as a DevOps fundamental. The preferred solution for these individuals is a policy one, do not allow individuals who have left the company to have access, and have comprehensive rules for user behavior in place. One of the preferred policies is least privilege, ensuring users never have more access than needed to do their job. Then, the policy solutions can be mitigated by technical signaling when bad behavior happens rather than stopping an event that may be good in some contexts.

How to secure the platform

Several standard approaches exist to secure platforms effectively through technical means. The first approach, as referenced, is to implement SSO tools using proven user directories. After that, encryption methods can go a long way towards securing data, preventing password misuse, and protecting code, even in production. Finally, as part of the platform's operational construct and security tools, the implemented gadgets prevent new security problems from reaching the platform or proliferating across the functions. Gadgets include scanners across the platform, monitoring deployed applications, and pipeline tools that prevent errors from reaching production.

Single-Sign-On (SSO)

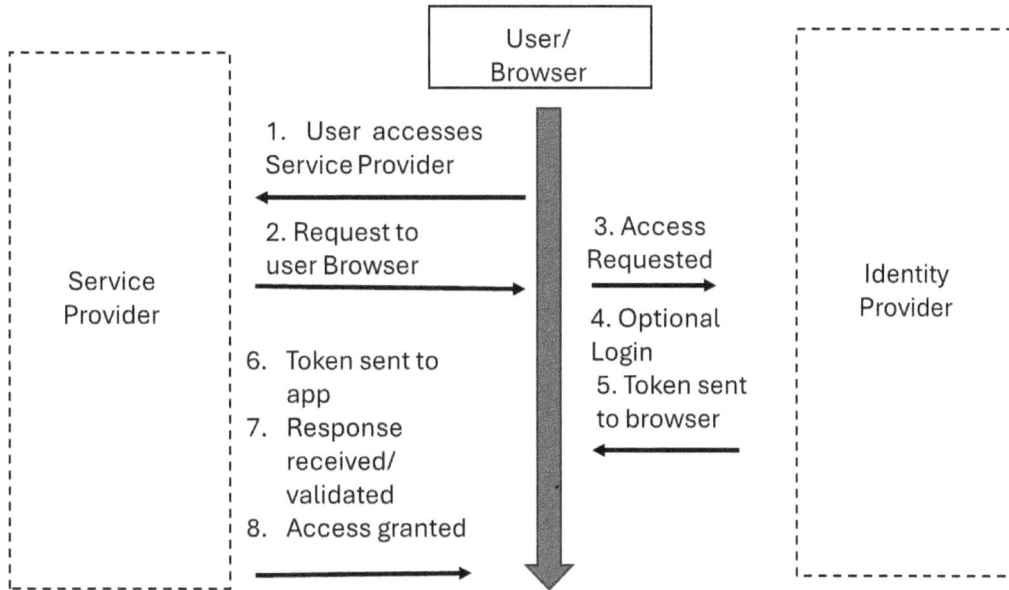

SSO applications create an authentication method that allows users to access multiple websites with one set of credentials. The converse to this is password managers that require different communication but store all elements in the same place. A sample of the SSO process appears in *Figure 7.2*.

Single Sign On

Figure 7.2 – SSO process

Password managers would arrive before the connection began, providing input in *stage 4* for the **Optional Login**. The **Identity Provider** allows a primary connection or verifies more advanced access based on the password. The returned token then tells the service provider what properties to release. These identity properties often align with the SSO through an authentication protocol, typically either a **Lightweight Directory Access Protocol (LDAP)** or **Secure Assertion Markup Language (SAML)**.

LDAP provides an industry standard to manage directory information. These functions are frequently separate from establishing a token, but verify a particular login has the permissions to use a token. As a process, a platform can establish an LDAP directory with user names and attributes, and then each user can log in. LDAP can divide into simple authentications, where a correct name and password connect a user, or integrate with a **Simple Authentication and Security Layer (SASL)**. SASL solutions require authentication before matching users against the overall directory.

LDAP is widely available, and some top-performing programs are **OpenLDAP** or **Apache Directory Server**. These then pair with administrative tools such as **Apache Directory Studio, Jxeplorer Java LDAP browser**, or **LDAP Admin Tool** to manage accounts on those directories. One set of tools creates the initial process and the other manages tools for those implementations.

SAML implementations work with identity providers to verify users. They then provided an XML authentication exchange to confirm the user. The benefit of this over LDAP is that SAML typically occurs outside the domain while LDAP functions are within the domain. It may be possible to use both in establishing LDAPs within a particular cluster or cloud, while using SAML tokens for external access. The SAML authentication can then be connected to the directory for verifying which services are available at particular locations.

The top question for the platform may be *which SSO I should use*? The answer is that one depends on a particular capability rather than any specific software in a platform. Multiple tools are available; one should look for the tool with the most integration across the capabilities you need. These functions in the collaborative and deployment environments use the SSO. In any case, identity within the SSO should be encrypted at rest or in transit to prevent outside users from observing passwords.

Encryption basics

All the discussion about encryption leads to a quick return to basic standards. Encryption has three basic forms: symmetric, asymmetric, and quantum keys. **Symmetric encryption** uses a single key to encrypt and decrypt the data. This model is known as **"Secret Key" encryption** because one must prevent third parties from seeing the key. The strengths include speed and cryptographic strength but the weakness is one must exchange keys before communicating securely. Two types of symmetric encryption exist; **block**, where set bit chains are encrypted through a secret key, and **stream**, where data encrypts during streaming without being retained in system memory. One of the challenges is that every key usage leaks some data about the encryption. Just like old-school cryptography, the more coded messages one has, the easier to find the overall key. Symmetric keys do not include metadata about creation dates, user practices, or life spans, making it necessary to use **key management systems**. Examples of symmetric systems include Triple Data Encryption (3DES), Advanced Encryption Standard (AES), Data Encryption Standard (DES), and Rivest Cipher 4()RC4.

Asymmetric keys depend on public and private keys and appear in *Figure 7.2*, which details SSO practices. This practice is also known as public key encryption. The asymmetric encryption process is slower, and the keys are much larger in overall bits. At a high level, the system uses a pairing between public and private keys to decode messages. **Transport Layer Security** (TLS) and **Secure Socket Layer** (SSL) systems use partial asymmetric approaches, with users obtaining a public key from a website and then linking to their private key to maintain security. Symmetric keys primarily use 128 or 256-bit functions, while asymmetric keys must be 2048 bits or more. Examples of asymmetric keys include Diffie-Hellman, **Elliptic Curve Cryptography** (ECC), El Gamal, **Digital Signature Algorithm** (**DSA**), and **Rivest-Shamir-Aldeman** (**RSA**).

Quantum encryption is an advanced topic and remains more theoretical than practical for day-to-day operations. These methods currently occurs in either **Quantum Key Distribution** (**QKD**) or **coin flipping**. In QKD, participants exchange polarized photons. The unique quantum properties mean any observation of the photon changes the properties of the other. Thus, any eavesdropping would affect the key received at either end and break the sequence. Coin flipping uses an agreement between users on polarized filters rather than the actual state, ensuring that only one valid key exists for the two users.

Another important consideration with quantum computing is its potential impact on key decoding. **Grover's algorithm**, a quantum search technique, significantly reduces the number of items that need to be examined—from a typical (N/2 – 1) items, where N is the number of items in a set, in classical search to just the square root of N items in the quantum context—making key searches far more efficient. This means if one is randomly trying 1,000 possible options for a key, classical computing must try 499 alternatives, while a quantum approach requires only 37. This drastically reduces the time to commit brute-force decryption against public or private keys. One way to ensure all data is successfully encrypted is by putting suitable scanners and testing tools inside the pipeline. Even the best security on the local platform requires network management to ensure those moving onto one's platforms are secure.

Scanners and pipelines

Security scans within the pipeline are part of the overall DevSecOps concept. Implementing these tools prevents harmful code from reaching production. A typical scanning package within a pipeline includes static testing to confirm coding practices, functional tests to verify elements, dependency scans to verify all called classes and objects exist, and run-time tests to verify that code runs as intended.

When moving past the initial pipeline, developers frequently use **smoke testing**. Smoke testing originated with mechanical engineering, as when activating new devices, they did not catch on fire, smoke, shake, or malfunction. Scans can also include regularly assessing deployed code to ensure new CVEs do not create vulnerabilities. The entire inventory of platform operations requires evaluation on a regular timeframe. New code testing occurs during development, but scanning on a weekly, quarterly, or other periodic timeframe prevents errors from reaching baseline capabilities.

Pipelines should incorporate security scans into multiple stages with different jobs configured across the *build*, *test*, *deploy*, and *operate* phases. At the build stages, scanners conduct static analysis to verify code and functional code blocks. During testing, dynamic scans can evaluate what elements code calls, what ports are in place and verify embedded secrets are either removed or encrypted. During deployment, security tools verify against existing dependency CVEs, and ensure only the appropriate and approved networks are connected. Each security item produces artifacts for comparison with diff tools to ensure all security risks are understood. To be clear, `diff` tools do not solve problems, only highlight changes in security posture from one pipeline run to the next.

One best practice is incorporating `diff` tools directly into the pipeline. This practice allows creating artifacts directly showing security changes rather than handling the process later. Another best practice is incorporating pipeline tools that generate SBOM documentation upon deployment. The SBOM shows all the software and versions incorporated within the deployed guide, and aids in completing later audits for the platform to obtain security certification.

Multiple operational tools are available as open-source or by a vendor to scan operational inventories. **OpenScap**, **Zed Attack Proxy (ZAP)**, **Snyk**, and **Anchore's Syft** or **Gype** are effective scanning tools. **Tenable's Nessus** and **Qualsys** focus on networks, while anti-virus companies like **McAfee**, **Norton**, and **BitDefender** offer more detailed looks at singular nodes or small networks. Again, combining multiple tools into the platform structure will create the best value.

Network management and security practices use

Securing the platform moves beyond the user experience portion to the networks and tools where platforms reside. Data and information move through channels, requiring secure practices to ensure adequate security. In this case, we are not talking about those on the platform but the path through which they reach the platform as the network tools. These include a variety of protocols such as **Transmission Control Protocol (TCP)**, **Internet Protocol (IP)**, **Hypertext Transfer Protocol (HTTP)** the most common as well as some others. Communication models can be point-to-point, client-server, or publish-subscribe but each involves handshakes within the network.

As an important background, Google initially drove the change from HTTP to HTTPS, a protocol using SSL, and then moved to TLS. The company began using HTTPS in 2008, implementing full-testing in 2014 and 2018, marking sites not using the HTTPS protocol as "Not Secure". HTTPS uses the SSL interaction, which exchanges certificates, based on a public key, between the browsers. Once the connection is verified, the web server uses the public key access to send a secret key and establish a secure connection. TLS is a newer and updated version of SSL, removing existing vulnerabilities. As mentioned above, in patching, even security protocols are constantly rewired and reconfigured by stakeholders to eliminate vulnerabilities.

Another important thing to remember across network management is the SYN-ACK handshake, expressing **synchronization (SYN)** and **acknowledgment (ACK)**. In a typical handshake, the user sends a synchronization message to the server using the TCP or HTTPS function with an initial sequence number. Synchronization contains an initial sequence number, and the server responds with its own sequence number. The system increments these numbers to create the ACK message. Exchanging functions verifies for both systems the establishment of a secure path. The challenge can be ensuring the establishment of the correct path when communicating. Network tools that help ensure that platform users take the right path are functions including firewalls, traffic monitoring, and zero-trust policies.

Firewalls

Firewalls are tools that prevent non-approved traffic from entering the service. They are security systems designed to prevent authorized access to or from an existing network. In considering a platform, typically, positions from firewalls would be after the initial user access and between any cluster sets. Firewalls fill a traditional security role in guarding against intrusion and signaling if a non-approved access is detected or approved. One can deploy firewalls as hardware, software, or cloud-based systems. These three can be configured at different points to secure different platform aspects.

The most common use for firewalls is preventing outside users from interfacing with private networks. In our platform design, the firewall would prevent unauthorized users from reaching the initial access point, and additional firewalls would prevent users from moving between clusters. As with other tools, the best firewall for the platform is the one that works best for your system.

There are some elements to choose from in picking the best firewall approach. The first is whether the system deploys as hardware, software, cloud, or some combination of those locations. For our platform installation, some factors to consider are compatibility, scalability, performance, and manageability:

- **Compatibility** addresses how well the firewall works with the platform systems. Compatibility can be found in operating systems, applications, hardware and security features. Firewalls need to seamlessly integrate and control traffic regardless of which system, or combinations of systems might appear.

- **Scalability** is also a top concern for platforms, as user numbers may vary quickly. Scalability within the firewall addresses the ability to rapidly scale between numbers of users. Firewalls must manage high user numbers but also be able to switch to other firewalls if the system becomes overwhelmed. Distributed Denial of Service (DDoS) attacks frequently seek to send more traffic than a firewall or server can handle, causing the system to shut down. Network Protocols play a key role in scalability, allowing systems to auto-detect limits, manage between firewall elements, and keep systems from failing.

- **Performance** is always important. One needs to assess how well a firewall works on the platform, how fast it passes traffic, and whether high availability exists. Each of these will vary from system to system and require testing for the expected platform load. This traffic point is an excellent spot to use Chaos Engineering to test for extreme loads. High availability with firewalls usually assesses if a secondary firewall will be activated when the initial load becomes too high. If a firewall load becomes excessive, the inability to move to secondary locations can impact user satisfaction through throttling traffic

- **Manageability**, the final category, reflects how easy a firewall is to use. In a cloud environment, using PaaS manageability might be a low concern as the same teams always manage that firewall. If one chooses to deploy a platform to multiple enterprise locations, this might increase in importance as one needs to train others in operation. The last part of manageability reflects how your selected firewalls contribute to traffic monitoring practices in the following paragraphs.

Multiple ways exist to manage these factors. As with other areas, conducting a subjective and objective scoring against firewall categories can provide a strong comparative measure.

Traffic management

Establishing good firewalls contributes to a solid **traffic management** process. Platforms are designed for multiple users, arriving from different locations and accomplishing different goals, so solid traffic management is essential. The key factors associated with traffic management are visibility, identifying user and organization habits, and establishing baselines. Once one sets these fundamental factors appropriately, the next step is finding appropriate remediation strategies.

- **Visibility** within traffic management should address OSI layers two through seven. The platform concentrates on layers three through six, but since firewalls control traffic, the visibility needs to extend past those to the initial layers connecting with functions. Expanding observable layers account for north-south traffic within the cloud and east-west traffic from cluster to cluster or cloud to cloud. Despite having firewalls, these benefit from using **Test Access Points** (**TAP**) and **Switch Port Analyzers** (**SPAN**) to help monitor traffic.

- **TAP**: Passive device that copies network traffic and sends it to a monitoring tool. PhanTap is one example available as opensource from GitHub

- **SPAN**: Forward copies of all incoming and outgoing packets from the existing switch to another port for analysis. Examples include the open-source tool WireShark which is a common favorite among those first learning network integration

Both devices act without disrupting the flow of traffic, merely creating visibility for secondary and tertiary tools. TAP placement occurs between any two connected infrastructure pieces, whether physical or virtual, and SPANs often appear in baseline network equipment.

The TAP captures inbound and outbound traffic, including all layer two and three packets. This device enables a full copy of multi-directional network traffic. SPAN ports tend to be more accessible and available at low user cost. The disadvantage of SPANs is that this traffic may not be prioritized and drops during high-traffic periods. The drop can then lead to holes in the visibility since the system does not achieve the full line rate. Combining the two systems provides a practical step into developing user behavior patterns.

- Establishing monitoring allows for *identifying user and organization habits*. These patterns allow one to rapidly differentiate between what might be an attack on the platform and what is standard behavior. One difficulty with behavior is that substantial data must exist before starting. in the next section, we discuss using AI/ML tools to facilitate analysis; however, the first step is using architectural diagrams to envision what items communicate with others and what the standard patterns look like. Advanced monitoring tools such as **DataDog**, **Honeycomb**, and **Salt** are options as their initial installation provides some basic behavior patterns for Day 1. Many of these may first seem like infrastructure management but offer the advanced analytics necessary for monitoring. These can then be modified as one's platform becomes more mature

- The priority for traffic management is to assess how different users implement the platform. Good monitoring practices show which tools are used most often, how those tools are used and identify bottlenecks within the platform. Accentuating standard monitoring tools with internal metrics occurs through virtual tools such as a personal favorite, **Open Telemetry** (OTEL).

  - **OTEL**: An open-source observability framework includes various tools, APIs, and **Software Development Kits** (SDK). Enables teams to instrument, create, collect, and then export telemetry data to other tools to understand system performance and behavior. OTEL was a **Cloud Native Computing Foundation** (CNCF) project that merged two earlier projects, OpenTracing and OpenCensus. As open-source, the tool is free to download, has extensive documentation online, and a wide user community. Documentation and community are two essential parts we always consider when adding open-source tools to our platform. OTEL aims to provide details about multiple steps that traditional traffic management may miss.

- The last traffic management step should be *establishing baselines*. Previously mentioned was using existing vendors to contribute and creating multiple collection points. Baselines originate from three primary sources: dev, test, and ops. First, those creating the platform have ideas about how traffic should flow based on the initial architecture. These baselines allow the creation of initial patterns to suggest traffic monitoring points. In the test phases, use cases allow experimenting with some patterns users might follow that the devs neglected. Testing use cases can include bad login attempts, moving incompatible formats between tools, or downloading data to personal devices.

Testing then moves to operations, the platform deploys with actual users who choose to ignore everything the devs thought or tested. Chaos engineering practices in the operations can help cover even unthought attempts. An old planning instructor once told us that tests are not complete until the system has been secured against an invasion by Elvis clones from Mars.

This naturally leads to how AI can enhance one's security deployments.

Leveraging AI for security enhancement

The most important part of AI for the security environment is gaining another set of eyes to help with risk management and mitigation. Attention economics is a concept that frequently applies in any business but, especially in software security. The concept details that the more areas one's attention has to deal with, the less attention is paid to any one item. In DevOps, attention economics expresses as context switching that occurs when one changes from one task to another, requiring a focused realignment. AI can be that security checker who never is distracted, cannot become bored with the repetitive work, and takes no coffee or lunch breaks. The below figure highlights all the potential places AI potentially integrates across the DevSecOps continuum.

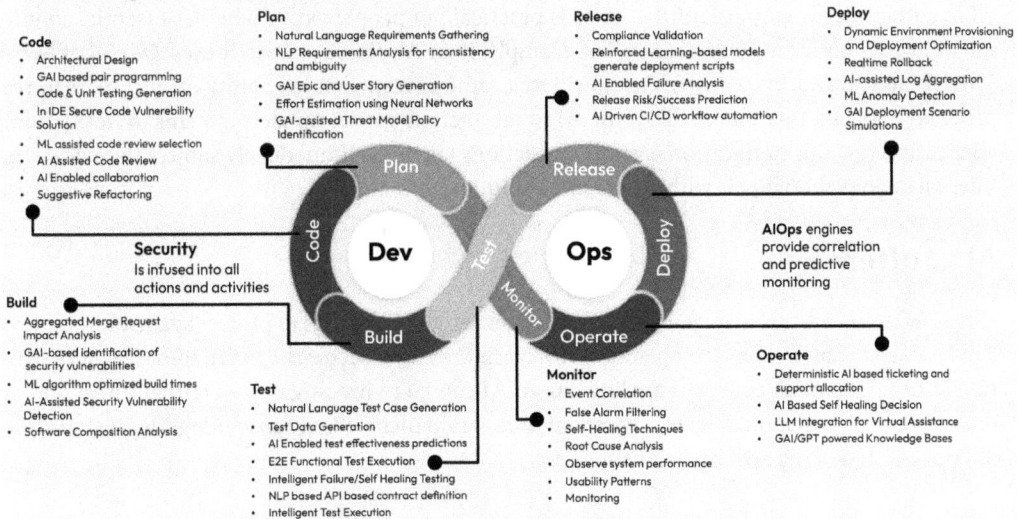

Figure 7.3 – AI in the DevSecOps continuum

Credit: Trac Bannon, Mitre Security Specialist

Think of all the daily security inputs, suggestions, and alerts. No human can spend enough time to identify, become familiar with root causes, and resolve all those issues. However, in working so much faster than the human brain, an AI system can help provide a step through funneling items into actions requiring human intervention, and those actions are solvable through AI automation. Choosing an AI integration requires careful evaluation of categories including security focus, usability, and scalability. After carefully training the AI/ML models, one can supply security as defensive or offensive approaches and apply these functions.

AI in defense

AI in defense means establishing tools that protect the existing virtual infrastructure and network connections. Defensive models are the most common use for AI tools today. Defensive-focused AI vendors include **Cylance**, **SentinelOne**, and **Vectra AI**. The process involves using a trained AI model to examine all the current behavior and alert to unusual processes. AI practices in defense focus on endpoint security and proactive defense. Designing endpoint solutions applies AI to monitoring user behavior, detecting malware, and implementing preventative defensive methods.

A clear distinction exists in defense between detecting bad behavior through analysis and automatically implementing solutions. The initial detection is simple for most AI devices with standard ML training paths as structured or unstructured training models. This implementation allows the AI to alert when items exceed or are about to exceed, what appears as a standard usage. The next step allows an AI to implement a solution to fix detected problems.

The implementation phase can cause some consternation for many organizations. The ability of the AI to automatically stop harmful activity is practical but people worry whether essential solutions might impact business performance. For example, if an AI detects a **Distributed Denial of Service** (**DDoS**) attack, and shuts down a port, will that same port impact the ability of customers to reach products? Solving this should allow the AI to take action but set up alert systems to notify human administrators. This notification ensures any actions taken are immediately subject to review. These internal actions should pair with AI offensive solutions.

AI in offense

When AI models are used to generate offensive security, the intent is to protect against future threats and investigate causes. Some companies specialize in these approaches; however, some legalities remain in question. The main concerns are how far an AI can go to investigate a potential threat and how one uses the information detected. Potential uses would include insurance filings, legal stop-orders, or criminal actions against malicious actors.

The best company for offensive AI security is probably **DarkTrace**, which specializes in real-time threat detection. Offensive AI solutions are likely to be more proprietary and require special knowledge. This means implementing offensive AI within the platform should not be preferred approach at the current time. Instead, organizations should contract with companies conducting offensive AI practices to provide information. This converts the AI from an offensive model to a defensive suggestion. These defensive notes would feed into the training databases for the platform and limit legal liability. AI is an exciting tool; much work will likely further these options over the next several years.

Summary

Our goal remains to help you better understand how to approach security in the DevOps cycle. Securing the platform by design requires understanding the design basics. Design basics include discovering security experience essentials by shaping platform ideation through parts, identity, presence, and opposites to form a better mental picture. The better you can define the issue, the more possibilities exist to define the ongoing interaction and envision long-term solutions.

We also went beyond the initial security design into the network interactions required to create an effective and secure platform. You must understand how the platform acts in isolation and those elements interact with the broader world. The related solutions include best practices for SSO, firewalls, and traffic management. Finally, we discussed potential areas to include future AI tools within the platform security construct.

In the next chapter, we build from these initial design constraints to explore some actual applications and use-case involved with platforms in the market.

> **Call to action**
> - Recognize the security concept behind your platform design.
> - Identify how your platform will conduct actions to guard and signal against malicious or insider events.
> - Model technology to support the initial ideation, and test those models.

Get This Book's PDF Version and Exclusive Extras

UNLOCK NOW

Scan the QR code (or go to `packtpub.com/unlock`). Search for this book by name, confirm the edition, and then follow the steps on the page.

Note: Keep your invoice handly. Purchase made directly from packt don't require one.

8

Real-World Applications and Case Studies

In this chapter, we will present case studies showcasing successful platform transformations and the integration of platforms with business strategies. This chapter also shares some anti-patterns and stories of failed platform transformations that underscore the value of strategic planning and how enterprises with considerable heritage applications and legacy technologies can face disruptions. One of the ways we can succeed in the feedback and improvement aspects of DevOps is by capturing lessons from previous implementations and incorporating them to support current operations. This chapter also examines potential future technologies and solutions that have not yet been fully implemented. Reading this chapter will enable you to understand successful transformations, identify areas that can delay a transformation, and prepare for technological changes that will impact platforms.

In this chapter, you will explore the key elements that contribute to both successful and unsuccessful platform transformations. You'll begin by understanding the components of a successful transformation, including how to establish meaningful metrics and track performance effectively. Then, you'll examine the factors that lead to unsuccessful transformations, learn to identify leading and trailing indicators of failure, and gain insights into how to better prepare for change. Finally, you'll delve into the role of evolving technology—understanding how it can impact a platform, when it's appropriate to implement changes, and how leveraging the right technologies can drive long-term success.

We will be covering the following main headings:

- Learning from successful platform transitions
- Evaluating unsuccessful transformations
- Best practices for platform success
- Innovating for new success
- Making technology leaps

Learning from successful platform transitions

You must be able to identify a strategy based on clear inputs to ensure a successful platform transformation. Returning to the basics of what makes platforms succeed will prepare you to implement successful processes and technologies. The model we will evaluate here is the original pyramid that establishes capabilities for stability, security, adaptability, and scalability across functions for supporting, designing, developing, deploying, and operating (*Figure 8.1*). The detailed discussion of this model occurred in *Chapter 2*. Each layer and pillar plays a critical role in developing successful platforms.

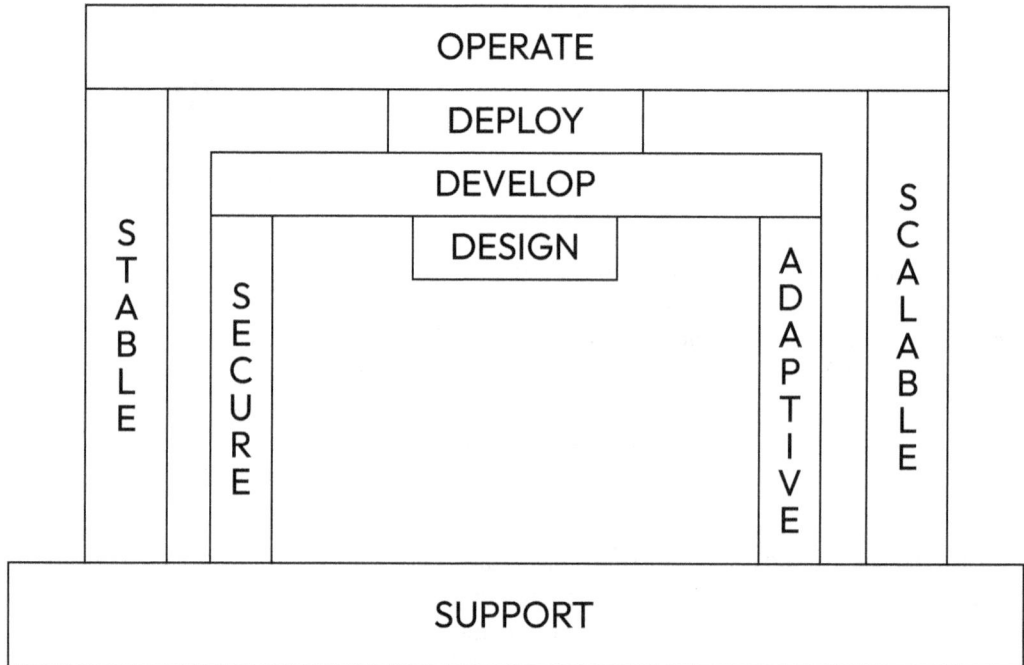

Figure 8.1: DevSecOps pyramid

When getting started with a new platform, there is an emphasis on the initial development, deployment, and operations while still ensuring you are adhering to the pillars of stability, security, adaptability, and scalability. It can be difficult to evaluate each area and assign detailed metrics as the requirements change from organization to organization. However, assigning an initial metric can help with determining practical barriers to improving a platform or moving to a different provider.

One standard metric used across multiple organizations is indicators to establish levels of performance. These include assessments such as availability on the network, response time to outages, query times for users, and resource utilization:

- **Service-Level Agreements (SLAs)**: These are strategic-level discussions between the customer and the provider.

- **Service-Level Objectives (SLOs)**: These are the mid-level operational tasks to notify the organization when something exceeds bounds. Many organizations often skip these mid-level connected points, especially smaller companies.

- **Service-Level Indicators (SLIs)**: These are the first worker-level notifications about tasks within the system.

An example SLA might be 99% uptime, an SLO is to track routine uptime over a set increment, such as a week, while the SLI would be the current status indicator. Each would likely appear on dashboards.

Designing these elements requires understanding what the platform needs for success. While considering each element provides an excellent path to success, we tend to skip SLOs. Coming up with mid-level objectives can be difficult for small companies, and even in large companies, they become simply an aggregate of SLI information. These aggregates directly relate to the SLA, rather than establishing distinct fields. Instead of adding to the ability to identify and remediate issues, SLOs become a painful thought exercise for many individuals.

The next section expands on some SLA formats to accelerate platform success.

Service-level agreements for Platform Engineering

The goal of any SLA should be to set the overall objective for the service provided. In our designed and engineered platform, our top objectives are as follows:

- **Development ease**: Measure the rate at which code is committed, new features are released, or code is replaced

- **Successful testing**: Evaluate test coverage, successful tests, or artifacts associated with release

- **Push to production**: Evaluate how many expected features are released to customers

- **Real-time support elements**: Evaluate the time to recover after failure, time to upgrade, and response time for help-desk elements

In establishing an SLA, six typical categories help ensure fidelity:

- **Define**: Establish what the customer needs. Examples include 99% availability, less than 48 hours of downtime per year, 4 hours to respond to a support call, 30 minutes to respond to an outage, multiple pipelines can run simultaneously, and all critical security vulnerabilities are remediated before production.

- **Document**: Create an interaction that regularly reports on SLA status. As these items are typically longer in duration, weekly, monthly, or quarterly reports are best as a summation of dashboard activity.

- **Agree**: Most critical to the SLA process is the agreement between the customer and producer that the agreed-upon SLAs measure the right metrics.

- **Monitor**: Any defined SLA requires monitoring. The monitoring itself occurs with the SLIs, but the SLA should define how monitoring occurs for each function. For example, the response to an outage might be per outage, or aggregated across multiple pipelines over time. Automated monitoring can reduce manual overhead, increasing the stability of the platform.

- **Measure**: The SLA should be defined to an acceptable level. While an initial SLA of less than 48 hours of downtime per year might be acceptable, noting downtime rates adds usability. If one has 30+ hours of downtime in the first quarter, the SLA might be inappropriately scaled.

- **Report**: The SLA should include a reporting mechanism. An SLA that alerts the customer of potential lapses might be ineffective if a mechanism exists to remediate those lapses. This category relates to the monitor and document steps. Most important here is assessing when a problem exists where the customer requires notification and when issues are handled internally. For example, if the average ongoing outage time is 25 minutes, it might be valuable to identify the exceptions that exceed 30 minutes, as well as confirming the average.

All of these aspects are beneficial when it comes to establishing SLIs as well. Each SLI constitutes a measurement that contributes to the SLA. The most important aspect here is creating automated systems tracking for the different aspects. If you are tracking an outage, the SLI will show the time it started, the time it stopped, who handled the issue, and perhaps a tier level for how difficult the challenge was to fix. The SLI would also show availability at the current time, potentially aggregating into the overall SLA. While SLAs and SLIs provide a sound foundation, much can be learned through examining some successful scenarios of platform transformation.

Successful scenarios

Several commercial platforms have successfully delivered a customer platform and enhanced value through rapid production. We will look at some examples in this section.

GitLab

One of the best DevOps platforms on the market is GitLab. The company expanded from the initial open source model developed in 2011 to create a business model, GitLab Inc., in 2014. The company uses a subscription model to offer differentiated product levels, although all are connected by similar SLAs and support. Gartner recognized GitLab as a leader in 2023 for their contributions to the DevOps Platform category. The company is entirely remote, with 1,800 team members across 60 countries and regions that support more than 1 million active users and 30+ million registered users.

What led to GitLab's successful transformation was an emphasis on stability, security, adaptability, and scalability. GitLab's transformation from the GitHub formats means many users are already familiar with the embedded tools. Including repository use as part of the basic pipeline framework emphasizes a continuation of previous skills. The basics for creating software with GitLab are the same as many students learn in computer science classes throughout high school and college.

These features are then integrated with platform governance when using either a free or purchased platform version. Secrets can be embedded and shared within a project but not outside the project. Individual access accounts shape access, with organizations able to purchase a cloud-based system or local servers. At the same time, this allows for shared pipelines, running multiple pipelines, and analytics. Governance then links security automation to assist supply chain awareness and routine upgrades. Multiple security scans and tools are supported.

In considering adaptability and scalability, GitLab offers faster CI pipeline builds by using previously constructed toolsets. These expansions augment speed and can build effective software that benefits the organizational value stream. The GitLab website contains numerous use cases of companies who have purchased their software and reached new heights:

- **Lockheed Martin (defense aerospace)**: Pipeline build speed increased over 80 times, thousands of Jenkins servers retired, and 90% less system maintenance time

- **CACI International (defense IT services)**: Security scanning speeds increased 13 times, labor and admin costs reduced by over 90%, and consolidated over 7 tools into a common platform

- **NVIDIA (advanced hardware)**: Enabled growth of over 51% during the first year and 99% uptime delivered for the overall platform

- **Carfax (vehicle retail)**: Reduced the toolchain from 12 tools to a single instance focused on feature delivery, created a 20% deployment boost over multiple years, and 30% of vulnerabilities identified earlier in the SDLC with secret detection as well as container and dependency scanning

Each of these companies experienced different successes. The common element between customers is that none had used a comprehensive platform before and integrating with GitLab created new success paths. Platforms are an enablement tool, allowing you to spend more time building and deploying software rather than focusing on platform construction.

One complaint about the GitLab platform is that while the code merges and pipelines work effectively, including the generative AI GitHub Copilot and the GitLab Duo application, the overall work management aspects are still lacking. The platform has incorporated GitLab Issues to mimic other work management systems but lacks some operational aspects. The platform expertly performs at the build and deploy levels, but operationalizing those functions to the larger organization still requires some work. One big gap is visualizing ongoing work through tools such as Scrum and Kanban boards or creating supplementary documentation for issues. Despite these issues, GitLab is an excellent example of a tool that sparked a platform design and then made that platform available to others as a completed woodshop, allowing a focus on needed items.

Netflix

On the other side of the model, a well-known company that successfully integrated platforms into daily practices is Netflix. Netflix was one of the first adapters in the broader marketplace for successful container and automated system use. Many of the initial chaos engineering practices, such as the **Chaos Monkey** deployment, originated with Netflix. Chaos Monkey and associated tools, known as the **Simian Army**, test the operational Netflix environments for errors that have not yet occurred but are eventual possibilities.

In 2020, Netflix took on a significant tooling reversion to bring its development workforce into a stable platform. Brian Leathern led these transformations. He found that the microservices architecture originally used was becoming increasingly fragmented as the company expanded. The platform goals were to manage multiple services, enable discovery, and allow context switching. An example of a workflow that created a problem was using Bitbucket to review pull requests, Spinnaker to check deployment pipelines, and Jenkins to analyze build failures, and then having multiple internal tools for metrics regarding operational status. Every deployment required manual pushes between tools, rather than using a consistent platform.

These multiple interactions became increasingly complicated as the architecture continued to grow. Not only were the operational tools difficult to use, but the wide variety meant developers were often unaware of new tools and processes added to the overall chain. One team's shortcuts on Bitbucket or Spinnaker, for example, might only appear in their local documentation. Further, solutions to common fixes were not distributed across the platform but only appeared in local implementations.

Netflix started by building a platform architecture and moving into a federated platform **Minimum Viable Product (MVP)**. A key aspect was not just moving existing experiences into a new platform, as might happen with a common **Single Sign-On (SSO)**, but ensuring full integration so that the tools communicate with each other. This communication enabled viewing the entire SDLC, not just a small portion, from a development perspective. One innovative concept was the ability to use collections, selecting multiple elements within the platform to build a customized workflow. These workflows were then still visible from every level.

One key takeaway from Netflix's experience, which remains ongoing, is that platforms must do more than consolidate business functionality. An effective platform must integrate workflows and create knowledge about new functions. During the transition, platform engineers must be able to show how the new platform reduces time and effort. The GitLab example showed multiple instances of reducing time and providing useful tools. A quick look through the Netflix TechBlog (www.netflixtechblog. com) reveals the many challenges faced during their platform implementation, however. Overall, Netflix continues to be successful, with gross profit margins routinely exceeding 35% across multiple quarters.

Successful transformations indicate clear wins for companies that have integrated Platform Engineering. Companies and organizations are always more willing to discuss successes than failures. Diving into unsuccessful transformations becomes more of an exercise in personal experiences with different instantiations rather than published use cases. The next section evaluates some aspects that lead to unsuccessful or incomplete transformations.

Evaluating unsuccessful transformations

Establishing SLAs and practical standards can lead to a successful transformation as you'll be focusing on stability, security, adaptability, and scalability. But those same focuses can also derail the transformation. An overemphasis on one area can leave a platform with some areas where it is high-performing but allow the rest to remain seriously out of balance. Sometimes, an unsuccessful transformation can be a matter of opinion rather than a practical application. Small things such as **User Experience** (**UX**), tool integration, and update processes can matter when promoting a platform for internal or external use. Examples of these challenges are provided here:

- **Small challenges**: Examples of these are user happiness, tool integration, and update processes. These affect time to production, UX, and support ticket metrics.

- **Large challenges**: Examples of these are lack of architecture and vision alignment, continually stuck in the in-progress stage, rather than done, with no working platform, separation from the user base, and no simple green-field to brown-field changes. In these cases, useful metrics are unavailable as users have not adopted platforms.

Recognizing potential challenges is a critical first step, but truly understanding those challenges is a required skill for a platform engineer. Each of these topics is discussed in detail in further sections.

Small challenges

These small challenges appear in the complete use case that follows on Atlassian. The reasons for this failure start with a poor UX based on developer unhappiness, high numbers of support tickets, and an increase in time to production. Fixing these issues requires making process and technical changes to the existing platform. Teams often fix these issues locally, but the challenge comes with communicating and integrating those fixes into the larger platform.

Users can be finicky, and small changes in an existing platform can create high levels of consternation. Any movement of standard elements between different areas requires assessment through models such as alpha-beta implementations. Examples include changing repository structures, providing new tool options, or proliferating local shortcuts. These require allowing a few users to test a beta implementation and provide comments before broader dissemination. This alpha-beta model prevents large changes from stalling user production as a result of changing common paths without a solid path for new training and documentation. These example methods can help resolve user dissatisfaction while another effective indicator is support tickets submitted and resolved.

Support tickets should always be a significant indicator of platform experience. Lacking a comprehensive support team is a crucial indicator of an unsuccessful transformation. DevOps states that the team that builds software runs it, but expanding from small teams to large user bases can compromise these improvements. Effective support models have three levels to help maintain DevOps improvements:

- **Tier 1**: Questions about platform usage with information present in documentation
- **Tier 2**: Changes in configuration requiring administrator assistance
- **Tier 3**: Bugs or new features

To clarify, a bug occurs when something should work based on the original delivery but does not, and a feature refers to when a user wants something that is not included in the initial scope. With new platforms, the initial Tier 1 ticket numbers will be high, and then those numbers likely convert into more Tier 2 tickets as users become more familiar with operations. Tier 3 ticket numbers should always be low as bugs usually appear in development and testing, while new feature suggestions help design the next steps.

The last common small challenge occurs with tool integration and update processes. When discussing GitLab, we saw the ease with which files and code can easily be associated with projects, be transferred into pipelines, and reach production. In poor platforms, you might see code contained in different areas than documentation and work progress managed on different tools, lacking connection. For example, coding work might be carried out in one tool and code changes reported in a different management tool, rather than the two being connected. This gap means that when a developer submits and merges new code, they must enter a new system log changes. Changing systems can slow down production and impact observability for the entire team.

Following tool integration is the platform update process. Continually updating software with DevOps standards requires constant updates. Update management should either be transparent to the user or occur at set times. Transparency involves notifying users when updates occur and providing high-level information and links to more details. These updates can be functional changes linked to new tutorials or security updates, or even communicating backend changes to improve performance. Regular updates create rapport with users, informing users about when ticketed problems and basic fixes will be addressed. When new security patches are released, users may deluge support functions with requests for updates. Staying ahead of this creates an effective platform. Despite fixing small changes, many platforms struggle with more significant and extensive issues.

Large challenges

As mentioned earlier, large challenges can include poor integration between vision and architecture, inability to reach a production platform, lack of user response, and no brown-field to green-field model. Each of these poses a severe problem, with any one derailing production but a combination turning a good platform vision into a continuous resource drain. Addressing these requires coordination across an organization, confronting top-to-bottom and bottom-to-top issues. A common error that occurs is no communication or feedback in DevOps existing in verified and effective channels. This analysis goes back to Conway's law, where systems produced by an organization tend to mirror the organization's structure, with hierarchical organizations creating hierarchical tools and flat organizations creating flat models.

An inability to complete the transformation effectively is common. This happens most often when teams try to build their platform. The transformation vision starts with the effective planning converted to architecture demonstrated in early chapters. Teams often develop a vision of what they expect but lack an architectural plan. One example is teams that have comprehensive week-to-week delivery schedules and excellent five-year plans but lack the middle section where deliveries connect to the overall strategy. Some engineers jump from large problems to immediate solutions without architectural integration. The result is excellent code in many different areas but either no comprehensive integration or numerous manual shortcuts required for success.

Another key factor can be misleading indicators during a standard metrics analysis. A platform may successfully enable one application to reach production but fail for others. While one application may deploy successfully, the Platform Engineering has failed. Successful platforms enable multiple applications to succeed by offering an integrated base with opinionated but not prescriptive solutions. Some companies can drive certain elements better on one platform than others, creating near-term success and long-term complications. We often see this appear on code-specific platforms such as Python or Java, or a function-specific one such as one for testing or security. These can be short-term fixes but fall short of the desired platform end goal.

One of the first indications that a platform failed during a transformation is user response. Deploying the initial platform involves the engineering build, coordinating **Infrastructure as Code** (**IAC**), and pushing products to production. When doing this, you must remember to measure the UX. Users tend to like using certain tools and functions. If you remove those functions, even if for a positive engineering outcome, users may decide not to use the platform. A common example is when platforms perform actions for the user without telling the user. This could result in the user duplicating code, for example, which could break the intended function. Platforms must focus on user happiness and be transparent in their functions. If we return to our woodshop example from *Chapter 2*, you could offer pre-cut wood lengths and demonstrate design elements, but users will want to see all the platform options. In technical terms, this can be as simple as offering a pull-down menu, or an approval button.

Another key area where many platforms fail is not offering sufficient instructions on use. This failure appears most commonly in changing brown-field to green-field solutions. Developers previously built an application and then want to migrate to a new platform. In building their application, developers may make choices that are no longer available. Good platforms must offer easy ways to align these models. Common failures in this area relate to programming languages, database schema, or testing versions. For example, an application may be promoted to production based on an earlier security test. The application no longer passes the pipeline when the platform includes the latest security versions. Notifying users of how development and production affects them and the associated platform solutions can mitigate these frustrations. Solution notification to users can be an area where GenAI solutions excel, automating the process rather than requiring manual solutions. The following two case studies are examples of where we have seen unsuccessful platform implementations.

Atlassian

Atlassian is known for offering one of the best starting points for companies managing a DevOps transformation. Tools such as Jira and Confluence are widespread throughout the commercial market. Jira offers a customized Kanban or Scrum solution that expands into project management across multiple levels. Some new instantiations of Jira Cloud even offer high-level management of multiple teams. Confluence offers documentation and notes that are fully interactive with the Jira solution and supplement those functions. However, in our opinion, Atlassian has a failed platform.

The company offers integrated solutions with other functions such as Bitbucket to manage code and SonarQube to address security. While each function appears on the platform, they lack proper integration. Bitbucket is part of the Atlassian suite but SonarQube is a recommended plugin requiring additional integration. Users pull Jira tickets and releases into Confluence, and vice versa, but the mechanics tend to be convoluted. Jira tickets are not easily connected to Bitbucket outcomes or SonarQube reports. This discrepancy forces developers to move through multiple windows and cut and paste data to attain a single source of truth. These single sources are more easily obtained by other platforms.

At the same time, linking the issues is not always communicated across the platform, creating a challenging work environment. Visualizing change in status may require launching a new application rather than being observed within the current window. Working with actual code from Bitbucket but having to log changes in other features becomes very difficult for the average user. The platform problems begin with the advanced knowledge required and continue through difficult and needlessly complex administrative tools. Users often require multiple administrative passwords across each tool, rather than using a shared admin account for all responsibilities.

One of the most common problems with Jira occurs in the workflow process. Bitbucket's pipeline elements do not automatically mirror to Jira and are even more difficult when GitLab is integrated into Atlassian tools. Additionally, many teams try to create their own workflows despite all projects being in a common organization. An example would be one team using stages of to-do, in-progress, and done, while another uses code1, deploy, revise, code2, test1, deploy2, and finished. Trying to resolve progress across these multiple teams becomes challenging. Bitbucket links may be copied into a Jira ticket but it requires switching functions to determine progress.

Another simple failure of Atlassian, in dealing with user satisfaction, is that despite multiple user requests, as evidenced by their community board, they have never included wildcard searches across their platform. A wildcard search is when a special character, such as *, is used before or in an alphanumeric string to find an item. This feature gap means that searching Atlassian requires knowing the exact name of the desired object. Without a wildcard search, users must search multiple combinations or scroll through filesystems to find the desired object. This small absence can cause high levels of frustration for users.

One final problem with Atlassian is the numerous security challenges. The company has had numerous failures over the years with multiple critical and high vulnerabilities released in the past 12 months. A single critical vulnerability can derail a system, but multiple vulnerabilities affect system performance and user attitudes. Each vulnerability is bad, but the first critical vulnerability of 2024 resulted in 39,000 access attempts across 18,000 ports from 600+ IP addresses in the first week. Some issues were fixed but many continue or have yet to appear. The sheer number of vulnerabilities suggests key gaps within the system with the potential for future exploitation.

Combining the lack of integrated solutions, workflow challenges, and user happiness highlights the key failures within the Atlassian tools. The systems may work well for a time but fail over the long term when adhering to key platform creation pillars. The platform's lack of integration challenges stability, a security problem is posed due to multiple vulnerabilities, user satisfaction declines, showing the lack of adaptability, and initially scalable, non-integrated workflows pose challenges as the system expands. Despite business successes, if you are looking at what not to do from a Platform Engineering perspective, Atlassian is that model.

United States federal government

From a personal perspective, in our experience working with **United States** (**U.S.**) federal programs and contractors, the government's software factories frequently demonstrate poor practices. Many problems originate not from the government workers or their capacity to deliver but from outdated administrative requirements. The **Federal Acquisition Regulation** (**FAR**), a massive document with 2,000+ pages across 37 chapters, supplements for various agencies, and then cost accounting standards, poses much of this challenge. Despite being updated over the years, the regulations are more geared toward the slower material and labor acquisition model, rather than being the fast-paced standard needed for delivering an effective platform, and the subsequent software.

Many government agencies experience personnel change at a high rate and cannot maintain progress. These changes occur at worker and management levels. One program we worked for saw regular turnover between 30% and 50% at all levels. This turnover created challenges in meeting team goals. In another instance, the key stakeholder insisted the key to progress was making no changes to the quarterly plan due to capacity maximization, but then personally added another 800 hours of required tasks within the first week. In other cases, turnover issues extend to leadership, who bring in new plans and ideas, overhauling previous work.

One key challenge in the government processes, accentuated by FAR, is the focus on labor hours rather than completion. The regulatory inability to correctly identify developing software versus completed deliveries places a premium on labor time rather than completed delivery. For example, an agency that wants a legacy database application migrated to a platform must hire developers for a set period rather than contracting them for a potential delivery. Visualizing this, it would mean hiring 8 developers for 40 hours a week over 12 months rather than allowing a company to suggest an application delivery at a set cost within six weeks. Considering that the standard developer rate is over $100 per hour, the cost would be $16M versus what might be a much smaller cost for the application.

Another challenge government platforms face is converting from brown-field to green-field systems. The U.S. government systems are so large and embedded that they cannot change small parts without breaking the entire system. A good platform's scalable and adaptive aspects exemplify constant improvement, but this can be impossible with some legacy systems. An excellent example is from the COVID era, when a state government needed to find COBOL developers to update an old system. This conversion had previously been required but data transfer and limited contractual opportunities presented as challenges.

At the same time, government regulations often require multiple human tests beyond the software capability of DevOps. One organization we are familiar with was contracted to provide user-requested updates quarterly. After the first two updates, the government organization reported that they could not perform testing and requested that the developers slow down with delivering updates, despite the stated and contractual requirement for update delivery. The requested slowdown would lead to producing one update every 6 to 9 months, leading to user dissatisfaction, threatening the ability to maintain security, and impacting software performance. As with DORA metrics, platforms aim to support continuous delivery when updates complete, not when a user is available for a two-week testing cycle.

These examples focused on U.S. government operations. When shifting to a different model, such as those used in China, we see that many of their platforms are state-sponsored. State-sponsored platforms are created using government funds and sold on the open market. At other times, China mandates the use of a specific platform, constraining user choice, as follows:

- Jihu replaces GitLab.
- Weibo replaces Twitter.
- WeChat replaces Facebook.
- Alibaba replaces Amazon.

The **Chinese Communist Party (CCP)** reverse-engineers platforms, ignores intellectual property constraints, and then empowers a Chinese production company. They also ban Western platforms, or any similar applications, allowing users only to implement Chinese solutions. Metrics are then skewed by state-mandated usage, with over one billion users adopting the platform. These state mandates are only successful in regions with authoritarian governments, rather than open competition, as factors other than security, scalability, adaptability, and stability drive usage.

Many government platform flaws are contractual. Others are a result of mindset. Previous chapters emphasized culture, leadership, and organizational standards and showed that Platform Engineering is not just a technical solution. Artificially slowing down platform delivery primarily impacts security and stability. However, the inability to respond to user requests promptly also challenges a platform's adaptability and scalability. It is not enough to purchase a platform transformation; in line with Conway's law, the organization must prepare for change. The following section highlights some best practices that can drive successful transformation and ways to recognize future trends.

Best practices for platform success

Recognizing some best practices that accelerate delivery, integration, and subsequent growth is key to ensuring successful transformation. This section identifies best practices, sets some initial guidelines, and proposes ways to ensure platforms remain current. A quick list of these best practices is as follows:

- Service platforms.

- Recognize growth limits.

- Don't build what already exists.

- Establish metrics.

The technology supporting platforms is constantly changing, and we must ensure a suitable mindset to anticipate these changes exists. There are multiple ways of incorporating changes; these best practices function as a guide rather than an exhaustive list. Let's delve deeper into them.

Service platforms

We should never forget that, despite the technological origins, humans build, operate, and use platforms. If a human uses a machine, it will require some form of service. Many organizations overlook this or attempt to divert support responsibilities to the purchasing customer. Some form of service should be readily available within a platform. Service examples are embedded knowledge bases, a common messaging system, routine notifications, and competent service staff.

Knowledge bases can take the form of notes pages and documentation. Readily available tools can convert code comments or Markdown language in repositories into clear documents. Along with this, systems can provide notifications for updates, downtime, or suggested training. Common metrics such as availability and usage are often hidden rather than shared with users. Sharing this knowledge builds confidence across multiple levels.

When these first support attempts fail, users should be able to reach a human or AI-driven service to address their issues. The support staff's first goal should be to identify problems as Tier 1, within the documentation; Tier 2, minor configuration changes; or Tier 3, a bug or feature. All issues should be tracked in an observable format for users and admins, such as ServiceNow or another ticketing system. This creates issue observability and allows rapidly aligning metrics. One key example of AI support is chatbots. These provide a place for users to ask questions and receive a tailored response that guides them through specific answers.

Recognize growth limits

Every new platform wants to be the most successful, with the widest adoption and the highest profit. These goals conflict with a platform's activity to deliver support. Successful platform implementations might follow the Netflix model as a user platform versus a development orientation, or GitLab where the service burden falls on the users. True DevOps Platform Engineering incorporates multiple areas. One of the hardest things is realizing that while scalability is important, there are also times when growth needs to be constrained.

All platforms might eventually support millions of users, but the growth occurs over time. You must realize the performance limits within the existing platform. Netflix grew from 24M subscribers in 2011 to over 220M in 2023; however, most growth areas maintained a steady pace of growth of 20% to 30% in any individual year. Any platform model should strive for a similar pace, expanding the capability to plan for and match customer growth. Customer growth is the best model to generate long-term value and profit. Research methods such as surveys gathering user feedback and market intelligence can help companies plan for what growth levels to expect. Unicorn-style growth is always hoped for but rarely achieved, and many companies would be incapable of handling growth of 100% or greater in a short period.

In our previous experience, a company was determined to succeed through offering a technical feature and spent thousands of hours and dollars achieving that capability. It was only after they had finished the development that they realized that only about 10 users would be using the feature, and the user count was unlikely to grow based on need. Growth should be carefully mapped and discussed. Small changes and features contribute to growth but require alignment to actual customer use. These alignments can be checked through UX metrics using surveys and operational metrics tracking usage.

Don't build what already exists

Many existing products are perfect for supporting platform development and deployment. Integrating tools can create early successes. Many of these tools either are open source or require minimal licensing fees. The first step when considering tool options should always be whether the tool is available through open source or licensed models. The best practice here is to recognize when you can rent, buy, and build when considering platform options.

Open source offers an answer, but not the only answer. Companies such as GitLab, Databricks, Elastic, MongoDB, and JFrog, among others, offer some portion of their code as open source. If a generic solution is the answer, these can be adopted into the platform early and switched to a paying model as growth increases. The ability to switch from open source to paid licensing by a provider makes this an example of the rent model.

Vendor lock-in is a common problem with the rent model. This means that if you wish to change data, architectures, or applications, they cannot be easily converted to a new model. The interoperability of many DevOps systems reduces how often true vendor lock-in occurs. A good application that leads to long-term success may be preferred by an organization over the ability to switch at some future date. This addresses the Agile and DevOps philosophies that teams must be able to change easily but those changes can also occur within a tightly coupled structure.

Buying software can be either an outright purchase or through a subscription model. Subscription models offer limited-time solutions but open the possibility of vendor lock-in when options are too constrained. For example, Atlassian offers subscriptions to build platform capability, but if you later switch, it requires moving databases. Limited or excessive fields can create challenges here. Buying delivers value if you intend to retain the software for an extended time. The best purchases are often security, resource management, and program management. Processes such as CI/CD, testing, and other deployments change frequently, and the rent model is more effective in creating immediate value.

The last option is building functions. These build options are often the last step when you believe an internal solution can achieve better than what is offered on the market. Platform Engineering can require a mix of an IAC and **Configuration as Code** (**CAC**) build that drives the integration of other rented or bought pieces. Rather than building each piece, modern platform architecture allows making those integrations proprietary without intensive preparation. One example might be purchasing a repository and SSO system with your organization creating an integration allowing SSO control of the repository. Integration builds tend to be lighter-weight constructions than full functionality.

Establish metrics

Metrics are always required for DevOps. These measurements should be tailored depending on what you want to achieve. Setting acceptance criteria within different builds should determine what metrics are later measured by the organization. The DORA metrics are excellent in initial development practices as they provide flow rates and capacity measurement, while later measuring repair and recognition times. You can supplement these metrics with additional statistics about usage, availability times, performance rates, security linkages, and others.

A common path for including metrics is the previously mentioned path to establish SLAs and SLIs for required items. These expand beyond the initial measurement to create a contract between the user and provider. Moving metrics from a measurement to a value-creating option is always a best practice. We discussed SLAs in detail earlier in this chapter.

It is important to remember with metrics that establishment often leads to gamification. In gamification, one is focused simply on achieving the metric rather than the underlying goal. You can rectify this by frequently evaluating metric success or establishing cross-referencing metrics. A good example is in code commits: if a metric requires more frequent commits, users may shrink the commit size; however, reaching the overall goal still takes the same time. You can compare the code commit frequency with time to customer and commit sizes. This allows for evaluating the best size to commit, and at what time, to reach customer value.

Innovating for new success

Though innovation can be considered a best practice, it deserves separate consideration. Innovation can often be narrowly constrained to the next technology hurdle, but all aspects of the platform matter. Business innovation can be just as important as fielding new technology since it can rapidly bring more customers. Too many companies tend to focus solely on building the latest technology, rather than improving internal practices. At the same time, a business model lagging behind technical solutions may be incapable of supporting either value or growth. Teams should encourage innovation through practices such as hackathons, regular downtime for special projects, employee training budgets, conference attendance, publication, and widespread experimental options.

One platform pillar that remains constant is stability. In considering innovation, people often struggle between differentiating **evolutionary changes** and **revolutionary changes**. An evolutionary change makes small steps from the current model, and a revolutionary change rewrites the underlying model. For example, BlackBerry moving from a number pad to a full keyboard on cell phones was an evolutionary change, but Apple's move from a cell phone to the full-scale smartphones of today was revolutionary. Finding a balance between adopting these changes is a key component of business. Historic examples of failures at multiple levels are IBM stating personal computers would never happen, Kodak rejecting digital film, Sears rejecting the change from catalog to e-commerce, Yahoo not buying Google in 1998 for $1M, and Atari viewing gaming as an individual rather than a shared process.

An important innovation discussion is recognizing the difference between **cutting-edge** and **bleeding-edge** technologies. Cutting-edge implies the newest solutions available on the market, while bleeding-edge is typically technology that is not widely available. An example of cutting-edge technology is television moving from tube to digital to LCD to LED, and then multiple generations, improving pixel count, color, and transmission. A current bleeding-edge technology might be quantum networks, neural-linked devices, or multi-purpose AI assistants. Each technology realizes a problem but does not currently have the market or operations to support wider-scale adoption.

Platforms should attempt to include cutting-edge solutions while researching the bleeding edge but not expect customer adoption. Bleeding-edge solutions, despite increased capability, can often be derailed by things such as common formats or usability. Some examples are conflicts between laser disc, Beta, and VHS formats or audio with records, 8-tracks, cassettes, and CDs in the video recording industry. Both areas then faced a challenge with the growth of digital media and streaming transmissions.

Striking the right balance between innovation and usability sets the stage for understanding how to thoughtfully adopt and integrate new technologies.

Making technology leaps

Understanding technological change is the first step in implementing change through integration and adaptation. This leads to the question, what type of technology should I consider next? Everyone wants to find the next big thing, but rarely does a revolutionary change occur. Evolutionary platform technology focuses on several components: compute improvements, storage growth, and UI interaction. Each of these offers benefits but should be considered against the overall strategy.

Compute

The first improvement for a platform deals with improving capacity to compute. Additional compute generally costs more money and deals with adding additional cores either to on-premises servers or through virtual machines. Changing from a CPU core to a GPU core improves the ability to deliver specialized actions. One other factor might be adding quantum cores. While adding quantum sounds difficult, capabilities such as Amazon Braket enable using quantum machines without purchasing these solutions. Other upcoming changes include the following:

- **Graphene-based transistors**: Graphene uses one-carbon-atom-thickness materials with increased connectivity, rolled into tubes, and uses less space and energy. These tubes can be combined with other 2D materials to increase transmission speed. Graphene nano-tubes are expected to reach the market within the next five years.

- **Neuromorphic:** Technology involving neuromorphic systems calls for replicating human brain architecture. The difference in problem-solving would require significantly less energy than traditional models. This technology lags as most attempts to mimic biological processes still involve internet protocols removing the advantage from the improved structures.

- **Optical transmission:** Transmitting with optical methods uses photons rather than electrons, mapping data with light-intensity levels, and varying levels to perform calculations. Realized optical methods could improve efficiency and decrease power but challenges remain with integration and portability.

Storage

Storage may not be as widely needed in basic Platform Engineering as dealing with data coming across the platform. At some point, applications, especially AI/ML applications, require more data to be successful. Making that data accessible to the platform creates challenges, especially as the data produced extends into the terabyte and petabyte ranges. Estimates suggest the world's production of data exceeds 400 million terabytes daily. Most platforms do not require these levels, but being prepared means you can offer customers advanced capabilities:

- **DNA data storage**: Converts existing data from a binary base 2 into a DNA-based base 4. This allows increasing the overall capacity so much that some researchers believe the world's storage needs could be met with a cubic meter of powdered E. coli DNA. Challenges to this mode involve reading and writing with proteins.

- **Diamond data**: This involves using lasers to store data in nanoscale diamonds with laser pulses. These techniques are read-write capable, and a single, 5 cm diamond wafer can store up to a billion Blu-ray discs, or about 25 exabytes.

- **Blockchain**: Blockchain storage has been around for a while but only for specific and limited functions. Extending successful blockchain into different and streaming data would improve the security and confidentiality of systems. Blockchain storage improvements are more likely to emerge from software solutions than user-driven suggestions.

User interface

The last major area to improve platforms through technology is the user interface. While the user interface may seem peripheral, improvements in how individuals interact with platforms can create an enormous market advantage. A good example is Netflix, where the change from a mail-based system to on-demand streaming improved users' ability to access and view data. Some of the top trends in the user interface are highlighted here:

- **Interactive 3D**: This user approach appears in many science fiction movies but its applications are wide-ranging This would enable a user to view, edit, and work in 3D spaces, rather than being confined to a traditional monitor and keyboard configuration. Its implementation would mean making movements to access and configure platform applications, such as a hand signal to call code, run pipelines, and apply testing results.

- **Virtual and augmented reality interfaces**: These solutions are similar to interactive 3D but confined to a specific element. For example, 3D glasses can give the appearance of interaction without requiring a full 3D display. Augmented reality allows suggesting additional interactions, possibly by optical or audio inputs, to suggest changes within viewed applications.

- **Virtual assistants**: Many virtual assistants exist today in the form of chatbots, and other guides. You may even think of voice-activated integrations such as Siri or Alexa as virtual assistants. The next improvement, especially for platforms, will likely be AI tracking daily activities to suggest improvements. For example, think about an AI system that understands a worker's ability and can make tailored suggestions, notifying of additional training when they exceed certain parameters for time or quality with applications.

Preparing for the future involves a blend of implementing best practices and preparing for new technology. Best practices are people and process improvements such as providing service, creating growth opportunities, and updating metrics. Technological changes require recognizing the next steps for compute, storage, and UI improvements, such as quantum computing, DNA storage devices, and virtual chatbots. These techniques were demonstrated in the preceding best and worst case studies as the organizations attempted to achieve accelerated Platform Engineering.

Summary

Beginning with successful transformations, this chapter introduced SLA frameworks as a guideline for DevOps success. Incorporating an SLA establishes guidelines between the user and customer, enabling the determination of success or failure. While SLAs can be largely similar between different platforms, successful platforms such as GitLab and Netflix incorporated multiple paths to reach overall success.

Conversely, unsuccessful platform transformations fail to address small and large platform construction challenges adequately. Small challenges tend to be technical or operational, such as the failure of a tool, poor service, or bad metrics. Large challenges are more strategic, with platforms unable to align vision with architecture and the inability to make deliveries on time. DevOps is all about continuous value, so anything impacting that delivery can cause failure. The transformation failures highlighted included Atlassian and government processes.

Finally, the chapter concluded by identifying some high-level best practices and upcoming technological improvements for platform innovation. Platforms need to grow through increased value and an expanding customer base. Realizing this requires building effectively, incorporating existing technology, measuring success, and keeping up with innovation. Best practices provide guidelines to measure future success. Once challenges are identified, the following step requires ensuring that testing and measurement processes exist to maintain continuous success. The next chapter examines testing models in development, quality assurance in delivery, and successful operating platforms.

Call to action

- Establish SLAs and SLIs driven by your strategic goals for the platform.

- Routinely evaluate others in the field to learn from their successes and failures.

- Search new technological advances for what revolutionary and evolutionary advances exist.

Further Reading

- GitLab Corporate History: `https://handbook.gitlab.com/handbook/company/history/`

- Lockheed Martin Customer Analysis: `https://about.gitlab.com/customers/lockheed-martin/`

- Gitlab CACI Use Case: `https://about.gitlab.com/customers/caci/`

- Gitlab NVIDIA Use Case: `https://about.gitlab.com/customers/nvidia/`

- Gitlab Carfax Use Case: `https://about.gitlab.com/customers/carfax/`

- Zhou, H., Zhao, C., Conh, H., Huang, L. Man, T. and Wan, Y. (2023) "Optical computing metasurfaces: applications and advances". *Nanophotonics.* `https://doi.org/10.1515/nanoph-2023-0871`

- Lee, S. Y. "DNA Data Storage Is Closer Than You Think". Scientific American.com. `https://www.scientificamerican.com/article/dna-data-storage-is-closer-than-you-think/`

- City College of New York (2023) "Optical data storage breakthrough increases capacity of diamonds by circumventing the diffraction limit". Phys.org. `https://phys.org/news/2023-12-optical-storage-breakthrough-capacity-diamonds.html`

Get This Book's PDF Version and Exclusive Extras

UNLOCK NOW

Scan the QR code (or go to packtpub.com/unlock). Search for this book by name, confirm the edition, and then follow the steps on the page.

Note: Keep your invoice handly. Purchase made directly from packt don't require one.

9

Testing, Quality Assurance, and Operations

Platform solutions build beyond the basics to offer standardized pipelines and testing processes. Successfully implementing these processes generates repeatable **Bodies of Evidence** (**BoEs**) that allow measuring all software against the same standard. BoEs are the documents, artifacts, and processes that demonstrate to external auditors or other interested parties that security and quality exist. Often, we fall into the trap of thinking that because an application performs a unique function, we should test for different standards. Implementing best practices ensures quality across the product and allows for continual success.

In this chapter, we'll explore how to design and implement effective test strategies within the platform, covering key areas such as development, operations, security, and performance. We'll also learn how to create robust metric strategies that optimize both platform performance and the applications built on it. Additionally, the chapter will cover how to architect recovery strategies that promote resilience and scalability, ensuring the platform can withstand disruptions. Finally, we'll examine how to coordinate incident response operations to enhance reliability and maintain the integrity of both applications and data.

We will cover the following main headings:

- Best practices for testing platforms
- Metrics, monitoring, and performance optimization
- Platform incident management and recovery

Technical requirements

There are no technical requirements as such. Familiarity with testing options such as Robot Framework and SonarQube may be valuable. Knowledge of metrics integration using tools such as Grafana, Prometheus, and **OpenTelemetry** (**OTel**) will also be helpful.

Best practices for testing platforms

Throughout software development, business applications, and even sports, you will hear about the importance of testing to success. Testing allows you to determine whether a planned solution can meet the needed goals and carry out the required strategies. In our basecamp structure, testing occurs primarily in the design, develop, and deploy phases, with opportunities in the operate and support phases as well.

Each set of testing best practices offers some known areas for success. These testing practices are aligned roughly with our overall platform vision. Not all testing is internal as some methods may expand to user groups or operational surveys. Practices and metrics may differ slightly across different levels, such as software development, cloud management, or sales, such as **Net Promoter Scores (NPSs)**. For reference, the NPS is a user experience metric that uses survey questions to ask customers how likely they are to recommend the product. This NPS can be valuable but falls outside the normal testing paradigm. The NPS illustrates how an external practice, gathering user feedback, can contribute to developing internal practices.

The first step of any design is writing the test case. Common to DevOps, and essential for Platform Engineering is using **test-driven development**. Test-driven development means the first step in achieving success requires developing the test that will demonstrate success. For example, if setting a password policy requiring 8 different characters and no more than 20 characters in total, you would create a test with these parameters first. The following list clarifies the elements needed to design and execute successful testing:

1. **Designing the initial test case**: Password must include 8 different characters with no more than 20 characters in total.

2. **Analyzing the testing requirements**: Define what app framework will be used for the test.

3. **Setting up a test environment**: Establish where testing will occur.

4. **Analyzing software or hardware needs within the environment**: Ensure the environment has enough capacity for the test.

5. **Listing criteria for the system to respond**: The criteria are at least 8 different characters and no more than 20 characters in total.

6. **Listing testing methods**: List out the methods being used for testing.

7. **Designing the full test case and subordinate functions**: Design the full use case, including elements such as what types of characters are allowed.

8. **Running tests and studying the results**: The results may be as expected or they may show errors or unusual outcomes. An example is a flickering test where different results occur due to time-based system changes that were not part of the testing process.

One of our favorite testing approaches is **Robot Framework**. Robot Framework is an open source automation model allowing for test automation. It integrates with numerous tools and libraries.

Tests can be established as an initial case and computed against tabular cases, and the results can be measured. Robot Framework elements do not provide a range of answers or alternative solutions, only whether the desired test passes or fails on the criteria. In our password example, any password with fewer than 8 different characters, or more than 20 characters in total, would result in the test failing. Using automation, strings of random elements are created to test these criteria.

Testing should involve checking the initial flow, gathering feedback, and improving outcomes. A key consideration is how well the test environments mirror the production environment. The less difference, the more effective the tests tend to be; if there is more difference, more tests are needed. Automated tests run constantly and help expedite the process. Manual tests take more resources and take longer to identify problems. Do not forget about the impact of Conway's law on testing: if you do not carefully plan, testing will resemble the larger organizational processes and you may not find the end solution. As an example, testing that verifies a streamlined messaging format may miss hierarchical approvals required by the parent organization. The test might be successful, but the outcome skips important steps that affect the final product. This is a reminder to ensure the delivered functions match expectations through testing. The following sections include some best practices and examples of various tests, beginning with development.

Development tests

Development tests are the most simple and fundamental types of tests. These tests generally occur without external users, and there is no need for complicated architecture. The key to successful development tests lies in breaking pieces down to their fundamental level and understanding each piece. Think of development testing like preparing to create something in a woodshop: you find all the components, lay out the correct pieces for assembly, and ask a friend whether the design makes sense. The following list highlights some common development tests:

- **Unit testing (automated)**: Unit testing assesses the smallest pieces of code that can be logically isolated from another unit. Across multiple languages, this means isolating functions, subroutines, libraries, methods, and properties. Unit testing can look for areas such as correctly used variables, reuse of code segments, and correctly written code.

- **Code quality (partially automated)**: Agile, DevOps, and XP rely on using code quality checks, starting with paired programmers. Automated systems, especially generative AI, can expand on those code checks. The quality checks are a subjective assessment determining how well the delivered code matches typical code by the team. Tests here seek to isolate the smallest areas to determine reliability, maintainability, testability, portability, reusability, defects, and complexity.

- **Code reviews (largely manual)**: Direct review of code should be less than 400 lines with an inspection rate of less than 500 lines per hour, never for more than an hour. Good code tests establish a process to fix defects, foster a positive code review culture, and practice lightweight reviews. Generative AI, such as GitHub Copilot or OpenAI Codex, can assist by suggesting areas for code improvement. You can employ roles with **Large Language Models** (**LLMs**) to frame responses by asking as coder with 20 years of experience, which elements of the tested code can be reduced.

- **Static analysis (automated)**: Static tests are the automated debugging tests that are carried out before the program runs. This ensures the code is in the right **Software Development Kit (SDK)** and analyzed against coding rules. Static testing can discover some early vulnerabilities and bugs through software such as SonarQube, Veracode, and HP. These tests eliminate individual security problems, such as open ports and embedded secrets, at the easiest time to fix.

Development tests provide only a portion of the needed information. Once development testing occurs, the completed software expands to integration test to ensure new features work across the broader platform.

Integration tests

Integration practices aim to link feature elements together and bring those individual development code elements into further construction. Some integration can happen early in development, but platform integration focuses on making pieces work individually and then in aggregate with other platform elements. These tests and practices ensure information can be transmitted across coding elements, that the needed functions are carried out from start to finish, and that you can revert elements without breaking the program. Finally, initial performance tests happen within integration testing, especially to determine whether new code is better or worse at carrying out defined functions.

You should aim to make each integration test automated. Designing for automation within execution allows code to be executed prior to any testing verification. . When the code executes, it should be relatively simple so that a no- or low-code option can be engaged to execute all the integration tests. The test can then provide a complete answer to all potential problems, rather than requiring an individual to constantly execute the tests. Integration tests are also best completed in testing or preproduction environments, showing all processes work effectively before moving on to production. Integration testing best practices are as follows:

- **Data testing (automated)**: Evaluate the information with which the code interacts. Going back to our password example, integration data testing examines whether code can be called from a directory and then verifies the code samples against other functions.

- **End to end, or E2E (automated)**: Test the application workflows from beginning to end. This integration test checks whether a password is accepted, whether the user has permission to access the right program, and whether they can retrieve or store data within that application. E2E testing is often combined with data testing for best results.

- **Regression (automated)**: Regression testing requires running functional and non-functional tests after a change. This practice verifies that deployed changes can return to an earlier state when necessary. Regression and reversion are key incident response elements, but only if they work. Regression is also essential when bugs are found and fixed.

- **Performance (automated)**: Integration tests are the first place to examine how well code works. Setting performance tests means looking at memory usage, how long functions require, and which elements of a program are slow, and then establishing comparisons to desired outcomes.

Performance tests are run with software such as Apache JMeter, WebLOAD, and BlazeMeter; however, most are not free. With careful metrics, you can build effective analysis to conduct mostly free performance tests but remember the longer-term performance primarily derives from user experiences.

Software processes, having been successfully developed and integrated across the platform, can then go through delivery testing. Integration testing involves reviewing the commonalities between elements of the testing and production environments. Delivery testing involves verifying these commonalities.

Delivery tests

Delivery code means a feature is almost ready for prime time but requires one last check. Delivery processes occur at the end of the pipeline, during beta testing, for example, A/B deployments or even canary deployments. These tests are typically less automated as some parts need to be conducted by distinct user groups separate from developers. User personas can be automated – generative AI can make excellent templates – but there remains no substitute in these tests for actual users. The following list highlights some possible delivery tests:

- **Functional (partially automated)**: Performs input versus output tests in black-box form. During this phase, the code is not tested as individual items but as a set where one input produces exactly one output, and that one output traces to one input. This practice ensures functions are performed correctly.

- **Dynamic (partially automated)**: Dynamic tests seek to find errors when the code runs. Again, the emphasis on delivery means you do not look for code errors but errors in the function's outputs and inputs. Rather than having set use cases, this option allows for various inputs during execution. These tests require tight integration with functional testing.

- **Red/blue team (blended processes)**: Red teams are attackers and blue teams are defenders. This test designates a set team to defend a function and one to attack, then compares the results at the end of a cycle. Modern execution sometimes advocates for a purple team as a mix that can perform attack and defense. As a cultural practice, red teams tend to win, so changing the team composition from time to time can be beneficial to morale. Hiring an experienced red/blue team can be expensive.

- **Operational testing (manual)**: Operational tests are also known as user-acceptance tests. These are where either a single user or a team of users tries to use the new software. Operational testing is a more formal expression of dynamic tests than beta testing or A/B deployments. The chosen team might be proficient in the desired function, or it may consist of new users who receive training at the time. The best output from these tests is careful reports and user stories about the platform's performance. Operational tests may be unnecessary if other tests are performed correctly, but some customers prefer a final, hands-on acceptance test.

Once delivery tests are complete, only one area remains before users can access fully tested software as a valuable product.

Production tests

Old-school computer programmers might say production tests are not needed as all flaws are caught beforehand. The modern DevOps pace means this no longer holds true. If testing is a reasonable process during development, integration, and delivery, the same quality testing should occur in production. Production tests, especially on the platform, ensure users are not bending parameters into new and untried formations. The following list highlights some common production tests:

- **Runtime security (automated)**: Runtime security tests are those that run on the actual deployed software. The key is implementing instrumentation to create observability and telemetry across the system. Runtime implementations check for items not noticed during initial production, such as **Common Vulnerabilities and Exposures** (**CVEs**) released after the code reaches deployment. Good runtime testing ensures security flaws do not surprise the software development or operations team.

- **Reversion (manual or automated)**: Similar to regression testing, reversion testing ensures a full rollback can be done on production software. This ensures that the entire platform can be successfully returned to an earlier state when a bug reaches production. Key aspects of this test include data integrity, user databases, and minimal downtime. Automated solutions with A/B testing can be set to revert when certain performance metrics are reached automatically.

Integrating tests from delivery to production creates a solid foundation for quality software. Each step emphasizes different areas, which is only possible as the software reaches the next step. As a final best practice, tests should always be run to completion in each section as it is easier to fix multiple errors at once, rather than fixing them as they occur. If you fix an error immediately after it is identified, there could be subsequent errors after the initial fix. For example, an error in code that prevents compiling must be found before testing in production; without the earlier testing steps, you'll spend longer trying to find minimal errors. Fixing problems early reduces the amount of time needed to resolve those changes once they reach production. One way to track testing effectiveness is through metrics, monitoring, and performance optimization.

Metrics, monitoring, and performance optimization

Every company wants to deliver more faster, increase customer value, and return a profit to stakeholders. Every DevOps business understands core metrics. More advanced organizations will possess the skill to identify the known unknowns behind the metrics. Gaining initial metrics leads to some understanding but additional details can be derived. Subsequent metrics should be scoped tightly and focused on acceleration and provide clear feedback. This section emphasizes how small changes to achieve some metrics can be deconstructed to provide advanced solutions.

There is software that provides metric solutions by managing data across a platform. This software also allows you to select advanced metrics with multiple comparison levels. Metrics are defined by first asking some basic questions, which lead to some universal, basic metrics. Then, you can formulate more advanced metrics, and finally, convert those numbers into positive actions.

The first questions

Many often question why using metrics matters at all, as all individuals in the process understand what is being done and what remains incomplete. Metrics provide a quantifiable and repeatable source of observability by measuring multiple processes and driving actionable solutions. The first element of a metric is a process or action to be measured, such as how many code commits a team makes. These can be expanded to select daily, weekly, or other time integrations to ensure the best time management. The key to early metric development is to assess the correct time frame to measure something. For example, if you are looking at website traffic to indicate website success, you may want to know whether the traffic hits were within hours after posting a new promotion or throughout the year.

People might question why a quantifiable tracking mechanism is needed, especially in small teams. Most individuals make bad decisions if they do not have quantifiable metrics. People who make decisions tend to overestimate their ability to predict correctly. This problem frequently occurs in scheduling tasks; you may predict that a project will take six months but it in fact takes a full year. Human prediction capabilities are so bad that scientists have found that 77% of randomly generated linear models make better decisions than individuals. Examples of decisions include completion times, guilt or innocence, fixes required, or proposed solutions. Metrics ensure decisions are less random.

Numbers provide the repeatable component for linear judgments. If we know our development team's performance last week and the week before, then we know that increasing that number by 100% in the following week with no other changes is a bad decision. Another similar decision is buying more cloud space for a projected service increase – thankfully, many of those operational decisions are now handled by load balancers. These technical load balancers also use metrics; they just make decisions about metrics without human intervention. These paths lead to options in using generative AI to monitor actions about metrics.

All metrics must spur action. If a metric cannot result in an action, it is not useful. The options we discuss next start with the basics and then expand into options for immediate action. If we return to the earlier commit problem, a basic metric might look at the number of commits per day. Expanding that metric might indicate commits per developer, lines of code per commit, time from the previous commit, or the type of function the commit provided. Each of these could drive a more specific action to resolve changes. You might instruct a slow developer, ask a fast developer to make more complete solutions with more lines, explore context switching between the team, or find more complicated functions. Each of these metrics then provides a path to make decisions to improve the metric based on organizational goals and value streams. Basic metrics allow for more detailed investigation while advanced metrics point squarely at the problem.

Basic metrics

Everyone should be familiar with the most basic metrics outlined by the **DevOps Research and Assessment (DORA)** organization. These four metrics, commonly used for software development, are deployment frequency, mean time to change, mean time to recover, and change failure rate. Let's cover them briefly:

- **Deployment frequency**: How often new code is deployed into production. Measured by deployments over time.

- **Mean time to change**: The time required for a new idea to become production code. Includes deployment frequency measurements. Measured in average time.

- **Mean time to recover**: The time to recover a production system to stable if bad or unstable code is deployed. Measured in average time.

- **Change failure rate**: The number of bad code elements that are allowed to reach production. Measured in percentage of bad code elements over good code elements.

These initially seem to be excellent metrics but are intended for more mature software organizations. Starting with these metrics can leave an organization wondering how to improve. For more detailed information, you can check out the DORA site: `https://dora.dev/`.

One important area of note among these metrics is that three out of the four are measured in time, with the last measured in percentage. The main point is how each drives additional action. The scope of each element highlights how they are high-level measures of success but are not useful as individual measures or for computing an aggregate score.

All metrics derive from the initial questions: what do you need to know and what happens afterward? This might be about security, production times, or user happiness. It is important to consider whether the metric actually answers the question even when it appears complete. For example, a metric stating that there have been no security breaches might only be tracking known security breaches or defining security breaches within a narrow parameter. While metrics address what seems to be the current need, they should be carefully studied before implementation to ensure real progress.

Measurements guide the development of metrics. The DORA metrics provide a single measurement either of a point in time or across a set period. For those computations to matter, you must also set a desired rate. The metric would drive further action. For example, if the change failure rate is 15%, does that number fall above or below the organization's expected number? In some instances, these SLAs can set rates. Another measurement could be measuring change failure during testing, pre-production, or the actual production environment. In building an effective metric, you might tolerate 15% failure during testing, 3% in pre-production, and less than 1% in actual production.

The other key element depends on deployment numbers within the same period. If a company deploys to production hundreds of times daily, higher failure numbers might be more acceptable as they are likely to be changed by the following deployment. If a team deploys over 100 times per day, each percentage of failure only indicates one piece of deployed code. This raises a common question about the use of raw numbers versus percentages. If a team averages three deployments monthly, the change failure rate would be 0%, 33%, 66%, or 100%. This creates much more variance in how you approach the metrics. In this case, you must directly compare the deployment frequency to the change failure rate for an accurate assessment.

These discussions can be further complicated when you consider value stream metrics. Some might suggest that value stream metrics should merely echo the DORA metrics. Value streams are derived initially from Lean manufacturing and consider the period from when material enters a process to when you receive value from the customer. DevOps often considers that deployed code is purchased code, but merely pushing code to production does not always generate revenue. These considerations should address how many users access production code, or broader operational metrics such as how code affects performance, user happiness, or other factors.

A simple example would be if new code is required for a company promotion event, time to deployment does not matter if the code is not completed before the event. Failure rates do not matter as the event is never launched, delayed, or canceled. Understanding how metrics affect overall value and success is critical to determining the right tests to guarantee development is done correctly and on time.

One question we always receive is how to make sure that your metrics are the right ones. In answering this question, we have found a simple framework from our days in intelligence operations to drive this discussion. The basic model is as follows:

1. **How do I know what has happened?** If requiring a number for measurement, what element must be present to observe or deliver those numbers? For example, is a system reporting uptime computed by server uptime, web availability, or just when the software is running? Differences in those numbers can require drastically different solutions.

2. **If I know what has happened, what comes next?** If the numbers are accurate, what should the next step be? Should the mean time to change decrease if the deployment frequency is high? If deployment frequency increases while the time to change increases, what action should be taken?

3. **Are the assumptions true?** Were correct assumptions made about the metric? Does the reporting tool assigned deliver the right information at the right frequency to contribute? For example, if the deployment frequency derives from a monthly timeline but the time to change is assessed quarterly, will the relationship between the items still stand?

4. **Do conclusions follow the assumptions?** You should consider whether conclusions about events follow the natural flow of the assumptions. If the conclusion is that value increases because deployment frequency increases, does that hold true if the change failure also increases?

5. **Compare apples to apples, not oranges to elephants.** You must ensure that the items measured are capable of comparison. When measuring deployment frequency, if one team must meet a security standard and the other produces open source, can you compare those rates when selecting improvement actions?

Coming up with answers to these questions for every metric can take some work. We would write them out for every problem when we started using this guideline. Writing out answers addresses questions two, three, and four in providing visual verification for what you are thinking. Writing also addresses the core metric issue that metrics are quantifiable and repeatable. Working through a standard process ensures all metrics meet the requirements, avoiding poor metrics in the system. The next section explores using these guidelines to decompose existing metrics to guide actions.

Decomposing a metric

Decomposing any metric requires starting with the current situation. The most important part of decomposition is supporting the shared vision and objectives of the platform. While the metrics needed may be entirely new, chances are that an existing metric fills part of the need. If, by some awful chance, the team does not currently have any metrics, then looking at the SLA can provide guidance on which metrics support operations. If you do not have an SLA, then looking at the acceptance criteria for the functions being built can provide a starting point. Thankfully, we now know the basic pillars and levels to guide our foundational construction in building a platform.

Change requires understanding those initial elements. If, for example, we want to explore the stability of our design process, that provides an initial metric. Previous chapters suggested that the design phase should only take up about 10% of the time required for the full value stream. Most teams conduct design during planning events, planned for about 4-8 hours of the 80-hour sprint. This provides an initial assurance that tasks are being completed efficiently. You may want to add to those measurements by determining how long a developer spends on a design once a ticket reaches their workflow bucket.

Obtaining additional data for decomposition can occur in multiple ways. You may use surveys to highlight areas that conflict with the known process. You can supplement this process with individual interviews or sensing sessions. A sensing session is when one gathers multiple individuals to ask about a particular topic. The key to this qualitative process is using the same questions across multiple interviews. When you use different questions across interviews, you can get a lot of data, but it becomes difficult to compare the individuals' contributions; you are making an oranges to elephants comparison. Between the surveys and interviews, you can often find where the existing metric falls short of the data needed to create action. The following list provides a quick look at how you might compose questions to decompose the DORA metric mean time to change:

- **How long does it take to complete an action?** How is this measured? Do you use story points, stories completed within an epic, the entire epic, or delivery to the customer? Is completed work measured against how much work remains in progress?

- **Are constraints identified?** The high-level evaluation of average time often does not show what is slowing down the various areas. Assigning reasons such as lack of time, blocked by other items, or not prioritized can show why the mean time might be changing.

- **Who built it?** If all tasks are assigned to a team, do we measure change at the team, individual, or product level? Does the metric include complexity as the denominator of time required? For example, can the comparative time between more and less complex tasks be seen? Can you compare the knowledge and skills assigned to the team to the desired output?

- **How are different features compared?** Where does priority scaling fall into the metric? You want to ensure high-priority items are completed faster than lower-priority items. When comparing different team success rates, are you factoring in the complexity of the problems assigned?

- **Never forget about security impacts.** Having a fast mean time to change helps, but as earlier, with the change failure rate, does the time to change include later security impacts? You should assess how long is spent in the production pipelines on security, and how that compares to overall production timelines.

If reading closely, you will see how these decomposition questions mirror the earlier questions about a metric. If a metric is underperforming but the action is unclear, we suggest using a physical or virtual whiteboard to ask the team questions. These questions help suggest where decomposition is needed to design accurate metrics, create action, and allow the platform to succeed.

Monitoring for metrics

Once you establish metrics, the next step suggests how you might monitor those metrics and provide active alerting. The primary success involves using dashboards to compile different information but create observability. The most important point to consider about dashboards is that they are a starting point for discussion, rather than a finishing point. Many organizations use dashboards to share information but never move past this. Dashboards create a snapshot, a compilation of various data, and some easy alerts in line with needed information. The next step integrates tools such as OTel from the CNCF, building heartbeats or pulse checks, and incorporating metrics into the SLIs, SLOs, and SLAs.

OTel combines tools, APIs, and SDKs into an open source observability framework to instrument, generate, collect, and export telemetry data. Most telemetry data consists of logs, traces, and metrics within the system. The example shown in *Figure 9.1* from the OTel documentation demonstrates how OTel may be configured.

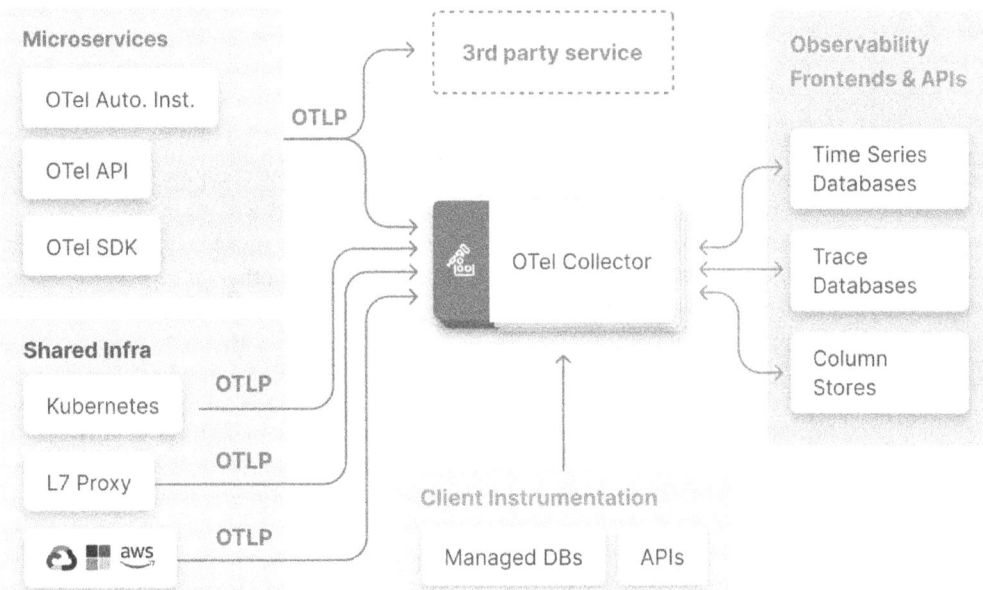

Figure 9.1: OTel architecture

You can see the various elements within OTel combined with other elements. As an open source option, OTel is one of our favorite tools for designing initial formats. The system instruments code with APIs, gathers SDK data, analyzes data by sampling to reduce errors, provides the required context, exports data, and allows for more filtering with an established backend. One advantage of OTel is exporting filtered data to tools such as Grafana, Prometheus, or Elastic to provide the needed data rapidly. Another common solution for OTel implementation is using the open source Jaeger tools.

Telemetry solutions can implement quality, time, or application metrics. These elements look for a push to collect as a heartbeat or a pull to collect as a pulse check. A **heartbeat** refers to metrics collecting data at a continuous rhythm with constant awareness while a **pulse check** requires an action to verify that progress continues. An example of the two elements is provided in *Figure 9.2* by comparing Prometheus and InfluxDB.

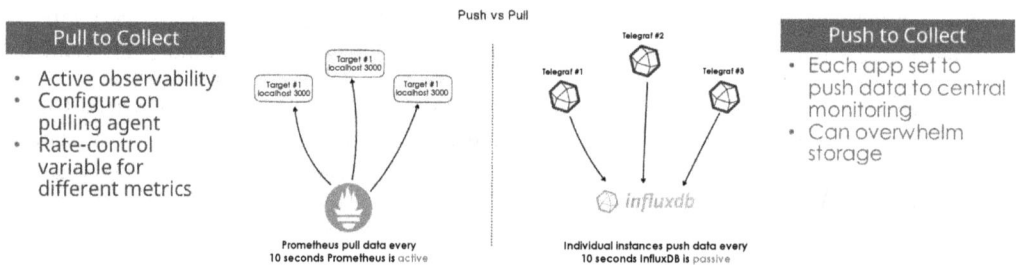

Figure 9.2: Push and pull with metrics

You can see how Prometheus allows pushing data while InfluxDB pull data into the collected format. The difference allows monitoring different elements depending on the compute and storage within the platform. Push metrics can help when contributing to pipelines while the pull metric can be more effective in SSO environments. Applying a push metric solution means every time the pipeline runs in the platform, it pushes data into the metric collection. On the other side, pull data can assess security tools by verifying that user logins are communicated to the larger platform. This pull data supports the observability that all users have authenticated tokens and that API calls are using the latest patches and upgrades.

All combined metric data should be observable through dashboards within the SLA frameworks. Dashboards can show different time frames but allowing monitoring supports implementing comparative decisions. Dashboard design can rapidly scale for different time frames, data, and frameworks. For example, you can set a dashboard to show platform time available, build a Pareto chart demonstrating which apps are available, and then compare through a scaled metric the individual applications and platform availability. Linking metric types through monitoring allows knowing how to optimize actions and when metrics require a change.

Optimizing metrics

The last element when considering metrics is realizing when a metric is no longer valuable. Teams frequently become attached to their metrics, reporting statistics even when they no longer create value. Metrics are designed to create discussion and inspire action; when a metric no longer achieves that goal, it is time to move on from it. This distinction can be especially difficult when metrics seem positive or were gamified in a way to achieve the metric without creating additional value.

One great example of a metric that can be gamified occurs in **story points** for DevOps teams. Story points describe how complex an issue may be, and a potential time for completion. If an issue has two story points, it is twice as complex as an issue with one and may take twice as long. If the metric is how many story points a team completes, some teams may make issues seem more complicated so that they complete a higher number of points. The solution to optimize the metric is rather than using story points, the measurement can be how many of the planned tasks are completed during a sprint. While story points may help team management, the higher percentage of planned versus done tasks allows for more accurate comparison.

Important to optimizing metrics is remembering that no metric should occur in isolation. Each of these metrics can relate to another for improved situational awareness. The math seems straightforward if the desired SLA is less than 1% of bugs released to production, and the metric is the bugs released to production. You should consider the secondary effect that if all code remains held until bug-free, the time to production might increase as every element waits until it is perfect. This summarizes the preceding thought pattern about detailing not just metrics but also the assumptions around those elements.

Metrics are typically posted on dashboards, reviewed during meetings, and cited by employees. Common metrics become cultural frameworks and sometimes express organizational values. A commonly held truth, expressed as a metric, can become a known fact, regardless of other elements surrounding the metric. One friend used to always quote, "50% of the people who quote statistics are right 100% of the time." This type of expression underlies the need to constantly review and update metrics. Optimization best practices require reviewing metrics regularly, not for the information contained but whether the metrics still answer the desired question.

The next section addresses how metrics can be used to inform incident management and recovery.

Platform incident management and recovery

Platforms are a customer-supporting operation, making incident management and recovery a critical component of success. Incident management should address all potential positive and negative issues, as the main goal remains supporting the customer with a successful platform experience. Normal delivery teams support an incident management response firing after an event is noticed whether internal or external, and platforms are no different. Previous discussions about tiered support, SREs ensuring various SLAs are met, and security concerns are all important elements of managing platform incidents. Each of those discussions highlighted metrics to further define how you handle incident resolution over time.

The first step in any incident process is implementing a ticketing system. These systems may use software such as Jira Service Management, ServiceNow, GitLab issues, or even a spreadsheet tracker. The primary concern with selecting ticketing should be the number of issues and the level of observability. If a system receives one to two issues daily, spreadsheets might be practical, but automation becomes essential as that number scales. Automation in incident response ticketing allows rapid triage, assigning resources, and quick resolution for easy problems. A reminder of the tiers has been provided here:

- **Tier 1**: Issues resolved through existing documentation and improved practices.

- **Tier 2**: Issues requiring a change in configuration, such as connections, ports, repositories, or software versions.

- **Tier 3**: Issues representing a bug, something that should work but does not, an issue, or a desired new capability.

Some incident notifications arise from observability on the system, but others occur through regular reporting. For example, phishing attacks, using a spam email to try and get targets to click links, are often reported by employees. Aggregating these reports and gaining observability over the ticketing system can reveal where an incident is occurring to a security team.

The platform incident response should use metrics to highlight significant areas. Metrics are derived from the SLAs and SLIs, depicting effective platform operations. When those metrics slide, the root cause analysis can reveal the need for a broader intervention. Incident response processes typically use some standard process alignment, such as preparation, identification, containment, eradication, lessons learned, and communication. Each step requires a checklist, dedicated to platform operations to resolve incidents.

Essential to incident response is the preparation phase. This preparation constitutes dedicated practices where teams assemble to address simulated issues. A smoothly running incident response requires practice. You never see professional sports athletes commit to a game without practice; the same applies to platform operations. The teams must know who is involved and have a place to practice and a set group of procedures to follow. These practice sessions should be held at least quarterly and should not be postponed or canceled due to actual events. The temptation is to skip an incident response practice when it occurs shortly after recovery from an actual incident. While there is no substitute for real-world actions, the practice helps create the success paths for those incidents.

One important point to note about incidents is that the work is not over even after resolution. The full response is incomplete until all systems recover to the pre-incident operations. In the platform, you will likely have multiple users, with different levels of information, all needing restoration. The 3-2-1 mantra applies here where platform data is backed up on three different media sources, in two physical locations, and with one option located offline. You can regularly test those backups through reversion and regression testing. These test models help demonstrate success before an operation becomes critical.

Typically, testing is seen as development while incident response activities are operations. In the platform, you can merge these two elements. Tests are key to development, but running tests in operations to verify activity creates observability. Observability then leads to incident awareness, early operations to eliminate problems, and successful recovery. True learning takes place in the DevOps model in creating flow, feedback, and continuous improvement in multiple areas. The next chapter combines all the technical DevOps solutions to provide a structure to create high-performing platform teams.

Summary

The platform evaluation in this chapter started with some of the tests and practices you can use to evaluate a platform. Samples of many different tests were introduced, with a path to success. These tests were then followed by a discussion of metrics. Metrics can be complicated but establishing a metric remains relatively simple. The basic metric framework for any question evaluates how you know and any assumptions around those metrics, and ensures comparisons between metrics are made accurately.

The chapter moved on from those initial metrics to more advanced processes involving decomposing, monitoring, and optimizing metrics for later success. The last step expressed how to set up incident responses within the platform. Incident response includes not just negative outcomes but developing a framework to deal with every potential issue a platform may encounter. Good incident response makes use of effective testing. The next chapter takes those sound technical foundations and expands into how you can build a high-performance platform team.

Call to action

- Practice writing and executing test cases to verify platform elements

- Examine the metrics typically used and determine whether they provide sufficient information to take corrective action

- Hold a training session for the incident response team

Part 3: Accelerate Deliver Business Value and Lead the Future

This part focuses on turning platform engineering into a strategic advantage. We will connect platform outcomes to business value, drive continuous improvement, and lead with a forward-looking mindset. This is where mastery comes into focus—where technology, teams, and leadership converge to deliver measurable enterprise impact.

This part has the following chapters:

- *Chapter 10, Building High-Performance Platform Teams*
- *Chapter 11, From Vision to Reality: Mastering Enterprise Platform Engineering*

10
Building High-Performance Platform Teams

Building high-performance teams in Platform Engineering is essential for sustained innovation and operational excellence. This chapter will guide you through creating, nurturing, and maintaining such teams, ensuring your organization meets industry standards and sets new benchmarks. Leveraging the practical and effective **5Es framework—Empathize**, **Empower**, **Engage**, **Entrust**, and **Equip**—we will explore continuous strategies to sustain high performance.

In this chapter, we'll explore the key components of building and sustaining a high-performing Platform Engineering team. We'll begin by examining the essential roles and organizational structures that form the foundation of an effective team. Next, we'll delve into hiring strategies, highlighting the critical skills, competencies, and approaches needed to recruit top talent that aligns with your organization's goals. Finally, we'll discuss how to sustain high performance over time through continuous learning, adaptive leadership, and fostering a culture of recognition and growth.

We will be covering the following main headings:

- Structure of a high-performing Platform Engineering team
- Hiring for a high-performing team
- Nurturing and developing the team
- Sustaining high performance
- Career development and progression

This chapter's insights and practical guidance will transform how you build and sustain high-performance Platform Engineering teams. It is your handbook for driving lasting success and elevating your organization to new heights.

Technical requirements

This chapter does not necessitate specific technical skills but benefits from a solid grasp of Platform Engineering principles, team dynamics, and organizational behavior. Understanding organizational structures, team topologies, and cultural dynamics will enhance the application of the content. Familiarity with industry practices in hiring, team development, and performance management is valuable. Prior knowledge of Platform Engineering and team dynamics, as discussed in earlier chapters, is essential for fully appreciating the insights provided.

Structure of a high-performing Platform Engineering team

In today's competitive digital landscape, a Platform Engineering team's structure is crucial for organizational success. A well-designed team boosts efficiency and innovation and aligns seamlessly with business objectives, driving transformative outcomes. Let us explore the critical elements of a high-performing Platform Engineering team, providing actionable insights to revolutionize your organization's platform capabilities. By implementing these strategic components, leaders can cultivate a team that consistently delivers exceptional results and propels the organization to new heights.

Team composition and roles

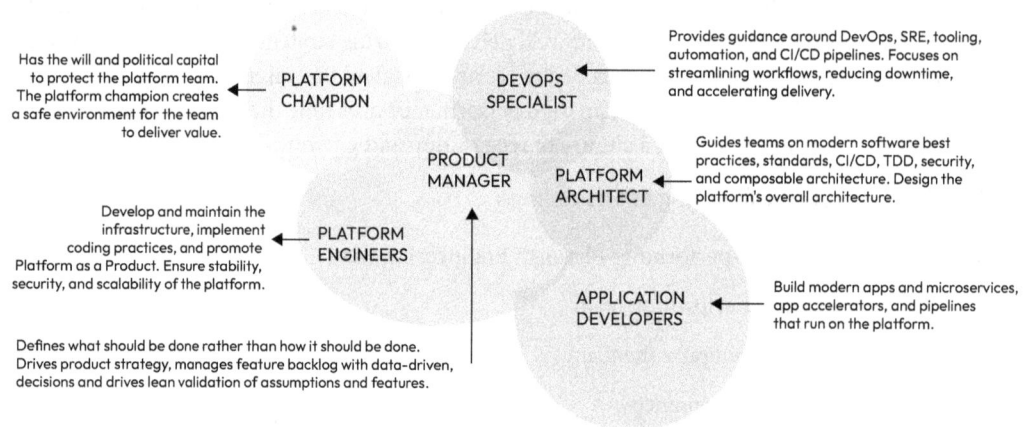

Figure 10.1: Composition of a high-performing Platform Engineering team

The success of a high-performing Platform Engineering team hinges on clearly defined roles with meticulously outlined responsibilities and expectations. In the following subsections, we will explore a few critical roles within a Platform Engineering team and provide actionable insights for leveraging these roles to drive organizational success.

Platform Champion

The **Platform Champion** is a pivotal figure tasked with creating an environment where innovation thrives, and the platform team can operate effectively:

- **Responsibilities**: The Platform Champion advocates for the team at the highest organizational levels, secures essential resources, and drives strategic initiatives aligning with the company's broader goals. They navigate internal politics to ensure the platform team is shielded from unnecessary obstacles and can focus on delivering value.

- **Skills**: Key skills include strategic vision, leadership, influence, and a deep understanding of the organizational landscape. They must also be adept at stakeholder management and capable of articulating the platform's value to senior executives.

- **Insight**: The Platform Champion should regularly facilitate cross-departmental meetings to enhance alignment with broader business objectives. This practice ensures that the platform team's initiatives are well integrated into the company's strategic roadmap.

Product manager

Product managers are the strategists of the platform team, ensuring that the team's efforts align with market demands and organizational goals:

- **Responsibilities**: The product manager defines what needs to be achieved, manages the product strategy, maintains the feature backlog, and validates features through data-driven decisions. They must bridge the gap between technical execution and business strategy, ensuring that the platform evolves to meet both user needs and business objectives.

- **Skills**: Essential skills include product management, strategic planning, data analysis, and excellent communication. They must be able to translate complex technical concepts into business value and vice versa.

- **Insight**: Incorporating continuous customer feedback loops into the product development process ensures that the platform remains relevant and valuable. This iterative approach helps the team stay agile and responsive to market changes.

Platform engineer

Platform engineers are the architects of developer productivity, responsible for building, maintaining, and evolving platforms that empower teams to deliver with speed and reliability:

- **Responsibilities**: These engineers design and implement tools such as **Backstage**, **GitHub/ GitLab**, and **CI/CD pipelines**, creating golden paths for developers. They also promote the **platform as a product** concept, ensuring the platform is robust, secure, and capable of scaling to future needs. Their work often overlaps with infrastructure teams, especially in managing complex cloud environments.

- **Skills**: Proficiency in coding, infrastructure management, SRE principles, and automation tools is essential. Familiarity with developer experience platforms and cloud-native technologies is critical to streamline workflows and enhance platform usability.

- **Insight**: Regular upskilling and hands-on experience with emerging technologies enable platform engineers to deliver cutting-edge solutions, ensuring developer satisfaction and organizational agility. *Platform as a product* focuses on treating the platform like a product for internal customers (developers), emphasizing usability, feedback loops, and continuous improvement, which is key to maximizing productivity and fostering innovation.

DevOps specialist

DevOps specialists are enablers of operational efficiency, bridging development and operations by designing scalable solutions that support multiple teams:

- **Responsibilities**: DevOps specialists create and maintain golden paths by integrating tools such as Jenkins, Kubernetes, and Terraform into cohesive workflows. They design CI/CD pipelines that cater to the needs of multiple teams, solve complex authentication and **role-based access control** (**RBAC**) challenges, and build dashboards that provide actionable insights for monitoring and optimization. Their role extends beyond individual teams, focusing on delivering scalable, standardized solutions that streamline workflows across the organization.

- **Skills**: Expertise in DevOps tools, infrastructure automation, **continuous integration/delivery** (**CI/CD**), and security best practices is critical. A deep understanding of multi-team development workflows and cross-functional collaboration enables them to address broader organizational needs.

- **Insight**: By establishing and maintaining internal communities of practice, DevOps specialists can share standardized workflows, governance policies, and best practices, fostering consistency and efficiency across development teams. This collaborative approach supports operational excellence and accelerates delivery at scale.

Platform architect

Platform architects design the structural framework of the platform, ensuring it supports scalability, security, and maintainability:

- **Responsibilities**: Platform architects provide guidance on software best practices, CI/CD, **test-driven development** (**TDD**), and security. They also design the platform's overall architecture, ensuring it can scale efficiently and securely.

- **Skills**: Key skills include software architecture, security best practices, and TDD. They must foresee potential scalability issues and design solutions that mitigate these risks.

- **Insight**: Collaboration with application developers is crucial to ensuring that architectural decisions are practical and aligned with the team's technical capabilities and limitations.

Application developers

Application developers within the platform team focus on building internal tools and services designed to enhance developer productivity and streamline workflows:

- **Responsibilities**: They create internal applications, microservices, app accelerators, and CI/CD pipelines tailored to the needs of development teams. Their goal is to provide reusable, scalable, and efficient solutions that enable other developers to deliver business value faster.

- **Skills**: Proficiency in application development, microservices architecture, and pipeline creation is essential. Familiarity with developer experience tools and internal platform requirements is critical for delivering impactful solutions.

- **Insight**: Fostering creativity through hackathons and collaborative innovation initiatives allows application developers to refine internal tools and services continually, ensuring they remain relevant and effective in supporting evolving developer needs.

Defining and optimizing the roles within a Platform Engineering team is crucial for driving efficiency, innovation, and alignment with business objectives. We should recruit individuals with the necessary technical skills and alignment with the organization's strategic vision for each role. Fostering collaboration and continuous development within these roles ensures the Platform Engineering team operates at peak performance, delivering exceptional value and driving organizational success.

Yet, even the most skilled team will fall short without the right organizational structure. The framework in which these roles operate is the foundation that enables high performance, agility, and strategic alignment.

Leveraging industry frameworks and guidelines

Building high-performing Platform Engineering teams benefits immensely from established industry frameworks and best practices. Two highly regarded resources in this domain are the **Team Topologies** framework and the CNCF Platform Engineering team guidelines:

- **Team Topologies**: Authored by Matthew Skelton and Manuel Pais, this framework introduces four fundamental team types and three interaction modes designed to streamline team structures and enhance collaboration. The *Enabling Team* and *Platform Team* concepts are particularly relevant for Platform Engineering. They provide guidance on structuring teams to focus on delivering self-service capabilities and enabling streamlined developer workflows. Adopting these principles ensures that teams are aligned with organizational goals, fostering innovation and minimizing friction.

- **CNCF Platform Engineering guidelines**: These guidelines emphasize creating **internal developer platforms** (**IDPs**) that centralize tools and workflows. IDPs drive consistency and efficiency across development teams by integrating golden paths, automation, and governance into a unified interface. The CNCF approach also underscores the importance of treating platforms as products, focusing on developer satisfaction and measurable outcomes.

By integrating these frameworks, organizations can optimize team alignment, improve collaboration, and deliver robust, scalable platforms. This approach empowers platform teams to operate at peak performance while adhering to industry best practices and fostering a culture of continuous improvement.

Organizational models

Choosing the right organizational model for the Platform Engineering team is crucial for success. The selected structure directly impacts the team's efficiency, agility, and alignment with business goals. The three most common organizational models are **centralized**, **decentralized**, and **hybrid**.

Centralized teams

Centralized teams consolidate Platform Engineering resources within a single department. This model ensures consistency and streamlines decision-making. Let's look at them closely:

- **Advantages**:

  - **Consistency and standardization**: Centralized teams implement consistent standards and best practices across the organization, minimizing variability and integration issues. This consistency ensures that all processes adhere to the highest quality standards, nurturing a culture of excellence.

  - **Simplified coordination**: With a single point of control, it's easier to coordinate projects and allocate resources efficiently. Centralized decision-making accelerates the implementation of strategic initiatives, eliminating the friction caused by disparate approaches.

  - **Focused expertise**: Concentrating expertise in one area fosters deep specialization and knowledge sharing. This concentration leads to a more robust skill set within the team, driving innovation and technical excellence.

- **Challenges**:

  - **Potential bottlenecks**: Centralized teams can become bottlenecks, slowing response times due to overloaded resources. This can stifle innovation and impede the rapid deployment of critical solutions in a fast-paced digital environment.

  - **Reduced agility**: This structure may need more flexibility to respond quickly to the unique needs of different business units. The centralized model can sometimes lead to a one-size-fits-all approach that may only suit some scenarios.

> **Note**
> Google's centralized model enhances quality and reliability through consistent practices and tools, ensuring high standards are maintained across the organization. By centralizing its Platform Engineering team, Google can enforce uniform standards and best practices, improving the quality and reliability of its platform services.

Centralized models work best when standardization and consistency are paramount. However, leaders must be vigilant to prevent bottlenecks and ensure that the centralized structure does not stifle innovation. Regularly reviewing workflows and resource allocation can mitigate these risks.

Decentralized teams

Decentralized teams embed Platform Engineering resources within various business units, offering greater agility and tailored solutions. Let's analyze them:

- **Advantages**:

  - **Enhanced agility**: Decentralized teams can rapidly respond to the specific needs of their respective business units, enabling quick iteration and adaptation, crucial for maintaining competitiveness in dynamic markets.

  - **Autonomy**: Empowering individual business units fosters a sense of ownership and accountability. This autonomy can boost motivation and innovation as teams feel more directly connected to the outcomes of their work.

  - **Closer collaboration**: Proximity to end users allows for better understanding and alignment with business unit goals. This direct interaction with stakeholders ensures that the solutions developed are highly relevant and user-focused.

- **Challenges**:

  - **Inconsistency**: Without strong central governance, decentralized teams might develop divergent practices and tools, leading to integration challenges. This lack of standardization can increase complexity and the risk of inefficiencies.

  - **Communication barriers**: Ensuring effective communication and collaboration across decentralized teams can be complex. Disconnected teams may need help sharing knowledge and aligning on common goals.

> **Note**
> Amazon's two-pizza team model promotes agility and responsiveness. Each team remains small enough to be agile and focused on delivering specific business outcomes, allowing Amazon to maintain a high level of innovation and speed.

Decentralized models thrive in environments that prioritize speed and customization. However, leaders must implement strong communication and governance frameworks to maintain team alignment and consistency. Regular cross-team meetings and integrated reporting systems help bridge potential gaps.

Hybrid models

Hybrid models combine centralized oversight with decentralized execution, aiming to balance the benefits of both approaches. Let's understand them better:

- **Advantages**:

  - **Strategic oversight**: A central team provides governance, sets standards, and ensures consistency across the organization. This strategic oversight helps align decentralized efforts with broader organizational goals.

  - **Operational flexibility**: Decentralized execution allows business units to adapt quickly to local needs while adhering to overarching standards. This balance ensures that teams can innovate rapidly while maintaining high quality and consistency.

- **Challenges**:

  - **Complex governance**: Balancing central control with decentralized autonomy requires robust governance frameworks. Effective governance must ensure that decentralized teams adhere to strategic goals without stifling agility.

  - **Coordination effort**: Effective communication and coordination mechanisms are essential to avoid misalignment and inefficiencies. Leaders must establish clear protocols for decision-making and conflict resolution.

> **Note**
>
> Pivotal's hybrid approach balances consistency with localized agility, providing strategic oversight while allowing business units to adapt and innovate. This approach ensures that all teams align with the company's strategic goals while remaining flexible to address specific challenges.

Hybrid models offer the best of both worlds, combining the strategic alignment of centralized models with the agility of decentralized teams. However, they require a sophisticated approach to governance and communication to function effectively. Leaders must cultivate a culture of transparency and collaboration to ensure that all teams work harmoniously towards common objectives.

Ultimately, the choice of organizational model—whether centralized, decentralized, or hybrid—depends on your organization's specific needs, culture, size, and complexity. Understanding these factors is crucial when selecting the right model for long-term success.

Choosing the right model

Selecting the appropriate model involves assessing your organization's size, complexity, and needs:

- **Organizational size and complexity**: Larger, more complex organizations might benefit from a hybrid model combining centralized governance and decentralized execution. This approach can address the diverse needs of various business units while maintaining strategic alignment.

- **Business needs**: Evaluate the specific requirements of your business units and their need for responsiveness and customization. Understanding the unique demands of each unit can guide the choice of model.

- **Existing culture**: Consider your current organizational culture and how well it aligns with centralized, decentralized, or hybrid approaches. Cultural fit is critical for the successful implementation of any organizational model.

When selecting an organizational model for Platform Engineering, organizations must evaluate their size, complexity, and culture to ensure alignment with their operational needs. The following is a decision matrix to guide this process:

Criteria	Centralized model	Decentralized model	Hybrid model
Size	Best for small to mid-sized organizations with fewer teams and a need for streamlined governance	Suitable for large organizations with autonomous teams	Ideal for medium to large organizations balancing central control with team autonomy
Complexity	Works well for simple, less complex platforms with minimal dependencies	Effective in managing highly complex, domain-specific requirements	Best for complex platforms requiring standardization and customization
Culture	Aligns with hierarchical or governance-focused cultures	Fits well with innovative and autonomous cultures	Fits collaborative cultures that value both governance and team flexibility
Benefits	Ensures consistent governance, toolsets, and processes	Empowers teams to innovate and adapt quickly	Offers a balance of centralized control and team agility
Challenges	Risk of bottlenecks and slower adaptability	Potential for tool and process fragmentation	Requires clear communication and robust coordination mechanisms

Table 10.1: Comparison of Centralized, Decentralized, and Hybrid Platform Team Models

Here are a few examples of choosing the right model:

- A start-up with fewer development teams and limited resources might opt for a centralized model to ensure uniformity and simplicity.

- A global enterprise with diverse teams working on domain-specific platforms could benefit from a decentralized model that allows autonomy and agility.

- A mid-sized company scaling its operations might find the hybrid model most effective, balancing consistency with flexibility.

Once the correct model is chosen, we should ensure its effective implementation.

Implementation strategies

Clear communication, robust governance, and flexibility are vital to implementing the chosen model effectively:

- **Clear communication**: Establish transparent communication channels between centralized leadership and decentralized teams to ensure alignment and collaboration. Regular updates and feedback loops can keep all stakeholders informed and engaged.

- **Robust governance**: Implement strong governance frameworks to maintain consistency and standards while allowing flexibility. Governance should facilitate rather than hinder team performance.

- **Flexibility and adaptability**: Be prepared to adjust the model based on feedback and evolving business needs. Continuous improvement should be a core principle of your organizational strategy.

Choose the suitable organizational model for your Platform Engineering team to maximize its value delivery. The structure should align with your strategic goals and improve operational efficiency. Assess your organization's needs and implement the chosen model effectively to create a high-performing Platform Engineering team that delivers value and aligns with your business outcomes.

Aligning teams with business outcomes

Aligning Platform Engineering teams with business outcomes ensures that every effort drives organizational success. This alignment maximizes impact, optimizes resource utilization, and enhances collaboration across the business. Next, we'll examine the key elements of maintaining strategic focus, the essential role of leadership in ensuring alignment, and the best practices for measuring and sustaining performance. These areas are crucial because they ensure that Platform Engineering initiatives contribute directly to the organization's broader goals, driving technical excellence and business success.

Strategic focus

Alignment with business objectives ensures that Platform Engineering efforts are strategically focused and value-driven. The following focus areas illustrate how strategic alignment drives efficiency, optimizes resources, and strengthens cross-functional collaboration:

- **Strategic relevance**: Platform teams should focus on delivering solutions that indirectly support strategic goals, such as driving developer efficiency, reducing time-to-market, and enabling innovation. For instance, a platform team implementing self-service CI/CD pipelines reduces developer wait times, allowing faster feature delivery aligned with product launch timelines. Team misalignment, such as investing in niche tools unused by development teams, can waste resources and hinder organizational goals.

- **Resource optimization**: By prioritizing initiatives such as golden paths that standardize development workflows, platform teams ensure resources are allocated to solutions with maximum organizational impact. An example of misalignment is dedicating resources to building custom tooling when proven off-the-shelf solutions could deliver the same value faster and at a lower cost.

- **Enhanced collaboration**: Clear alignment fosters synergy between platform teams and business units. For instance, a platform team collaborating with product managers to create deployment pipelines that support Agile release schedules ensures mutual success. In contrast, a lack of collaboration can lead to delays, redundant efforts, or tools that fail to meet user needs.

Maintaining strategic focus is essential, as misaligned efforts often result in wasted investments, reduced efficiency, and missed opportunities to create value. A product-centric, Agile approach enables platform teams to remain aligned with evolving business priorities, and this requires strong leadership to guide priorities, foster collaboration, and maintain alignment with business goals.

Role of leadership

Leadership is pivotal in maintaining alignment. Leaders must articulate strategic goals clearly and translate them into actionable objectives for the Platform Engineering team. The following principles help ensure that teams remain focused, engaged, and strategically aligned:

- **Vision and direction**: Leaders must provide a clear vision that aligns with the organization's strategic goals. This vision guides the team's efforts and ensures they are strategically aligned.

- **Consistent communication**: Leaders must communicate strategic priorities regularly to the team. This ongoing dialogue keeps the team focused and informed about how their work impacts the broader organization.

- **Empowerment**: Leaders must empower teams to make decisions that support business objectives. This autonomy fosters a sense of ownership and accountability.

Strategies for alignment

Implementing structured goal setting and performance measurement ensures continuous alignment:

- **SMART goals**: Establish **specific, measurable, achievable, relevant, and time-bound** (**SMART**) goals. SMART goals provide clear direction and measurable targets for the team.

- **OKRs**: Use **objectives and key results** (**OKRs**) to align team efforts with organizational objectives. OKRs provide a framework for setting and tracking ambitious yet achievable goals.

- **KPIs**: Define **key performance indicators** (**KPIs**) that measure the impact of Platform Engineering efforts on business objectives. KPIs provide tangible metrics to assess performance and alignment.

Feedback and adaptation

Maintain regular feedback loops and adaptation to ensure alignment over time. The following approaches support continuous improvement and strategic focus:

- **Regular reviews**: Conduct regular performance reviews to assess progress toward goals. These reviews provide an opportunity to realign efforts and address any deviations.

- **Feedback loops**: Effective feedback loops keep platform teams responsive and continuously improving. Automated dashboards in tools such as Grafana or Power BI provide real-time insights into platform usage and developer satisfaction. Weekly retrospectives foster continuous learning by addressing successes and challenges. Quarterly surveys and feedback channels in tools such as Slack streamline input from stakeholders, ensuring that feedback is timely, actionable, and integrated into workflows for sustained progress.

- **Continuous improvement**: Foster a culture of continuous improvement. Encourage the team to regularly evaluate their processes and adjust to enhance alignment and performance.

Aligning Platform Engineering teams with business outcomes is an ongoing journey that requires clear vision, strong leadership, and continuous adaptation. Leaders ensure success by focusing on strategic relevance, optimizing resources, and fostering collaboration. Using SMART goals, OKRs, and KPIs, alongside a culture of feedback, keeps Platform Engineering agile and aligned with evolving business needs.

These principles come to life when we look at real-world success stories. Netflix, in particular, offers a compelling example of how aligning Platform Engineering efforts with business outcomes can drive continuous innovation, scalability, and global success.

Case study – Netflix

Netflix's innovative approach to infrastructure and tooling provides valuable lessons in operational excellence, but it also highlights distinctions between DevOps practices and modern Platform Engineering. The following is a reframed exploration of their strategy and insights relevant to Platform Engineering.

Modular tooling and operational agility

Netflix is renowned for building modular, developer-focused tools such as **Chaos Monkey** and the broader **Simian Army** to test system resilience and failure handling. While these tools are a hallmark of advanced DevOps practices, their integration into a platform that can be universally consumed across teams—a hallmark of Platform Engineering—remains a separate challenge. Netflix's success lies in fostering team autonomy and accountability through its *operate what you build* culture, which ensures developers take end-to-end responsibility for their code.

Cloud adoption and tooling enablement

Netflix's migration to **Amazon Web Services** (**AWS**) enabled rapid global scaling and operational efficiency. However, this decision underscores potential risks, such as over-reliance on a single cloud provider, which could lead to vulnerabilities in cost management or service availability. Platform Engineering teams would focus on mitigating such risks by implementing cloud-agnostic tooling, centralizing governance, and providing consumption guardrails through an IDP.

Quantifiable benefits

As a result of the migration and implementation of advanced Platform Engineering practices, Netflix achieved several significant, measurable outcomes that directly contributed to its operational efficiency and business success, including the following:

- **Subscriber growth**: By early 2024, Netflix added 9.3 million subscribers, achieving its strongest start since 2020.

- **Global reach**: In 2023, Netflix had 238.3 million subscribers worldwide.

- **Operational efficiency**: With about 70 operations engineers post-cloud migration, Netflix eliminated the need for a traditional network operations center.

Platform engineering's role in Netflix's ecosystem

While Netflix excels in modular DevOps tooling, a Platform Engineering lens would emphasize consolidating these tools into cohesive workflows accessible through a unified interface, ensuring adoption and usability across the organization, as in these examples:

- Building golden paths that integrate resilience testing into CI/CD pipelines for consistent adoption across teams.

- Creating a centralized portal where developers can seamlessly access deployment tools, Chaos Engineering frameworks, and monitoring dashboards.

- While autonomy drives innovation at Netflix, challenges may arise in maintaining consistency across teams. Platform Engineering could address this by balancing autonomy with centralized guidance, ensuring that tools and processes align with organizational goals without stifling innovation.

Key takeaways

The principles that underpin Netflix's success offer valuable insights for any organization seeking to build resilient, innovative Platform Engineering teams. Here are the key takeaways from Netflix's approach:

- **Clear vision and direction**: Aligning team efforts with strategic business goals drives focused execution.

- **Empowerment and autonomy**: Decentralized decision-making fosters innovation and agility.

- **Continuous improvement**: Regular performance measurement and feedback ensure alignment and adaptability.

- **Centralized accessibility**: Integrate modular tools into a single, developer-centric platform to drive usability and consistency.

- **Guardrails, not roadblocks**: Empower teams with tools that include baked-in best practices for security, scalability, and compliance.

- **Cloud-agnostic strategies**: Reduce reliance on a single cloud provider through cloud-agnostic solutions and governance.

- **Autonomy with alignment**: Foster team autonomy while ensuring alignment with organizational goals through clear standards and workflows.

Netflix's strategy showcases how DevOps and resilience engineering practices laid the foundation for operational success, while Platform Engineering elevates this further by creating unified, scalable systems that enhance usability and efficiency. By integrating tools such as Chaos Monkey into standardized workflows and making them universally accessible through centralized platforms, Platform Engineering ensures that best practices are consistently applied across teams. This approach fosters innovation and autonomy and strengthens alignment with organizational goals, enabling Netflix to maintain its competitive edge in a rapidly evolving technological landscape.

Aligning Platform Engineering teams with business outcomes maximizes impact and drives organizational success. Clear goals, empowerment, and continuous feedback loops ensure strategic alignment and high performance. The next step involves strategic hiring practices to build a high-performing Platform Engineering team, which includes identifying critical skills, implementing effective hiring strategies, and fostering diversity and inclusion.

Hiring for a high-performing team

Building a high-performing Platform Engineering team is vital for organizational success. It starts with hiring individuals with technical expertise and soft skills that foster collaboration and innovation. This section focuses on identifying essential skills, implementing effective strategies, and promoting diversity in hiring. By aligning hiring practices with organizational goals, leaders can attract and retain talent to drive transformative outcomes.

Identifying key skills and competencies

Assembling a high-performing Platform Engineering team requires a strategic understanding of the essential skills and competencies. Here are the critical technical and soft skills that leaders should focus on to identify and attract the right talent.

Foundational skills and competencies

A successful Platform Engineering team thrives not only on technical expertise but also on a shared mindset and cultural values. The following qualities are essential for engineers to contribute effectively and drive long-term platform success:

- **Understanding outcomes**: Engineers must deeply understand business outcomes and their importance. This ensures that technical solutions align with strategic goals and deliver real value to the organization.

- **Commitment**: Commitment to the team's success and the platform as a product is essential. Engineers invested in the platform's long-term success contribute more meaningfully and are motivated to drive continuous improvement.

- **Builders, not heroes**: The focus should be on long-term solutions rather than firefighting. Engineers should proactively build resilient systems that prevent issues rather than reacting to problems as they arise.

- **Ability to fail**: It is vital to have a culture that allows for failing fast, failing often, and failing cheaply. Engineers must be comfortable sharing their failures publicly to learn and grow from them, fostering an environment of continuous improvement.

- **Entrepreneurship**: Engineers should be comfortable with rapid experimentation and pivoting fast. This entrepreneurial mindset encourages innovation and agility within the team.

- **Technical attitude**: Comfort with adopting new technologies, refactoring, **infrastructure as code** (IaC), and coding is crucial. Engineers must stay current with the latest advancements to keep the platform cutting-edge and competitive.

Technical skills

Technical proficiency forms the backbone of a high-performing Platform Engineering team. These are the non-negotiable skills that every team member must possess:

- **Cloud-native technologies**: Mastery of tools and platforms such as Kubernetes, Docker, and serverless computing is essential. Familiarity with cloud platforms such as AWS, Azure, or Google Cloud is crucial for building scalable and efficient systems.

- **CI/CD**: Expertise in CI/CD pipelines using tools such as Jenkins, GitLab CI, and CircleCI ensures rapid, reliable, and automated deployment of software updates.

- **Automation**: Proficiency in automation frameworks such as Ansible, Terraform, and Puppet streamlines infrastructure management, reduces errors, and enhances efficiency.

- **Programming and scripting**: Strong skills in programming languages (e.g., Python, Go, and Java) and scripting languages (e.g., Bash and PowerShell) enable engineers to develop robust solutions and automate repetitive tasks.

- **Security**: A deep understanding of security best practices and tools is necessary to ensure platform integrity and compliance and safeguard against potential vulnerabilities and threats.

Soft skills

Soft skills are equally important, fostering a collaborative and innovative team environment. These competencies ensure that technical expertise translates into effective teamwork and problem-solving:

- **Communication**: The ability to articulate ideas clearly and collaborate effectively with team members and stakeholders is fundamental. This ensures that everyone is aligned and working toward common goals.

- **Problem-solving**: Strong analytical skills are essential for identifying and resolving issues quickly and efficiently. Engineers must be able to think critically and develop creative solutions to complex problems.

- **Adaptability**: The technology landscape is constantly evolving. Engineers must be adaptable, willing to learn new technologies and methodologies, and able to navigate organizational changes.

- **Teamwork**: It is crucial to be able to work well in a team and support and learn from colleagues. A collaborative mindset ensures that the team functions cohesively and can tackle challenges collectively.

Understanding critical skills and competencies is essential, and observing how industry leaders implement these principles offers powerful insights. Let us examine the strategies employed by some companies to develop high-performing teams and achieve exceptional results.

Approaches that some companies have taken

Examining how top companies approach team building provides valuable lessons in crafting a high-performing Platform Engineering team. Here are some of the strategies these industry leaders have used to build effective, resilient teams:

- **Amazon**: Amazon prioritizes problem-solving abilities and cultural fit in its hiring process, using behavioral interview questions to assess candidates' past handling of complex situations. The company values a customer-centric approach and seeks candidates who thrive in a fast-paced, ever-changing environment. Amazon emphasizes the importance of learning and curiosity, ensuring its engineers continually strive to improve and innovate.

- **Google**: Google emphasizes a blend of technical prowess and collaborative skills in its hiring process. It focuses on candidates who demonstrate a strong foundation in software engineering, cloud technologies, and automation, along with excellent communication and teamwork abilities. This approach ensures that new hires contribute effectively to technical and team dynamics.

- **IBM**: IBM uses a comprehensive approach to identifying key skills, combining technical assessments with evaluations of soft skills. They use simulations and role-playing exercises to see how candidates perform in real-world scenarios. IBM's commitment to diversity and inclusion is reflected in its hiring practices, which aim to build teams that reflect the diversity of its global customer base.

- **Meta**: Meta prioritizes both technical skills and cultural fit in their hiring process. The interview process involves multiple stages, including resume screening, recruiter phone screening, technical phone screening, and onsite interviews. During onsite interviews, candidates face rigorous technical and behavioral questions. Meta emphasizes system and product design skills, especially for senior roles, focusing on scalability, reliability, and efficiency. Behavioral interviews assess cultural fit, problem-solving abilities, and leadership qualities. Meta looks for candidates who are proactive, adaptable, and able to thrive in a collaborative environment.

- **Microsoft**: Microsoft focuses on hiring for a growth mindset and technical excellence. Their interviews include coding challenges and scenario-based questions to evaluate a candidate's problem-solving skills and adaptability. Microsoft also strongly emphasizes diversity and inclusion, ensuring that their teams benefit from a wide range of perspectives and ideas.

- **VMware (Pivotal)**: VMware (formerly Pivotal) focuses on candidates' ability to solve complex problems and their cultural fit within the organization. Their hiring process includes coding challenges, system design interviews, and behavioral interviews. VMware emphasizes continuous learning and innovation and seeks candidates who are passionate about technology and eager to drive transformation. They value a collaborative mindset and the ability to work well in cross-functional teams. VMware also prioritizes diversity and inclusion, ensuring their teams benefit from various perspectives and ideas.

These examples demonstrate how targeted hiring practices can enhance a team's performance. With these insights, let us examine specific strategies for effectively hiring and integrating talent to develop a high-performing Platform Engineering team.

Effective hiring strategies

Attracting and hiring top talent for a high-performing Platform Engineering team requires strategic, well-defined approaches. Here are some actionable strategies that can serve as a handbook for leaders aiming to build and nurture exceptional teams. By implementing these strategies, organizations can ensure they hire the right individuals to drive innovation, efficiency, and growth.

Developing comprehensive job descriptions

Clear and detailed job descriptions are the foundation of effective hiring. When crafting a compelling Platform Engineering job description, it's important to focus on the elements that attract the right candidates and set clear expectations. Consider the following key components:

- **Key responsibilities**: Clearly define the role's main tasks and responsibilities, emphasizing their impact on the organization. This helps candidates understand what is expected and how their contributions will drive business outcomes.

- **Required skills**: List the technical and soft skills necessary for the position. Be specific about the expertise needed in areas such as cloud-native technologies, CI/CD, automation, programming, and security.

- **Company culture**: Highlight the company's culture, values, and what makes it a great workplace. This strategy helps attract candidates who are not only technically proficient but also an excellent cultural fit.

Structured interviews and technical assessments

Using structured interviews and technical assessments ensures a fair and thorough evaluation of candidates' abilities and fit:

- **Structured interviews**: Develop consistent questions evaluating technical skills and cultural fit. Use behavioral interview techniques to understand how candidates have handled situations in the past. This list can include questions about problem-solving, teamwork, and adaptability.

- **Technical assessments**: Use coding challenges, technical tests, and problem-solving scenarios to evaluate candidates' technical abilities. These assessments should simulate real-world tasks and challenges that candidates will face in the role.

Atlassian's multi-stage hiring process

Atlassian employs a rigorous multi-stage hiring process comprising initial screening, technical assessments, and behavioral interviews to ensure alignment with their collaborative and innovative culture, attracting and retaining top talent. The process filters out candidates who do not meet basic requirements, assesses coding skills and problem-solving abilities, and evaluates past experiences and teamwork capabilities. This approach helps Atlassian build technically strong, cohesive, and collaborative teams.

Leveraging behavioral and situational questions

Behavioral and situational questions can provide deep insights into a candidate's capabilities and fit within the team:

- **Behavioral questions**: These questions assess past behaviors to predict future performance. Examples include, "*Tell me about a time when you faced a significant challenge in a project and how you overcame it*," and "*Describe a situation where you had to work closely with a difficult team member.*"

- **Situational questions**: These questions present hypothetical scenarios to help candidates understand how they would handle specific situations. Examples include "*How would you handle a critical system failure?*" and "*What steps would you take to integrate a new technology into the existing platform?*"

Diversity and inclusion strategies

Diversity and inclusion are critical for fostering innovation and a supportive work environment. To build a more diverse and inclusive Platform Engineering team, organizations should adopt intentional hiring practices that foster equity and representation. The following strategies support a fair and welcoming recruitment process:

- **Bias training**: Provide training for hiring managers to recognize and mitigate unconscious biases. This ensures a fair hiring process and promotes diversity.

- **Inclusive job descriptions**: Use inclusive language in job descriptions to attract a diverse range of candidates. Avoid gendered language and phrases that may discourage particular groups from applying.

- **Diverse interview panels**: Ensure interview panels are diverse to provide different perspectives and reduce bias. This also signals to candidates that the company values diversity and inclusion.

Example – IBM's comprehensive approach

IBM has implemented diversity initiatives such as unconscious bias training and diverse hiring panels, resulting in a more inclusive workforce and driving innovation and employee satisfaction. This commitment has strengthened IBM's position as a leader in technology and Platform Engineering.

IBM actively seeks candidates from diverse backgrounds and experiences, using advanced analytics to track diversity metrics and ensure alignment with diversity goals. By fostering an inclusive culture, IBM leverages diverse perspectives to drive innovation and improve decision-making across the organization.

Continuous improvement and feedback loops

Hiring strategies should evolve based on feedback and changing needs. The following approaches help optimize the process and enhance the candidate experience:

- **Regular reviews:** Conduct regular reviews of the hiring process to identify areas for improvement. Use metrics such as time-to-hire, quality of hire, and candidate satisfaction to assess effectiveness.

- **Candidate feedback:** Gather feedback from candidates about their experience during the hiring process. This can provide valuable insights into what's working well and what needs to be improved.

- **Adapt and innovate:** Stay updated with the latest hiring trends and technologies. Adapt your strategies to incorporate new tools and techniques to enhance the hiring process.

Organizations can refine their hiring processes and build stronger teams by embracing continuous improvement and feedback loops. Companies such as Meta and VMware have implemented these strategies effectively, offering valuable insights into how real-world practices can drive success.

Case study – Meta's rigorous screening process

Meta's hiring process evaluates candidates based on their technical skills and cultural fit through multiple stages, including technical phone screening, onsite interviews with system and product design questions, and behavioral assessments. This approach ensures a thorough evaluation of candidates' technical abilities and alignment with Meta's culture.

The process begins with an initial resume screening, followed by a recruiter phone screening to discuss the candidate's background and interests. The technical phone screen assesses coding skills and problem-solving abilities in a real-time collaborative environment. Onsite interviews include multiple rounds of system and product design interviews, while behavioral interviews focus on cultural fit and alignment with Meta's core values.

This approach selects the most capable and culturally aligned candidates, emphasizing real-world problem-solving and adaptability, which are crucial for maintaining Meta's innovative edge. Meta builds cohesive teams that are aligned with the company's values by focusing on technical excellence and cultural fit.

Case study – VMware's collaborative hiring approach

VMware emphasizes problem-solving skills and cultural fit in its hiring process, which includes coding challenges, system design interviews, and behavioral interviews. The company seeks passionate and innovative candidates who drive transformation and continuous learning.

Candidates undergo an initial screening involving real-world coding challenges, followed by system design interviews to assess their ability to architect scalable, secure, and efficient solutions. Behavioral interviews aim to evaluate problem-solving skills and cultural fit. VMware values candidates with a passion for learning and a collaborative mindset who can be part of a technically proficient team aligned with the company's values and culture.

VMware's approach prioritizes cultural fit and continuous improvement, ensuring teams are innovative, cohesive, and supportive and contribute to the company's success.

Ten effective interview questions

Consider incorporating these ten profound and thought-provoking questions to structure an effective interview process. These questions evaluate technical skills and cultural fit, providing immense value to the interview process:

Technical problem-solving: "Describe a complex technical problem you solved in your previous role. What was the problem, how did you approach it, and what was the outcome?"

System design: "How would you design a scalable and reliable microservices architecture for a new platform feature? Explain your thought process and the technologies you would use."

Cloud-native expertise: "Discuss a project where you used cloud-native technologies (e.g., Kubernetes and Docker). What challenges did you face, and how did you overcome them?"

Automation and CI/CD: "Explain your experience with CI/CD pipelines. How have you implemented and optimized these processes in past projects?"

Security practices: "What are some of the security best practices you follow in your work? Can you provide an example of how you ensured the security of a platform or application?"

Team collaboration: "Describe a time when you had to work closely with a difficult team member. How did you handle the situation, and what was the result?"

Adaptability and learning: "How do you stay current with new technologies and industry trends? Can you provide an example of a new technology you recently learned and applied?"

Intrapreneurship: "Tell me about a time when you had to rapidly experiment and pivot your approach. How did you manage the process, and what was the outcome?"

Failure and improvement: "Describe a project or task where you failed. How did you handle the failure, what did you learn from it, and how did you apply those lessons in future projects?"

Cultural fit and values: "What aspects of our company's culture and values resonate with you the most? How do you see yourself contributing to and enhancing our culture?"

Diversity, equity, and inclusion

Diversity, equity, and inclusion (DEI) play a crucial role in building high-performing teams and driving innovation. Embracing diverse perspectives leads to better problem-solving and decision-making, ultimately contributing to organizational success. By prioritizing DEI, organizations can unleash the full potential of their workforce and ensure a fair and equitable hiring process.

The importance of diverse teams

Diverse teams bring a wealth of perspectives and experiences that fuel innovation and creativity. By including individuals from various backgrounds, organizations can tackle challenges from multiple angles, leading to more robust solutions. Fostering diversity and inclusion within Platform Engineering teams not only supports equity but also drives measurable business benefits. The following outcomes highlight the value of building diverse, inclusive teams:

- **Enhanced problem-solving**: Diverse teams are better equipped to address complex problems by bringing various perspectives and approaches. This diversity of thought enhances creativity and leads to more innovative solutions.

- **Increased employee satisfaction**: An inclusive work environment where all employees feel valued and respected improves morale and retention. Employees are more likely to be engaged and committed when they see themselves represented and appreciated within the organization.

- **Better decision-making**: Studies have shown that diverse teams make better decisions as they consider a more comprehensive range of factors and potential outcomes. This leads to more effective and strategic decision-making.

Concrete strategies for inclusive hiring processes

Organizations must implement strategies that actively promote diversity and mitigate bias to create an inclusive hiring process. To create a more equitable and inclusive hiring process, organizations should implement targeted strategies that reduce this bias and support fair evaluation. The following practices can significantly enhance diversity and fairness in recruitment:

- **Mitigate bias through training**: Provide training for hiring managers to recognize and counteract unconscious biases. This ensures a fair hiring process and promotes diversity. Bias training helps managers understand their implicit biases and develop strategies to counteract them, leading to more equitable hiring decisions.

- **Craft inclusive job descriptions**: Use inclusive language in job descriptions to attract a diverse pool of candidates. Avoid gendered language and phrases that may discourage certain groups from applying. Inclusive job descriptions signal to potential candidates that the organization values diversity and is committed to creating an inclusive work environment. Studies have shown that women and **underrepresented minorities** (URMs) are often more critical of their qualifications and may refrain from applying if they don't meet all listed requirements. Including statements encouraging applications from candidates who meet most but not all criteria can help mitigate this effect.

- **Ensure diverse interview panels**: Assemble diverse interview panels to provide different perspectives and reduce bias. Diverse panels are better equipped to assess candidates from different backgrounds, leading to more balanced, fair hiring decisions.

- **Implement blind hiring practices**: Reduce bias by implementing blind hiring processes that remove names and other identifying details from resumes. This practice ensures a focus on candidates' skills and qualifications, leading to more objective hiring outcomes.

- **Standardize interviews for fairness**: Use structured interviews with standardized questions to ensure consistency and fairness. This approach minimizes unconscious bias and ensures all candidates are evaluated based on the same objective criteria.

Case study – VMware's commitment to DEI

VMware strongly emphasizes diversity, equity, and inclusion throughout its hiring process and has implemented several initiatives to ensure a fair and inclusive process. VMware offers a strong example of how organizations can embed diversity and inclusion into their hiring processes through the following best practices:

- **Diverse hiring panels**: VMware ensures its interview panels are diverse, including individuals from various backgrounds and experiences. This helps to provide different perspectives during the evaluation process and reduces the risk of bias.

- **Bias training**: VMware provides comprehensive bias training for its hiring managers to help them recognize and mitigate unconscious biases. This training is integral to the company's commitment to creating an inclusive work environment.

- **Inclusive recruitment practices**: VMware actively seeks to attract a diverse pool of candidates through targeted recruitment efforts. The company partners with diverse professional organizations and attends events that focus on underrepresented groups in technology.

VMware has created a more inclusive and equitable hiring process by implementing these strategies. This commitment to DEI has strengthened the company's workforce, leading to higher levels of innovation and employee satisfaction.

Addressing implicit bias in the hiring process

While explicit biases are often recognized, implicit biases can persist and impact the hiring process. Acknowledging and addressing these challenges is crucial to ensuring an equitable environment:

- **Implicit bias**: Unconscious biases can negatively impact the evaluation of candidates from underrepresented groups. This can lead to unfair assessments and missed opportunities to hire talented individuals.

- **Systemic barriers**: Systemic barriers, such as lack of access to professional networks and educational opportunities, can disadvantage certain groups in the hiring process. Organizations must actively dismantle these barriers and create a more equitable hiring process.

Strategies to overcome these challenges

Organizations can implement several strategies to overcome these challenges and create a more inclusive hiring process:

- **Active recruitment**: Actively seek out and recruit candidates from underrepresented groups. Partner with diverse professional organizations and attend events focusing on diversity in technology.

- **Mentorship programs**: Implement mentorship programs to support the professional development of employees from underrepresented groups. These programs help bridge the gap and provide opportunities for growth and advancement.

- **Inclusive culture**: Foster an inclusive culture where all employees feel valued and respected. This includes providing ongoing DEI training and creating open dialogue and feedback opportunities.

Embracing diversity, equity, and inclusion in the hiring process is not just a moral imperative but a strategic one. By fostering an inclusive environment and implementing fair hiring practices, organizations can unlock the full potential of their workforce, drive innovation, and ensure sustainable success. Leaders can create a more inclusive and equitable work environment by emphasizing the importance of diverse teams and delicately addressing the challenges faced in the hiring process. In the next section, we will explore practical strategies for team development, focusing on creating a learning culture, managing performance, and fostering career growth.

Nurturing and developing the team

Building a high-performing Platform Engineering team goes beyond hiring the right individuals; it requires a strategic approach to nurturing and developing these talents. The 5Es framework—*Empathize, Empower, Engage, Entrust*, and *Equip*—provides a comprehensive methodology to foster a thriving, innovative, and resilient team. This section delves into the 5Es framework, emphasizing its profound impact on team development and how leaders can implement it to drive success.

Empathize

Empathizing with your team is the foundation of effective leadership. An empathetic leader understands the needs, challenges, and aspirations of their team members, creating a culture of psychological safety and trust:

- **Psychological safety**: Establishing a safe environment where team members feel comfortable expressing ideas, concerns, and mistakes without fear of judgment or retribution is crucial. This openness encourages creativity and innovation. Pivotal, now part of VMware, is renowned for its culture of psychological safety. By fostering an environment where failure is viewed as a learning opportunity rather than a setback, Pivotal has been able to maintain high levels of innovation and employee satisfaction.

- **Understanding individual needs**: Regular one-on-one meetings and feedback sessions help leaders stay attuned to individual team members' needs and motivations, allowing for tailored support and development opportunities. At Netflix, managers frequently engage in candid conversations with their team members to understand their career aspirations and challenges, fostering a supportive and growth-oriented environment.

Empower

Empowerment involves enabling teams to take ownership of their work and make decisions that drive the organization forward. Empowered teams are more engaged, motivated, and productive. The following approaches highlight how leading companies foster autonomy and ownership:

- **Delegating authority**: Trusting team members with significant responsibilities and decision-making power fosters a sense of ownership and accountability. This delegation is essential for developing leaders within the team. Atlassian, for instance, empowers its engineering teams by decentralizing decision-making, allowing them to manage their own projects and innovate freely.

- **Product- or service-centric focus**: Encourage teams to think from a product- or service-centric perspective, understanding the broader impact of their work on the organization and its customers. This focus aligns their efforts with strategic goals. Spotify's autonomous squads are a prime example, where teams are given the autonomy to manage their products, driving innovation and accountability.

Engage

Engagement is about fostering open communication and collaboration within the team. Engaged teams are more cohesive, innovative, and resilient in the face of challenges. The following practices help foster a communicative environment that supports productivity and engagement:

- **Open communication**: Promote a culture of transparency where information flows freely and team members feel heard. Regular team meetings, town halls, and feedback channels are vital for maintaining this communication. Microsoft's regular "pulse" surveys help gauge employee sentiment and encourage open dialogue, leading to continuous improvement in team engagement.

- **Improving the signal-to-noise ratio**: Ensure communication is clear, concise, and relevant, minimizing distractions and misunderstandings. Tools and practices that streamline communication can significantly enhance team efficiency. Trello, for example, uses its platform to keep communication organized and focused, reducing noise and improving productivity.

Entrust

Entrusting your team means giving them the autonomy to determine how to achieve their goals. This trust fosters innovation and a strong sense of responsibility. The following practices help leaders foster a sense of purpose while giving teams the freedom to excel:

- **Defining the "Why"**: Clearly articulate the purpose and objectives behind tasks and projects. When team members understand the "why," they are better equipped to determine the "how" and drive toward meaningful outcomes. Amazon's leadership principles emphasize the importance of leaders communicating the broader purpose and vision, ensuring team alignment and motivation.

- **Avoiding micromanagement**: Allow team members the freedom to approach their work in their own way. This autonomy encourages creative problem-solving and boosts morale. GitLab's remote work culture and trust in employees' self-management exemplify how reducing micromanagement can lead to high performance and job satisfaction.

Equip

Equipping your team with the right tools, resources, and training is essential for their growth and success. A well-equipped team is capable, confident, and ready to tackle any challenge. The following strategies help create an environment where teams can thrive and grow:

- **Collaboration tools and learning resources**: Provide access to the latest tools and technologies that facilitate collaboration and productivity. Invest in continuous learning opportunities such as workshops, courses, and certifications. Salesforce offers extensive learning resources through Trailhead, ensuring that employees are well equipped to excel in their roles.

- **Work-life balance**: Support a healthy work-life balance to prevent burnout and ensure sustained productivity. Flexible working arrangements and wellness programs can significantly contribute to team well-being. Adobe's focus on work-life balance through its wellness initiatives and flexible work policies has been instrumental in maintaining high employee satisfaction and performance levels.

The 5Es framework offers a robust, holistic approach to nurturing and developing high-performing teams. By empathizing with team members, empowering them to take ownership, engaging them through open communication, entrusting them with autonomy, and equipping them with the necessary tools and resources, leaders can create an environment where their teams thrive. Implementing the 5Es framework enhances team performance and drives organizational success, making it an indispensable strategy for any forward-thinking leader.

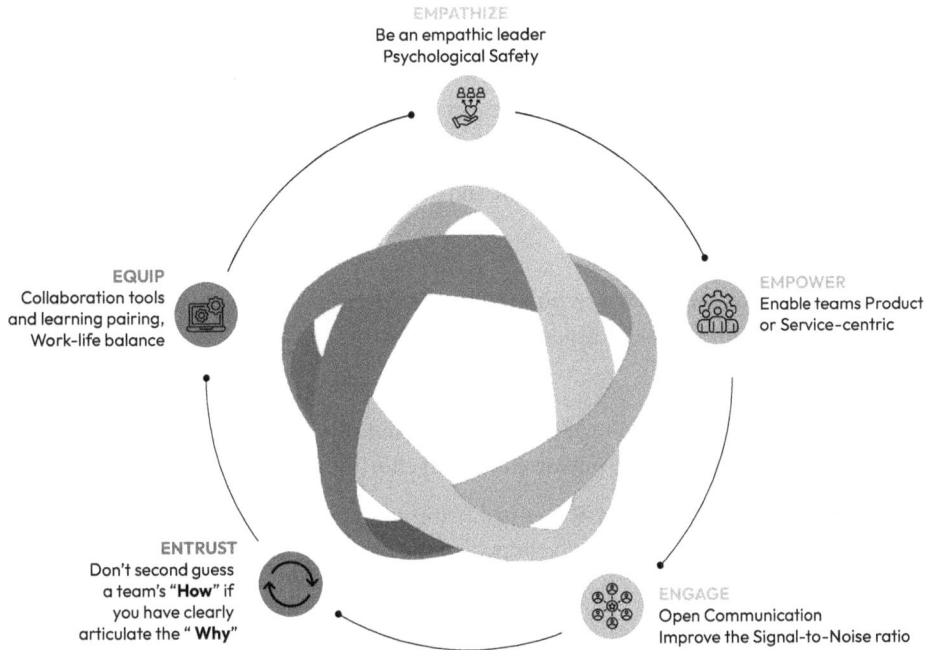

EMPATHIZE
Be an empathic leader
Psychological Safety

EQUIP
Collaboration tools
and learning pairing,
Work-life balance

EMPOWER
Enable teams Product
or Service-centric

ENTRUST
Don't second guess
a team's "**How**" if
you have clearly
articulate the "**Why**"

ENGAGE
Open Communication
Improve the Signal-to-Noise ratio

Figure 10.2: The 5Es framework

Implementing the 5Es framework

Rolling out the 5Es framework in a Platform Engineering team can transform it into a high-performing, innovative, and cohesive unit. Here's a comprehensive example of how a company can implement this framework, highlighting the specific actions taken and the benefits derived from each step.

1. **Empathize**

   Action: Establish regular one-on-one meetings and feedback sessions with team members to understand their needs, challenges, and career aspirations.

   Implementation:

   - **Psychological safety**: Create a safe space for team members to express their thoughts and concerns without fear of judgment. Leaders can achieve this through regular check-ins and an open-door policy.

   - **Understanding individual needs**: Use these sessions to gather insights into what motivates each team member and any obstacles they face in their work.

Benefits:

- **Increased trust and openness**: Team members feel more comfortable sharing ideas and concerns, leading to higher engagement and collaboration.

- **Tailored support**: Leaders can provide personalized support and development opportunities, helping each team member to grow and perform at their best.

2. **Empower**

Action: Delegate significant responsibilities and decision-making authority to team members to foster a sense of ownership and accountability.

Implementation:

- **Delegating authority**: Assign critical projects and allow team members to make key decisions. Encourage them to take initiative and lead efforts.

- **Product or service-centric focus**: Encourage teams to think from a product or service perspective, understanding the impact of their work on the organization and its customers.

Benefits:

- **Enhanced motivation**: When team members feel empowered, they are more motivated and engaged.

- **Improved innovation**: Empowered teams are likelier to experiment and innovate, driving continuous improvement and creativity.

3. **Engage**

Action: Foster open communication and collaboration within the team to ensure everyone is aligned and working toward common goals.

Implementation:

- **Open communication**: Hold regular team meetings and town halls and create feedback channels to ensure information flows freely and everyone's voice is heard.

- **Improving the signal-to-noise ratio**: Use tools and practices that streamline communication, making it clear, concise, and relevant.

Benefits:

- **Better alignment**: Clear and open communication ensures that everyone is on the same page and working toward common objectives.

- **Higher engagement**: Regular interactions and feedback mechanisms keep the team engaged and motivated.

4. **Entrust**

    Action: Provide team members the autonomy to determine how to achieve their goals, fostering innovation and responsibility.

    Implementation:

    - **Defining the "Why"**: Clearly articulate the purpose and objectives behind tasks and projects. Ensure that team members understand the broader impact of their work.

    - **Avoiding micromanagement**: Allow team members the freedom to choose their approach to work. Trust them to deliver results without constant oversight.

    Benefits:

    - **Enhanced innovation**: Autonomy encourages creative problem-solving and innovative thinking.

    - **Increased responsibility**: Team members feel more responsible for their work, leading to higher quality and efficiency.

5. **Equip**

    Action: Provide team members with the tools, resources, and training necessary for their growth and success.

    Implementation:

    - **Collaboration tools and learning resources**: Ensure that the team has access to the latest tools and technologies that facilitate collaboration and productivity. Invest in continuous learning opportunities such as workshops, courses, and certifications.

    - **Work-life balance**: Support flexible working arrangements and wellness programs to prevent burnout and ensure sustained productivity.

    Benefits:

    - **Enhanced capabilities**: Access to the right tools and resources enables team members to perform their tasks more efficiently and effectively.

    - **Sustained productivity**: Supporting work-life balance helps prevent burnout and ensures that team members remain productive and engaged.

By implementing the 5Es framework, a company can transform its Platform Engineering team into a high-performing, innovative, and cohesive unit. Each action within this framework addresses specific needs and fosters an environment where team members can thrive. The result is a capable, confident, deeply engaged, and motivated team to drive organizational success. Embracing the 5Es framework is a strategic move that will benefit the team and the organization significantly. Next, we will explore strategies for sustaining this high performance over the long term.

Sustaining high performance

The 5Es framework empowers us to build and nurture high-performing teams. Achieving and maintaining high performance requires continuous care and strategic actions. High performance demands an ongoing commitment to fostering team growth, innovation, and resilience. Let us explore actionable strategies to ensure sustained high performance. These insights will equip you with the tools to keep your Platform Engineering team thriving and consistently delivering exceptional results.

Continuous learning and development

Investing in continuous learning and development for your team to sustain high performance is imperative.

Action: Implement ongoing training programs, encourage professional certifications, and provide access to the latest industry resources.

Implementation:

- **Ongoing training programs**: Regularly scheduled workshops and seminars on the latest technologies and methodologies ensure that team members stay current with industry trends.

- **Professional certifications**: Encourage team members to pursue relevant certifications and provide financial support for these endeavors.

- **Access to industry resources**: Subscribe to industry journals, online courses, and conferences. Create a library of resources that team members can easily access.

For example, Google's focus on continuous learning is ingrained in its culture. Google offers various training programs and encourages employees to spend 20% of their time on projects outside their regular work, fostering innovation and continuous skill enhancement.

Benefits:

- **Skill enhancement**: Continuous learning keeps the team's skills sharp and relevant, allowing them to tackle emerging challenges effectively

- **Innovation**: Exposure to new ideas and technologies fuels innovation and creative problem-solving within the team

- **Employee retention**: Providing growth opportunities keeps employees engaged and reduces turnover

Performance metrics and feedback

Regular performance evaluations and feedback are crucial for sustaining high performance.

Action: Establish clear performance metrics and conduct regular performance reviews.

Implementation:

- **Clear performance metrics**: Define SMART goals for individuals and teams

- **Regular performance reviews**: Schedule quarterly or bi-annual performance reviews to provide constructive feedback and set new goals

- **360-degree feedback**: Incorporate feedback from peers, subordinates, and managers to provide a holistic view of performance

For example, Netflix uses a unique feedback system where employees receive regular feedback from peers and leaders. This system fosters a culture of continuous improvement and accountability.

Benefits:

- **Objective evaluation**: Clear metrics and regular reviews ensure performance is evaluated objectively and fairly

- **Continuous improvement**: Regular feedback helps identify areas for improvement and provides guidance on achieving it

- **Alignment with goals**: Performance metrics align individual and team efforts with organizational objectives, driving consistent progress

Recognizing and rewarding excellence

Recognizing and rewarding team members for their contributions is essential for maintaining high morale and motivation.

Action: Implement a recognition and rewards program that acknowledges individual and team achievements.

Implementation:

- **Recognition programs**: Establish programs to recognize outstanding performance, such as Employee of the Month awards or public acknowledgments in team meetings

- **Incentive programs**: Offer bonuses, promotions, or other incentives tied to performance metrics and achievements

- **Celebrating milestones**: Celebrate project completions, anniversaries, and other significant milestones to build a sense of accomplishment and camaraderie

For example, Salesforce has a comprehensive recognition program that includes spot bonuses, team celebrations, and formal awards. This program has been effective in maintaining high employee engagement and satisfaction.

Benefits:

- **Increased motivation**: Recognition and rewards boost morale and motivate employees to maintain high performance
- **Enhanced engagement**: Regular acknowledgment of contributions fosters a sense of belonging and engagement
- **Positive culture**: A culture of recognition and celebration strengthens team cohesion and loyalty

Adaptive leadership and agility

Leadership that adapts to changing circumstances and promotes agility within the team is crucial for sustained high performance.

Action: Develop adaptive leadership skills and promote an Agile mindset within the team.

Implementation:

- **Leadership training**: Provide training programs focused on adaptive leadership, emotional intelligence, and change management
- **Agile methodologies**: Implement Agile methodologies such as Scrum or Kanban to enhance flexibility and responsiveness
- **Empowering decision-making**: Encourage team members to make decisions and take initiative, fostering a culture of agility and adaptability

For example, Spotify's use of Agile methodologies within its engineering teams allows for rapid adaptation to market changes and continuous delivery of high-quality products. This approach has been instrumental in maintaining their competitive edge.

Benefits:

- **Enhanced flexibility**: Adaptive leadership and Agile methodologies enable teams to respond quickly to changes and challenges
- **Improved decision-making**: Empowering teams to make decisions fosters a sense of ownership and accountability
- **Sustained Innovation**: Agility promotes continuous experimentation and innovation, which is essential for long-term success

Building a collaborative culture

A collaborative culture is essential for fostering teamwork and innovation.

Action: Promote practices that enhance collaboration and teamwork.

Implementation:

- **Team-building activities**: Organize regular team-building activities to strengthen relationships and trust among team members

- **Collaboration tools**: Provide tools and platforms that facilitate accessible communication and collaboration

- **Cross-functional teams**: Encourage the formation of cross-functional teams to bring diverse perspectives to problem-solving

For example, Atlassian emphasizes collaboration through its team-building activities and uses tools such as Confluence and Jira to streamline project management and collaboration.

Benefits:

- **Enhanced teamwork**: A collaborative culture fosters better teamwork and synergy

- **Increased innovation**: Diverse perspectives and collaborative efforts lead to more innovative solutions

- **Stronger relationships**: Regular team-building activities strengthen relationships and trust within the team

Improving psychological safety and trust

Psychological safety and trust are foundational to a high-performing team.

Action: Foster an environment where team members feel safe to express ideas and take risks.

Implementation:

- **Open communication channels**: Ensure open lines of communication where team members can voice concerns and ideas without fear

- **Encouraging vulnerability**: Leaders should model vulnerability by admitting mistakes and encouraging learning from failures

- **Regular check-ins**: Conduct regular check-ins to gauge team morale and address any issues promptly

For example, Pivotal, now part of VMware, has been recognized for its strong emphasis on psychological safety, allowing team members to take risks and innovate without fear of retribution.

Benefits:

- **Higher engagement**: When team members feel psychologically safe, they are more likely to engage fully and contribute their best ideas

- **Increased innovation**: A safe environment encourages risk-taking and experimentation, leading to innovative solutions
- **Stronger team cohesion**: Trust fosters a supportive and cohesive team environment

Establishing work-life harmony and well-being

Work-life balance is crucial for maintaining high performance and preventing burnout.

Action: Implement policies that support work-life harmony and employee well-being.

Implementation:

- **Flexible working hours**: Offer flexible working hours to help employees balance work and personal commitments
- **Wellness programs**: Provide programs supporting physical, mental, and emotional health
- **Time off policies**: Ensure generous time off policies that allow employees to recharge and prevent burnout

For example, Adobe's focus on work-life balance through its wellness initiatives and flexible work policies has been instrumental in maintaining high employee satisfaction and performance levels.

Benefits:

- **Reduced burnout**: Supporting work-life balance helps prevent burnout and ensures sustained productivity
- **Improved well-being**: Wellness programs contribute to overall employee health and satisfaction
- **Higher retention**: Employees who feel supported in their work-life balance are likelier to stay with the company long-term

Organizations must commit to continuous learning, performance management, recognition, adaptive leadership, collaboration, psychological safety, and work-life balance to achieve high performance. Implementing these strategies ensures that Platform Engineering teams remain motivated, innovative, and high-performing long-term, driving consistent results and fostering a thriving and resilient organizational culture.

While high performance can be sustained through continuous learning and feedback, providing clear opportunities for career advancement is equally vital for keeping teams engaged, motivated, and aligned with long-term organizational goals.

Career development and progression

Sustaining high performance goes beyond day-to-day success—it requires a clear path for individual growth. By offering well-defined opportunities for career advancement, organizations can retain top talent and foster long-term commitment. In Platform Engineering, career development should continuously align with technical mastery and leadership potential. Throughout this chapter and the book, we've provided essential strategies to excel in interviews and prepare for Platform Engineering roles. These insights are designed to ensure that the right people join your team and have the tools to grow and thrive within it, which is the ultimate goal of career development and progression.

To help you progress in your Platform Engineering career, here are six actionable steps to continuously develop and grow. These proven strategies, successfully used by many professionals in the field, will help you build a strong foundation for long-term career growth and progression.

Embrace lifelong learning

In Platform Engineering, where technology and best practices evolve rapidly, the value of continuous learning cannot be overstated. It's not just about keeping pace with these changes but embracing them with a mindset of continuous growth and improvement. Here are practical ways to stay ahead:

- **Technical certifications**: Pursue industry-recognized certifications such as AWS Certified Solutions Architect, Google Cloud Professional, or Kubernetes Administrator. These demonstrate your commitment to mastering critical tools and technologies.

- **Specialized skills development**: Identify emerging technologies gaining traction in your industry (e.g., infrastructure as code, SRE practices, or AI/ML integration) and invest time learning them. Staying relevant means adapting to new advancements.

- **Internal knowledge sharing**: Actively participate in internal knowledge-sharing initiatives, such as lunch-and-learns, hackathons, or technical forums. This helps you learn and builds your reputation within the team.

Seek out mentorship and coaching

Career growth is rarely a solo journey. It's about building relationships with mentors and coaches, both within and outside your organization, who can provide the guidance and support you need to accelerate your career development:

- **Internal mentorship**: Identify senior engineers or platform leaders who can guide you through complex technical challenges and leadership development. Seek regular feedback and be open to constructive criticism—it's a critical part of growth.

- **Peer mentorship**: Don't overlook the value of peer mentorship. Engaging in code reviews, paired programming, and technical discussions with your peers sharpens your skills and builds mutual learning relationships.

- **Cross-departmental mentorship**: Look beyond your immediate team. Platform engineers who understand how their work integrates with other areas of the business (e.g., product development, sales, and customer success) gain a broader perspective and become more valuable leaders.

Take ownership and show initiative

Advancing your career often requires demonstrating leadership before officially being given the title. It's about taking ownership and showing initiative in every task you undertake. Here's how you can stand out:

- **Lead projects**: Volunteer to take on leadership roles in projects, even if they are outside your direct responsibility. This demonstrates initiative and your ability to manage complexity.

- **Solve problems beyond your scope**: Identify gaps or inefficiencies in your team's processes— whether they relate to automation, DevOps pipeline inefficiencies, or cross-functional communication—and propose solutions. Leaders are proactive problem solvers.

- **Drive innovation**: Suggest and implement new tools, frameworks, or practices that can improve the platform's performance. Engineers who consistently contribute to innovation signal their readiness for career advancement.

Define a clear growth path with your manager

Having a structured growth plan with your manager is crucial. Here's how to make the most of this relationship:

- **Regular career conversations**: Ensure that you have scheduled career discussions with your manager at least quarterly. Use these conversations to define clear goals, including short-term technical skills and long-term leadership competencies.

- **Set measurable goals**: Work with your manager to set SMART goals that align with your career aspirations. This could be mastering a particular technology or leading a key project.

- **Track your progress**: Keep a log of your achievements, skills gained, and projects completed. This helps in performance reviews, reinforces your growth trajectory, and provides tangible evidence when you are ready for a promotion.

Consider leadership as a path forward

Not every engineer aims for a leadership role, but for those who do, there are key steps to take:

- **Technical leadership**: Start by becoming your team's go-to resource for complex technical challenges. This doesn't mean being the smartest in the room but being the most reliable and collaborative.

- **Soft skills development**: Leadership is as much about soft skills as it is about technical prowess. Focus on developing communication, empathy, and conflict resolution skills, which are critical in managing teams.

- **Lead by example**: Whether you're in a formal leadership position or not, demonstrating a solid work ethic, accountability, and a positive attitude makes you stand out as a leader others will want to follow.

Leverage the tools from this book for career success

As outlined in previous sections of this chapter and throughout the book, we've provided substantial guidance on how to excel in Platform Engineering roles, from interview preparation to performance metrics. Here's a reminder of how to apply these insights to your career growth:

- **Ace the interview**: Refer to the earlier sections on behavioral and technical interview strategies. Practicing coding challenges, mastering system design questions, and preparing to articulate your problem-solving approach will set you apart from other candidates.

- **Focus on key skills**: As discussed in the hiring section, mastering critical Platform Engineering skills such as cloud-native technologies, automation, and CI/CD pipelines will fast-track your career progression.

- **Adapt and innovate**: Remember that career growth is not just about mastering the present but also about adapting to future trends such as AI/ML technologies. Stay curious, be flexible, and continually look for ways to innovate within your role.

By embracing continuous learning, seeking mentorship, taking ownership, and building a clear growth path, you, as a platform engineer, can unlock new opportunities for advancement. When aligned with technical mastery and soft skills, leadership roles can further propel your career growth. These steps, combined with the insights and strategies presented throughout this book, offer a roadmap for long-term success in Platform Engineering.

The journey to mastering Platform Engineering is about excelling technically and cultivating resilience, adaptability, and leadership. With these tools, engineers can drive both personal and organizational success. Remember, your growth is a journey, and every step you take brings you closer to becoming the leader your team and organization need.

Summary

This chapter has outlined the essential strategies for building and sustaining high-performance Platform Engineering teams. From structuring your team effectively to hiring the right talent and fostering continuous growth, we've provided a comprehensive guide to achieving excellence. Implementing the 5Es framework lays the foundation for long-term success, while continuous learning, adaptive leadership, and a culture of recognition and psychological safety ensure sustained performance. We have also explored how to advance your career and develop the leadership skills necessary to guide these high-performing teams to even greater success.

> Call to action
>
> **Embed continuous learning**: Implement programs and initiatives that promote ongoing education and skills development within your team. Encourage the pursuit of certifications, attendance at industry conferences, and participation in internal knowledge-sharing sessions.
>
> **Foster a collaborative culture**: Establish an environment where open communication, psychological safety, and teamwork are the norms. Utilize tools and practices that support teamwork and ensure all voices are heard, contributing to a more innovative and cohesive unit.
>
> **Adopt Agile and adaptive leadership practices**: Develop leadership skills that emphasize flexibility, responsiveness, and empowerment. Implement Agile methodologies to enhance team adaptability and decision-making capabilities, ensuring your team can swiftly navigate changing landscapes.

In the next chapter, we will connect all the insights and strategies discussed throughout this book. We will reflect on our transformative journey and understand how it all coalesces into a cohesive approach to enduring success in Platform Engineering.

Get This Book's PDF Version and Exclusive Extras

UNLOCK NOW

Scan the QR code (or go to `packtpub.com/unlock`). Search for this book by name, confirm the edition, and then follow the steps on the page.

Note: Keep your invoice handly. Purchase made directly from packt don't require one.

11

From Vision to Reality: Mastering Enterprise Platform Engineering

The final chapter of this book brings together the insights, strategies, and knowledge accumulated throughout our exploration of Platform Engineering. *Mastering Enterprise Platform Engineering* is not just a title. It is a clarion call to inspire and motivate you to apply these principles in your organization, driving transformation and achieving lasting success.

This chapter will wrap up the journey we've undertaken, emphasizing the importance of Platform Engineering in delivering business value and preparing for the future. By the end of the chapter, you will be motivated and equipped with the practical steps needed to implement what you have learned from this book. These steps are designed to drive transformation and help you achieve enduring success in your organization. This practical approach will instill confidence in your ability to apply Platform Engineering principles effectively.

This chapter empowers you to drive transformative change by embedding platform engineering into the core of your organization, cultivating a culture of agility, efficiency, and innovation. It guides you in delivering sustainable business value through the development of scalable and resilient platforms that enhance developer productivity and streamline workflows. Additionally, it prepares you to lead the future of platform engineering by leveraging AI, automation, and emerging technologies to stay ahead of evolving industry trends.

The strategies are in place, the vision is clear, and the opportunity is now. It's time to build, innovate, and lead. The evolution of Platform Engineering is just beginning. The real question is not whether AI and automation will redefine the future but who will shape it. Those who take action today will define the path forward.

We will be covering the following main headings in this chapter:

- From lessons learned to future wins

- Strategic planning and continuous improvement

- Delivering business value through Platform Engineering

- The future of Platform Engineering: 10 predictions for the next 5 years

- Seize the future: Your role in shaping Platform Engineering

From lessons learned to future wins

As we reach this pivotal point, we must recognize the transformative progress we've made. This book has been more than just a guide—it has served as your strategic compass through the complexities of Platform Engineering. Within these pages, we hope you have uncovered a wealth of insights, tools, and strategies, all designed to revolutionize your technical infrastructure and your organization's cultural and strategic fabric. This journey has been one of transformation, equipping you with strategies that reshape not only technology but also culture, operations, and business impact. Every insight and framework this book explores is a building block for driving meaningful change.

To build a resilient, scalable, and high-impact platform, we must first ensure our foundation is unshakable. The principles we've explored form the bedrock of effective Platform Engineering—guiding the path from initial adoption to enterprise-wide transformation. Let's distill these foundational elements and reaffirm the core strategies that drive success.

Foundations and principles

Platform Engineering is the cornerstone of modern digital enterprises, providing the structured foundation to scale, automate, and streamline software development and delivery. Its principles are deeply rooted in DevOps, cloud-native architectures, automation, and self-service enablement, ensuring that platforms remain resilient, flexible, and optimized for business agility.

Throughout this book, we have emphasized that Platform Engineering is not just about technology—it is about creating an ecosystem that empowers developers, removes friction, and accelerates business value delivery. From building **internal developer platforms (IDPs)** to automating **continuous integration and continuous deployment (CI/CD)** workflows and implementing scalable infrastructure, the principles of Platform Engineering help organizations move faster, reduce complexity, and enhance developer experience.

Core principles that drive Platform Engineering success are as follows:

- **DevOps as the foundation**: Platform Engineering extends DevOps principles by centralizing infrastructure, governance, and tooling into self-service capabilities. This enables teams to focus on development while reducing operational overhead.

- **Platform as a product mindset**: A successful platform treats developers as customers, ensuring that tools, workflows, and automation enhance productivity rather than creating additional friction. Measuring platform adoption and developer satisfaction ensures continuous improvement.

- **Architecting for scale and resilience**: Cloud-native architectures, containerization (Kubernetes), and declarative infrastructure management (IaC) enable scalable and resilient platforms that support enterprise-wide efficiency.

- **Automation and self-service**: Removing repetitive manual processes through CI/CD automation, golden paths, and IDP integrations reduces cognitive load for developers and accelerates feature delivery.

- **Security and compliance by design**: Integrating policy-as-code, automated security scanning, and access controls ensures that security is embedded within development workflows without slowing down innovation.

- **Continuous improvement and observability**: Implementing platform-wide telemetry, feedback loops, and performance monitoring ensures that engineering teams can optimize workflows based on real-world usage data.

By adhering to these principles, organizations reduce time-to-market, enhance reliability, and drive continuous innovation. This approach ensures that Platform Engineering is an enabler of operational efficiency and a strategic driver of business success.

Key insights include the following:

- Platform Engineering is the next evolution of DevOps, enabling centralized governance while maintaining team autonomy.

- A well-architected platform enhances developer experience, accelerates software delivery, and ensures long-term scalability.

- Automation, self-service, and observability are critical to platform success and adoption.

- Treating the platform as a product ensures that developer needs are prioritized, leading to better adoption and efficiency.

- Security and compliance must be embedded in platform workflows to maintain speed without compromising protection.

Cultural transformation

Cultural transformation is the foundation of high-performing Platform Engineering teams. A successful platform is not just a collection of tools and automation—it thrives on a culture that encourages innovation, fosters psychological safety, and aligns engineering efforts with business outcomes. Without this foundation, even the most advanced platforms risk becoming underutilized, rigid, or misaligned with organizational needs.

Here are some key insights:

- Culture defines the success of Platform Engineering. A generative, high-trust culture fosters innovation, efficiency, and developer satisfaction, while bureaucratic and control-driven environments create friction and slow progress.

- Platform teams must operate with a "platform as a product" mindset. By treating developers as customers, measuring adoption through **developer experience (DX)** surveys and **net promoter score (NPS)** scores, and continuously refining workflows, platform teams ensure their solutions drive business impact.

- The POWER framework accelerates cultural transformation. Organizations can build an ecosystem where Platform Engineering delivers measurable value at scale by focusing on purpose, outcomes, workflow optimization, empowerment, and reducing manual toil.

- Psychological safety fuels high-performance teams. A culture where failures are treated as learning opportunities rather than risks leads to higher innovation velocity and stronger collaboration. For example, Google's Project Aristotle found that psychological safety was the top factor in high-performing teams.

- Continuous measurement is key to cultural transformation. Organizations must track cultural and platform success through developer satisfaction scores, time-to-onboard, **change failure rate (CFR)**, and innovation velocity to ensure alignment with business goals.

Practical strategies for cultural transformation include the following:

- **Emphasizing DX**: Treat internal developers as customers. Conduct regular DX surveys, track NPS scores for platform adoption, and refine onboarding experiences. For example, Spotify's Backstage project was built to improve the DX by providing a centralized, self-service developer portal.

- **Promoting a learning culture**: Encourage internal hackathons, brown-bag sessions, and game days where teams experiment with new technologies without fear of failure. Psychological safety plays a key role—teams that feel safe to take risks and learn from mistakes innovate faster and build more resilient platforms.

- **Psychological safety and blameless postmortems**: Implement a culture where failures are learning opportunities, not career risks. Measure progress by tracking CFR and **mean time to recover (MTTR)**—two key indicators of how well teams recover from mistakes and improve over time.

- **Cross-team collaboration**: Platform teams should act as enablers, not gatekeepers. Create feedback loops between product, security, and infrastructure teams to align efforts with business priorities. Use innovation velocity—measuring the number of internal tools created—as a leading indicator of how well platform teams empower developers.

- **Continuous measurement**: The success of cultural transformation must be quantifiable. Organizations should track the following:

- Developer satisfaction scores (DX surveys and NPS) to gauge how well the platform serves its users.

- Time to onboard new engineers, measuring how quickly a developer becomes productive on the platform.

- Operational metrics such as MTTR and CFR to indicate resilience, stability, and iterative improvement.

Cultural transformation requires continuous reinforcement, leadership commitment, and iterative improvements. As organizations embed Platform Engineering within their strategy, a culture of empowerment, experimentation, and psychological safety drives sustainable success. AI is becoming an indispensable force in Platform Engineering to accelerate this transformation further, enabling automation, intelligence, and adaptive decision-making at scale.

AI in Platform Engineering

Integrating AI into Platform Engineering has revolutionized how organizations automate, optimize, and secure their platforms. From code generation and predictive maintenance to AI-driven security and real-time optimizations, AI is transforming how platforms are built and managed. Generative AI tools such as GitHub Copilot, GitLab Duo, and Amazon Q Developer enhance developer productivity, while machine learning models in AWS SageMaker and Azure AI enable proactive infrastructure monitoring and anomaly detection.

Companies leveraging AI in Platform Engineering have achieved faster software delivery, increased resilience, and enhanced security. Netflix's chaos engineering practices, powered by AI, have ensured service reliability at a global scale, while GitLab Duo's AI-driven workflows have streamlined CI/CD automation and security scanning. AI-powered analytics in Tableau and Power BI have enabled organizations such as Walmart and JPMorgan Chase to optimize business strategies, while AI-based cloud automation tools such as AWS Auto Scaling have driven sustainability and cost efficiency.

By embedding AI into Platform Engineering, organizations reduce operational complexity, improve decision-making, and enhance platform resilience. AI-powered solutions offer scalability, real-time optimization, and proactive threat detection, ensuring platform teams remain agile, efficient, and innovative. The future of Platform Engineering is AI-driven, and organizations that embrace these advancements will gain a significant competitive advantage.

Here are some key insights:

- AI is redefining Platform Engineering, from automation to intelligence. Traditional platforms relied on manual workflows; AI now enables self-optimizing, self-healing platforms that enhance efficiency and resilience at scale.

- Generative AI is not replacing developers—it's amplifying them. AI-powered tools such as GitHub Copilot and GitLab Duo remove developer toil, accelerating software delivery while allowing engineers to focus on high-value innovation.

- AI-driven security is a necessity, not an option. With evolving cyber threats, AI-powered anomaly detection and predictive security analytics are now critical components of secure software supply chains.

- AI transforms cloud infrastructure from reactive to proactive. AI-driven resource optimization, predictive scaling, and cost governance tools are replacing manual capacity planning, ensuring platforms are cost-efficient, scalable, and resilient.

- The future of Platform Engineering belongs to those who embrace AI now. Organizations that integrate AI into their IDPs, security frameworks, and operational workflows today will define the next era of technological leadership, leaving behind those who resist change.

AI is redefining Platform Engineering, driving smarter automation, intelligent infrastructure, and proactive security. The future will be shaped by AI-enhanced observability, self-healing systems, and real-time decision-making frameworks that eliminate inefficiencies and optimize operations at scale. Organizations that embed AI into their IDPs, security frameworks, and cloud operations will unlock unparalleled efficiency, ensuring continuous innovation and resilience. As Platform Engineering enters an AI-first era, investing in AI-driven platforms is no longer optional—it is the key to future-proofing infrastructure, streamlining developer experiences, and sustaining long-term competitive advantage.

Security and compliance

Security and compliance have been recurring themes, emphasizing their critical importance in the digital age. We explored best practices for integrating security into every stage of the development life cycle, from design to deployment. Understanding regulatory requirements and implementing continuous monitoring strategies were highlighted as essential to ensure your platforms remain secure and compliant. Maintaining robust security and compliance standards is non-negotiable in today's digital landscape.

We discussed how integrating security measures at every stage of the development life cycle can mitigate risks and protect sensitive information. Continuous monitoring and adherence to regulatory standards are essential for maintaining a secure and compliant platform. By prioritizing security and compliance, organizations can build trust with their stakeholders and ensure the longevity of their platform initiatives. Furthermore, adopting a proactive approach to security helps anticipate potential threats and vulnerabilities, minimizing the risk of breaches and ensuring the platform's integrity.

The key takeaways are as follows:

- **Best practices**: Integrating security at every stage of development is fundamental to protecting assets and maintaining trust.

- **Regulatory compliance**: Adhering to regulatory requirements is essential for avoiding legal pitfalls and ensuring operational integrity.

- **Continuous monitoring**: Ongoing monitoring and adaptation are necessary to maintain a secure and compliant environment.

Ensuring robust security and compliance lays the foundation for resilient and trustworthy platform operations. With these safeguards in place, organizations can now focus on scaling their platforms efficiently while maintaining optimal performance under increasing demand.

Scalability and performance

Our discussion on scalability and performance provided the tools and techniques needed to handle growing demands and maintain high performance levels. For instance, horizontal scaling involves adding more servers to your system to handle increased traffic, while vertical scaling involves upgrading your existing servers to handle more load. These insights are crucial for ensuring that your platforms can meet the needs of your users while maintaining efficiency and reliability. Scalability and performance are critical aspects of Platform Engineering that determine the platform's ability to support growth and deliver consistent user experiences while maintaining efficiency and reliability.

Optimizing load balancing was also discussed as a critical factor in maintaining high performance. By mastering these techniques, organizations can ensure their platforms are equipped to handle increasing demands and deliver reliable, efficient services to their users. Implementing these strategies not only enhances user satisfaction but also contributes to the overall stability and resilience of the platform, enabling businesses to thrive even during peak usage periods.

Here are some key insights:

- **Scaling strategies**: Effective scaling strategies are vital for accommodating growth and ensuring continuous performance.

- **Auto-scaling**: Dynamic resource adjustment through auto-scaling enhances operational efficiency and reliability.

- **Load balancing**: Optimizing load distribution is crucial for maintaining performance and preventing system overloads.

Achieving scalability and performance is only as effective as the teams that build and maintain the platform. Organizations must cultivate high-performance platform teams equipped with the right skills, culture, and strategic alignment to sustain growth and innovation.

Building high-performance Platform Engineering teams

Creating and sustaining high-performance Platform Engineering teams is crucial for driving innovation, efficiency, and long-term business impact. High-performing teams are not just assembled but intentionally built through strategic hiring, cultural alignment, and continuous development. Organizations that invest in well-defined team structures, clear roles, and leadership-driven enablement create environments where platform teams operate at peak efficiency, drive developer productivity, and align with business objectives. Organizations can cultivate resilient, high-performing teams that consistently deliver value by applying the 5Es framework—Empathize, Empower, Engage, Entrust, and Equip.

Successful platform teams are built on strong leadership, continuous learning, and a relentless focus on DX. The ability to attract, retain, and develop top talent while fostering an inclusive and psychologically safe culture sets the best platform teams apart. An empowered, engaged, and well-supported team enhances platform capabilities and accelerates business transformation.

Key insights are as follows:

- High-performing platform teams require a strong foundation in structure, culture, and leadership. Clearly defined roles, collaborative team dynamics, and a product mindset ensure that Platform Engineering efforts align with business objectives.

- Hiring for high performance goes beyond technical skills. Identifying candidates who demonstrate ownership, problem-solving abilities, and adaptability ensures that teams are technically competent, collaborative, innovative, and resilient.

- Sustaining high performance requires continuous investment in learning, leadership, and recognition. A culture of psychological safety, continuous improvement, and shared accountability keeps teams engaged, motivated, and aligned with strategic goals.

- Effective leadership is the driving force behind Platform Engineering success. Leaders must provide a clear vision, structured goal-setting (OKRs and KPIs), and empowerment while fostering an environment of experimentation and innovation.

- The best platform teams measure their impact and continuously evolve. Metrics such as DX scores, onboarding time, deployment frequency, and CFR provide tangible insights into team efficiency, platform adoption, and overall effectiveness.

High-performing platform teams don't just emerge—they are built with intention, investment, and continuous refinement. By combining structured hiring, leadership-driven alignment, and a culture of growth and accountability, organizations can create platform teams that consistently deliver business value and technological excellence. Those that prioritize collaboration, empower their teams, and embrace continuous learning will define the future of Platform Engineering.

The shift to Platform Engineering is a vital evolution that equips you with the strategic vision and leadership skills necessary to drive real impact. Each principle and strategy we've examined serves as a foundation, empowering you to create and manage platforms that are resilient, adaptable, and ready for the future. As we move forward, it's crucial to focus on the strategic planning and continuous improvement that will ensure these platforms not only meet today's demands but also set the stage for sustained success.

Strategic planning and continuous improvement

As we journey through the multifaceted world of Platform Engineering, it becomes clear that integrating various tools, techniques, and frameworks is essential for achieving maximum impact. This section will provide a cohesive strategy for implementing these insights in your organization, offering practical steps and solutions to overcome common challenges and ensure successful outcomes.

Platform Engineering is not just about adopting the latest tools or following the newest trends; it is about creating a holistic, integrated approach that aligns with your business objectives. It requires a deep understanding of the interplay between technology, processes, and people. By synthesizing the knowledge gained from previous chapters, organizations can create a robust and dynamic Platform Engineering strategy that drives continuous improvement and innovation.

The strategic role of Platform Engineering

At its core, Platform Engineering is about creating an environment where technology and business strategies converge. By implementing the right tools and practices, organizations can unlock new levels of innovation and efficiency. This strategic alignment ensures that every platform aspect—from development to deployment—contributes to the organization's overarching goals.

For example, adopting a Platform Engineering mindset can help businesses stay ahead of the competition by enabling faster response times to market changes, improving product quality, and enhancing customer satisfaction. It allows organizations to be more agile, adapting quickly to new opportunities and challenges, thus maintaining a competitive edge in an ever-evolving market landscape. This proactive approach is not only about keeping up with technological advancements but also about anticipating and shaping the future of the industry.

Additionally, the strategic role of Platform Engineering includes fostering cross-functional collaboration, breaking down silos, and promoting a unified vision across the organization. By integrating Platform Engineering into the core business strategy, organizations can ensure that technology investments drive meaningful outcomes, supporting growth and long-term success.

Building a cohesive business strategy

The first step in integrating Platform Engineering practices is to develop a cohesive strategy that aligns with your organization's goals. This strategy should encompass the selection of appropriate tools, the establishment of robust processes, and the cultivation of a supportive culture. Here's a roadmap to guide you:

1. **Assessment and planning**: Begin by thoroughly assessing your current infrastructure, workflows, and pain points. Identify areas where Platform Engineering can bring the most significant benefits. Develop a detailed plan that outlines the goals, timelines, and resources needed for implementation. This initial assessment helps identify gaps and opportunities and ensures that the strategy is tailored to the organization's specific needs.

2. **Tool selection and integration**: Choose the tools and technologies that best fit your organization's needs. This could include container orchestration tools such as Kubernetes, CI/CD platforms such as GitLab, and automation frameworks such as WSO2 Choreo. Ensure these tools are seamlessly integrated to create a unified platform supporting continuous delivery and operational efficiency. The integration of tools should be driven by a clear understanding of how they complement each other and contribute to the overall platform strategy.

3. **Process optimization**: Implement processes that streamline development and deployment workflows. Adopt practices such as **infrastructure as code** (**IAC**), CI/CD, and automated testing. These processes reduce manual intervention, minimize errors, and accelerate delivery cycles. Process optimization is an ongoing effort that requires regular review and adaptation to evolving business and technological landscapes.

4. **Cultural transformation**: Foster a culture that embraces change, encourages collaboration, and prioritizes continuous improvement. Empathic leadership and clear communication are crucial to transforming your team. Encourage cross-functional teams to work together, share knowledge, and innovate. Building a culture of trust and openness is essential for overcoming resistance to change and fostering a sense of ownership and accountability among team members.

Creating a roadmap for implementation

Creating a detailed roadmap is essential to ensure a successful Platform Engineering transformation. Here's a step-by-step guide:

1. **Define objectives**: Clearly define what you aim to achieve with Platform Engineering. Set measurable goals such as reduced time-to-market, improved deployment frequency, and enhanced system reliability. These objectives should align with the organization's strategic goals and provide a clear direction for the transformation effort. Establishing **key performance indicators** (**KPIs**) can help track progress and measure success.

2. **Develop a timeline**: Outline a realistic timeline for implementation, with milestones and checkpoints to track progress. Allow flexibility to accommodate unforeseen challenges and adjustments. A well-structured timeline helps maintain focus and ensure that the project stays on track. Regularly revisiting and adjusting the timeline based on project developments can ensure that the roadmap remains relevant and achievable. Involving key stakeholders in the timeline creation process can also help gain their buy-in and support for the project.

3. **Allocate resources**: Identify the resources required, including personnel, budget, and technology. Ensure that you have the necessary support from leadership and stakeholders. Effective resource allocation is critical for ensuring that the transformation efforts are adequately supported and can achieve the desired outcomes. Incorporating resource planning tools can help manage and optimize the use of resources throughout the project. This step should include contingency planning to address potential resource shortfalls and unexpected challenges.

4. **Monitor and adjust**: Continuously monitor progress against your objectives and adjust as needed. Use metrics and feedback to refine processes and ensure you are on track to achieve your goals. Regular review and adaptation are essential for maintaining momentum and ensuring continuous improvement. Establishing a robust feedback loop with stakeholders and team members can provide valuable insights for iterative improvements. Additionally, using advanced analytics and reporting tools can provide real-time visibility into project performance, enabling proactive adjustments.

Fostering a culture of continuous improvement

Organizations must move beyond static methodologies to thrive in an evolving digital landscape and embed continuous improvement as a core strategic function. This means establishing structured mechanisms for iterative learning, innovation, and feedback loops rather than treating improvement as an ad hoc initiative. Successful organizations proactively evaluate emerging technologies, optimize processes, and refine platform capabilities to maintain a competitive edge.

A culture of continuous improvement requires more than just adopting new tools—it demands a shift in mindset. Encouraging teams to experiment with emerging frameworks, refine operational models, and challenge the status quo ensures adaptability and resilience. Structured internal innovation programs, cross-functional hackathons, and investment in technical upskilling enable platform teams to push boundaries and turn incremental optimizations into transformational advancements. Netflix's chaos engineering, which fosters resilience by simulating failures, and the POWER framework for cultural transformation exemplify how structured experimentation can drive continuous improvement. Similarly, as discussed in earlier chapters, AI-powered predictive observability showcases how platforms can leverage intelligent automation to refine operations and improve reliability.

Collaboration is the catalyst for sustained improvement. Active participation in open source communities, industry working groups, and internal knowledge-sharing forums accelerates learning and ensures organizations remain ahead of evolving best practices. GitHub's InnerSource model, where organizations apply open source principles internally to foster innovation, is a prime example of how knowledge-sharing accelerates learning. Additionally, organizations such as Google and Microsoft, which institutionalize continuous learning through engineering excellence programs and post-mortem-driven development, demonstrate how structured improvement efforts translate into long-term success.

Platform Engineering is not just about delivering technology—it's about shaping an organization's ability to evolve. Strategic, data-driven continuous improvement transforms Platform Engineering from a support function into a value-generating powerhouse, enabling faster innovation cycles, greater developer satisfaction, and long-term business differentiation.

Delivering business value through Platform Engineering

Platform Engineering is not just about creating scalable infrastructure or streamlined workflows—its true impact lies in delivering tangible business value. Every decision, tool, and process must ultimately contribute to faster innovation, improved developer productivity, reduced operational overhead, and increased competitive advantage.

To successfully translate Platform Engineering investments into business outcomes, organizations must focus on three key areas: maximizing DX, operationalizing efficiency at scale, and driving measurable business impact.

Elevating developer experience as a business enabler

The most direct way to deliver business value through Platform Engineering is by enhancing DX. Developer productivity, velocity, and satisfaction directly impact product delivery timelines, feature innovation, and operational resilience. A frictionless developer experience leads to faster time-to-market, higher software quality, and better talent retention.

Key actions to maximize developer experience include the following:

- **Invest in IDPs**: Enable self-service workflows for developers by automating environment provisioning, deployment processes, and infrastructure access.

- **Minimize cognitive load**: Standardize development workflows with golden paths, well-documented APIs, and intuitive onboarding processes to reduce friction.

- **Streamline tooling and workflows**: Remove redundant tooling and ensure seamless integrations between CI/CD, observability, and security pipelines.

Organizations that prioritize developer experience as a business imperative have seen tangible results. Spotify's Backstage IDP reduced onboarding time for new engineers by 55%, allowing them to contribute to production faster. Google's DX initiatives cut deployment friction, leading to a 45% reduction in time spent on non-coding tasks. These improvements accelerate developer velocity, reduce burnout, and increase overall innovation capacity, reinforcing platform engineering's role as a key driver of business success.

Driving operational efficiency at scale

The second pillar of delivering business value through Platform Engineering involves optimizing resource utilization, reducing inefficiencies, and ensuring cost-effectiveness. A well-architected platform enables predictable scaling, improves infrastructure reliability, and automates repetitive operational tasks, freeing teams to focus on higher-value initiatives.

Key actions to optimize efficiency include the following:

- **Adopt FinOps and intelligent cost optimization**: Implement AI-driven observability, workload rightsizing, and auto-scaling strategies to optimize infrastructure spending.

- **Automate everything possible**: Use IaC, automated deployments, and self-healing mechanisms to eliminate manual interventions.

- **Enhance platform resilience**: Introduce continuous performance tuning, chaos engineering, and proactive monitoring to reduce outages and service disruptions.

Many leading organizations have leveraged Platform Engineering to drive operational efficiency at scale. Netflix's chaos engineering practices proactively test failure scenarios, ensuring platform resilience and minimizing customer impact during outages. Similarly, Uber's AI-powered FinOps approach optimizes cloud expenditures, leading to a 30% reduction in infrastructure costs while maintaining performance. When embedded within platform strategy, these examples highlight how operational efficiency directly translates to cost savings and improved service reliability.

Aligning Platform Engineering with business metrics

The final step in maximizing business value is ensuring that Platform Engineering aligns with key business KPIs and strategic objectives. It's not enough for platform teams to deliver outstanding technology—they must quantify their impact in terms that executives and stakeholders understand.

Key actions for business alignment include the following:

- **Define and track success metrics**: Align Platform Engineering KPIs with business outcomes such as deployment frequency, lead time for changes, and revenue impact from platform improvements.

- **Showcase business impact**: Regularly present data-driven insights on how platform initiatives accelerate innovation, improve reliability, and drive revenue growth.

- **Embed continuous feedback loops**: Collaborate with product, engineering, and leadership teams to iterate on platform priorities based on real business needs.

Organizations that successfully align Platform Engineering with business strategy create direct value for customers and stakeholders alike. Capital One's platform modernization efforts led to an 80% reduction in deployment time, accelerating digital banking feature releases and improving customer experience. Shopify's developer-centric platform investments enhanced engineering throughput, enabling faster feature rollouts and reducing time-to-market for merchants. These examples illustrate how Platform Engineering catalyzes revenue growth and competitive differentiation when strategically aligned with business priorities.

Platform Engineering is not just an infrastructure investment but a force multiplier that drives business agility, efficiency, and innovation. Organizations can ensure their platform investments yield measurable business value by focusing on developer experience, operational efficiency, and business alignment.

Companies that prioritize Platform Engineering as a strategic function—rather than a backend operational concern—position themselves to outpace competitors, deliver superior digital experiences, and future-proof their technology ecosystems.

As Platform Engineering matures, new challenges and opportunities emerge. AI-driven automation, predictive observability, and self-optimizing systems reshape how platforms are designed, built, and operated. The future of Platform Engineering will be defined by intelligent systems, adaptive infrastructure, and even deeper integration with business strategy. Organizations that embrace these advancements will not just keep up with industry shifts—they will lead the next wave of digital transformation.

The future of Platform Engineering: 10 predictions for the next 5 years

As technology accelerates, Platform Engineering is at a pivotal crossroads, poised to redefine how software is built, deployed, and managed. The next 5 to 10 years will see seismic shifts in developer workflows, automation, and platform capabilities, fundamentally reshaping the role of platform engineers, developers, and AI-driven automation. Here are 10 predictions we make about Platform Engineering and its long-term trajectory.

1. Developers will evolve into product architects, not just coders

The role of developers will shift away from writing boilerplate code and configuring infrastructure to becoming strategic product architects who focus on business logic, user experience, and system design. AI-powered agent-based development will handle repetitive coding, allowing developers to curate, orchestrate, and fine-tune AI-generated solutions rather than manually write every line of code. Low-code and no-code platforms will merge with traditional software engineering, creating hybrid development ecosystems where human expertise enhances AI-generated artifacts instead of replacing them.

> *By 2027, AI will be an integral co-developer, turning software engineers into high-level system designers who guide, validate, and optimize AI-driven code generation*

This shift reflects an industry-wide move toward DX as the ultimate productivity metric. Instead of measuring success by lines of code, teams will measure how quickly they can deliver meaningful features that solve real business problems. As AI tools take over mundane tasks—such as boilerplate code and environment setup—engineers will devote more time to architecting resilient systems, collaborating with stakeholders, and refining user experiences. This evolution boosts developer satisfaction and ensures a more substantial alignment between technology and business strategy.

How organizations can prepare

Organizations should invest in AI-powered coding assistants (e.g., GitHub Copilot or GitLab Duo) and promote design-thinking workshops encouraging developers to view their work through a product lens. Implement dual career tracks—one focusing on deep technical leadership and the other on product-focused system design—to accommodate varied skill sets and aspirations. Leaders must recognize and reward developers' architectural and strategic contributions, reinforcing the message that software engineering success is measured by impact, not just code volume.

2. The end of tool fragmentation: Integrated, self-service developer experiences

The current challenge of integrating fragmented DevOps and platform tools will give way to unified, intelligent IDPs that provide a seamless, self-service experience for developers. Cognitive AI layers will replace the need for manual tool orchestration, allowing engineers to define high-level intents while the platform autonomously provisions, secures, and optimizes infrastructure in real time.

> *Within three years, organizations that still rely on manually stitched-together DevOps tooling will fall behind. Fully integrated, AI-enhanced IDPs will become the gold standard, providing developers with an intuitive, frictionless experience*

Today's DevOps landscape is flooded with specialized tools for CI/CD, monitoring, security, and more. Although each tool is powerful, lack of integration often leads to manual handoffs, repeated configurations, and inconsistent governance. The future points to all-in-one platforms where these capabilities converge, guided by AI to simplify developer tasks. By abstracting complexity behind cohesive interfaces, developers will no longer waste time reconciling disparate systems.

How organizations can prepare

Adopt or build an IDP that unifies your CI/CD, observability, security, and infrastructure provisioning. Integrate AI-based recommendations to guide developers in selecting optimal build pipelines or security policies. Encourage developer feedback loops—through surveys and usage analytics—to refine the platform continuously. Make the platform a product: define product owners, set roadmap priorities, and measure adoption and satisfaction to ensure ongoing evolution toward seamless self-service.

3. Platform Engineering will shift from infrastructure to AI-driven orchestration

Platform Engineering will evolve beyond infrastructure provisioning and automation, becoming the central nervous system of intelligent, AI-driven orchestration. AI will dynamically optimize cloud resources, predict failures before they occur, and enable fully autonomous platforms that require minimal human intervention. Workflows will be intent-driven, where developers specify desired outcomes, and AI handles execution.

> *By 2030, AI-driven orchestration will make manual infrastructure tuning and operations obsolete, shifting Platform Engineering to governance, policy enforcement, and strategic automation*

The need for real-time, event-driven architectures will grow as businesses demand instant adaptability to workload spikes, cost optimizations, and security threats. AI will observe and act autonomously, rerouting workloads, mitigating risks, and enforcing governance in real time.

How organizations can prepare

Organizations must invest in AI-native platforms that support autonomous policy enforcement, AI-enhanced FinOps, and predictive maintenance. Adopt serverless-first architectures where possible, allowing AI to allocate resources dynamically based on demand forecasting models. Train platform engineers to think beyond infrastructure automation and embrace AI-driven orchestration and policy-based governance.

4. Security will become predictive and autonomous

Instead of reacting to security incidents, AI-powered security frameworks will proactively detect vulnerabilities, enforce compliance, and mitigate threats before they materialize. AI-driven anomaly detection will flag unusual behaviors across networks, applications, and cloud environments, significantly reducing the **mean time to detect (MTTD)** and **mean time to respond (MTTRespond)**.

> *By 2028, AI-powered security analytics, anomaly detection, and automated threat response will be the industry standard, with manual security management becoming obsolete*

Security tools will shift from rule-based detection to adaptive, learning-based models that self-tune in response to evolving threats. AI will continuously validate supply chain security, flagging vulnerabilities in third-party dependencies and ensuring secure code generation.

How organizations can prepare

Implement AI-driven security tools such as machine learning-powered **intrusion detection systems (IDSs)**, automated compliance auditing, and continuous attack surface monitoring. Foster AI security collaborations between DevSecOps and platform teams to ensure security is not just an afterthought but an integrated, autonomous process.

5. AI agents will replace traditional IT operations

Routine infrastructure management tasks—such as patching, monitoring, scaling, and failure recovery—will no longer require human intervention. AI agents will autonomously monitor systems, detect anomalies, and initiate self-healing responses, minimizing downtime and operational overhead.

> *By 2029, AI-powered IT operations (AIOps) will replace traditional human-driven infrastructure management, significantly reducing manual intervention in platform operations*

As AI matures, IT operations will transition from reactive to proactive, then fully autonomous. Self-healing architectures will detect patterns leading to failures and resolve issues before they impact users. Organizations will experience unprecedented levels of uptime and operational efficiency without human operators manually troubleshooting incidents.

How organizations can prepare

Invest in AIOps platforms such as Datadog, Dynatrace, and Splunk that integrate machine learning models to detect anomalies, forecast failures, and automate remediation. Train platform engineers to shift from hands-on troubleshooting to governance and oversight of AI-driven operations. Encourage a proactive IT culture, where teams focus on optimizing AI workflows rather than firefighting incidents.

6. Developer experience will overtake cost as the primary KPI for platform teams

While cost efficiency has traditionally been a primary KPI for platform teams, the next decade will see DX become the dominant measure of success. Organizations will prioritize developer satisfaction, productivity, and onboarding speed as the key indicators of Platform Engineering excellence.

> *By 2027, the best-performing engineering organizations will measure success by how well their platforms enable developers to ship high-quality code—not just by how much they reduce infrastructure costs*

A poor developer experience leads to friction, delays, and shadow IT, forcing teams to bypass internal platforms. In contrast, platforms with intuitive self-service workflows, minimal cognitive load, and precise documentation will drive adoption, efficiency, and innovation.

How organizations can prepare

Establish developer experience teams focused on continuously improving IDP usability, documentation, and automation. Use metrics such as lead time for changes (DORA), NPS for developers, and onboarding time for new hires to track progress. Make developer productivity a board-level priority, ensuring platform investments align with developer needs rather than just cost savings.

7. AI and observability will converge for predictive operations

Observability will evolve from passive monitoring to predictive, AI-driven operations. Platforms will leverage large-scale AI models to detect early warning signals, proactively resolve incidents, and automatically fine-tune performance based on user demand and system load. Full stack observability, powered by AI, will replace traditional monitoring dashboards.

> *By 2026, AI-powered predictive observability will be a standard in enterprise platforms, reducing downtime and eliminating the need for manual issue triaging*

Today's observability stacks rely heavily on logs, metrics, and traces, requiring human intervention to interpret signals, identify root causes, and remediate issues. AI-driven observability will shift from reactive troubleshooting to predictive intelligence, where machine learning models analyze historical data, real-time telemetry, and anomaly detection patterns to anticipate failures before they occur.

Instead of engineers responding to alerts, AI will automatically diagnose problems, suggest fixes, and, in many cases, execute remediations autonomously. This transformation will reduce **mean time to resolution (MTTResolution)**, eliminate manual triaging, and improve system reliability. Over time, AI-driven observability will become adaptive, dynamically adjusting infrastructure configurations to optimize performance without human intervention. Organizations will unlock a new era of reliability, efficiency, and operational intelligence by embedding predictive monitoring, automated diagnostics, and autonomous system tuning into platform operations.

How organizations can prepare

To stay ahead, organizations must adopt AI-driven observability platforms such as New Relic AI, Datadog Watchdog, Dynatrace Davis AI, and Splunk AIOps, which integrate machine learning for anomaly detection and predictive analytics. Instead of relying on static threshold-based alerts, engineering teams must shift toward context-aware, AI-driven incident prioritization, where critical failures are identified based on business impact rather than isolated technical anomalies. Automating **root cause analysis** (**RCA**) will also be essential, leveraging AI to correlate system dependencies and past telemetry data to pinpoint potential issues before they escalate. Furthermore, self-healing automation should be tightly integrated with observability tools, enabling AI to trigger remediation when predefined failure patterns are detected automatically.

8. Platform teams will standardize multi-cloud architectures

Organizations will move beyond single-cloud dependencies, embracing multi-cloud architectures with AI-driven workload orchestration and higher levels of on-premises clouds. Intelligent platforms will dynamically distribute workloads across clouds based on cost, latency, and regulatory requirements.

> *By 2027, organizations will treat multi-cloud as the default architecture, leveraging AI for intelligent workload placement and cost optimization*

The risks of vendor lock-in, cloud outages, and geopolitical instability will drive companies to design cloud-agnostic architectures. AI will automatically adjust resource allocations across AWS, Azure, Google Cloud, and edge computing environments, ensuring optimal performance and cost efficiency.

How organizations can prepare

Invest in Kubernetes, Terraform, and AI-driven workload orchestration tools that abstract away cloud provider dependencies. Train platform teams to design cloud-agnostic systems, leveraging service meshes, API gateways, and edge computing to distribute workloads efficiently.

9. AI will enable autonomous governance and compliance

The burden of manually enforcing security policies, compliance standards, and governance frameworks will be eliminated by AI-driven automation. AI will continuously monitor, audit, and enforce compliance in real time, reducing the risk of human error.

> *By 2035, AI-driven compliance enforcement will replace manual security audits, reducing regulatory risks and ensuring real-time adherence to industry standards*

Regulatory compliance today is often a reactive, time-consuming process. AI-driven policy as code, automated compliance scanning, and anomaly detection will enable real-time, proactive governance. Security and compliance teams will focus on high-level strategies while AI continuously enforces best practices.

How organizations can prepare

Adopt AI-powered security tools that automatically detect vulnerabilities, enforce policies, and audit compliance. Use continuous compliance monitoring platforms (e.g., Wiz, Lacework, or Prisma Cloud) to address risks proactively before they become incidents. Encourage a security-first culture where compliance is baked into development workflows, not treated as an afterthought.

10. The future of work: AI-enhanced, human-driven platform teams

AI will not replace platform engineers but fundamentally transform their roles. Instead of focusing on manual infrastructure management, debugging, and operational maintenance, platform teams will act as AI system architects, policy enforcers, and innovation enablers.

> *By 2028, AI will handle 80% of routine platform operations, allowing engineers to focus on governance, optimization, and AI-human collaboration*

Platform engineers will evolve into strategic enablers of AI-driven workflows, ensuring platform reliability, security, and developer productivity. The role will shift from manual execution to AI governance, balancing autonomous intelligence with human oversight.

How organizations can prepare

Train platform engineers in AI ethics, policy automation, and AI-augmented operations. Encourage collaboration between platform teams and AI researchers to refine AI-driven automation continuously. Redefine success metrics to measure AI's impact on efficiency, security, and developer enablement.

AI, automation, and continuous evolution will define the next five years of Platform Engineering. Organizations that embrace these trends will gain a competitive edge, improve developer experience, and unlock unprecedented efficiencies. The future belongs to those who leverage AI not as a replacement for human expertise but as a force multiplier—amplifying the capabilities of developers and platform teams alike.

Organizations that hesitate to adopt AI-enhanced platforms risk falling behind, burdened by manual processes, fragmented tooling, and outdated architectures. The imperative is clear: invest in AI-driven automation, prioritize developer experience, and build platforms that are intelligent, scalable, and future-proof.

The evolution of Platform Engineering is just beginning. The real question is not whether AI and automation will redefine the future, but who will shape it. Those who take action today will define the path forward.

Seize the future: Your role in shaping Platform Engineering

Platform Engineering is no longer just a technical discipline—it is the foundation for innovation, agility, and sustained business growth. The decisions made today will define the competitive landscape for years to come. Are you ready to lead the charge? The future belongs to those who seize opportunities, challenge the status quo, and create scalable, developer-centric ecosystems that drive real business value. The time to lead the charge is now. Are you ready?

Three fundamental shifts must occur to optimally harness the power of Platform Engineering: a commitment to continuous reinvention, the courage to embrace AI and automation, and a relentless focus on developer experience. These principles will define the next generation of high-performance engineering teams.

Continuous reinvention: Staying ahead in a changing world

The pace of technological change is accelerating, and what works today may not work tomorrow. High-performing organizations don't just adapt—they continuously reinvent themselves. This means breaking free from rigid legacy systems, challenging outdated processes, and fostering a culture of relentless experimentation. The ability to reinvent is not just a choice but a necessity in today's dynamic business environment.

Successful teams think beyond today's solutions and build modular and scalable platforms designed for continuous evolution. They cultivate architectural flexibility, ensuring their platforms integrate new tools, accommodate emerging technologies, and scale effortlessly as business needs evolve.

Organizations that invest in learning, challenge complacency, and create an environment where innovation thrives will define the future. The question is: Will you be one of them?

AI and automation: The new imperative in Platform Engineering

We are entering an AI-first era where automation is no longer a luxury but a business imperative. AI-driven observability, intelligent workflows, and self-healing systems will transform how platforms operate, allowing organizations to move from reactive maintenance to proactive innovation.

This shift isn't just about efficiency—it's about unlocking human potential. Platform teams can focus on strategic innovation rather than routine maintenance by automating repetitive tasks, reducing toil, and embedding intelligence into infrastructure. The most successful organizations will be those that leverage AI to augment human expertise, not replace it, ensuring that human creativity and problem-solving skills remain at the forefront of Platform Engineering.

To shape the future, organizations must prioritize investing in AI-driven automation today. It's not an afterthought but a core pillar of their platform strategy.

Developer experience: The key to sustainable innovation

The success of Platform Engineering is measured by its impact on developers. A frictionless, intuitive, and empowering developer experience is the key to accelerating software delivery, reducing cognitive load, and fostering innovation.

Organizations must rethink how they enable their engineers—shifting from rigid control to developer empowerment. IDPs, golden paths, and self-service automation will define the new standard for developer enablement.

The future of Platform Engineering is not about controlling developers—it's about unleashing them. Organizations prioritizing developer experience will see increased adoption, greater productivity, and faster innovation cycles. Those that don't? They risk developer frustration and shadow IT and operational bottlenecks that will hinder progress.

The evolution of Platform Engineering is deeply intertwined with the changing nature of applications and how they are built, deployed, and maintained. Platforms must adapt to meet new demands as software architectures shift toward distributed, event-driven, and AI-enhanced models. The next frontier lies in creating adaptive, intelligent platforms that support modern application development and anticipate future needs.

The evolution of platforms and applications

The boundaries between platforms and applications are rapidly shifting, leading to a future where development environments are increasingly modular, flexible, and responsive. This transformation is exemplified by the rise of composable architectures, where platforms are built from interchangeable plug-and-play components. This shift toward modularity allows developers to create and deploy applications with unprecedented speed and precision, perfectly aligning with the dynamic demands of modern markets.

As platforms continue to evolve, they will increasingly blur the lines between infrastructure and software, creating systems that are not just cohesive but also adaptive. This is particularly evident in the rise of serverless architectures, which abstract the underlying infrastructure entirely, allowing developers to focus solely on application logic. Industry leaders such as AWS Lambda, Microsoft Azure Functions, and Google Cloud Functions are already showcasing the potential of serverless technologies to automatically scale applications in response to demand, reducing costs and improving efficiency. These advancements will drive the development of more sophisticated tools that empower developers to push the boundaries of what's possible, ensuring that their applications meet—and exceed—the expectations of users and markets.

Emerging technologies such as quantum computing, edge computing, and 6G will further accelerate this evolution. These advancements will enable real-time processing and decision-making at the edge, reducing latency and enhancing user experiences. As platforms become more distributed and intelligent, they will support a wide range of applications, from smart cities to autonomous vehicles, driving transformative change across industries.

As the boundaries between platforms and applications continue to dissolve, the integration of emerging technologies will redefine how we develop, manage, and deploy solutions. By embracing these advancements and strategically positioning your organization at the forefront of this evolution, you ensure that your platforms are not only prepared for the future but are also driving innovation and delivering exceptional value. The choices you make today will determine your organization's ability to lead tomorrow—now is the time to act decisively and shape the future.

Building the future starts now

The organizations that will lead in the coming years are not waiting for the future to arrive—they are actively shaping it. Platform Engineering is the bridge between technology and business success, and those who invest in continuous reinvention, AI-driven automation, and developer-centric platforms will define the next decade of software innovation. This is not just about survival but about thriving and leading in the digital age.

The most forward-thinking companies are already laying the groundwork for intelligent, self-optimizing platforms, creating seamless developer experiences, and embedding AI into their operational fabric. They are not asking *if* but *how fast*. They understand that delaying innovation is just another way of falling behind.

But transformation doesn't happen by accident. It requires bold leadership, strategic execution, and the willingness to challenge conventions. Organizations that fail to adapt will be left struggling with inefficiencies, technical debt, and frustrated developers, while those that embrace this shift will drive unparalleled agility, efficiency, and market leadership.

This is the inflection point. The convergence of AI, automation, and Platform Engineering has created an unprecedented opportunity to reimagine how technology fuels business success. Organizations that seize this moment will survive, thrive, innovate, and lead.

The question is not whether Platform Engineering will evolve but who will drive that evolution.

Will you be the one to lead?

Summary

As we conclude our journey, it's essential to recognize the comprehensive blueprint this book has provided—from the initial vision to the tangible reality of mastering Platform Engineering This book has equipped you with a comprehensive strategy, from vision to reality, guiding you through foundational principles to advanced capabilities, and providing a roadmap to build resilient, scalable, and high-impact Platform Engineering practices. The insights and strategies shared here are not just concepts but actionable imperatives. The future belongs to those taking decisive steps, leveraging Platform Engineering as a force multiplier, and driving meaningful transformation. The blueprint is in your hands. Now is the time to execute, innovate, and lead.

Key takeaways

Here are the key takeaways from this book:

- **Platform Engineering as a competitive advantage**: Beyond efficiency, Platform Engineering is a strategic enabler that drives agility, accelerates innovation, and enhances developer experience, positioning organizations for long-term market leadership.

- **AI-driven future**: Integrating AI into Platform Engineering is not optional—it is the defining force of the next generation of platforms. Organizations that leverage AI for automation, observability, and decision intelligence will outpace their competition.

- **Ecosystem thinking**: The most successful platform teams don't just build tools; they cultivate ecosystems. By fostering collaboration, shared knowledge, and self-service enablement, they create a foundation for continuous growth and adaptability.

- **From vision to reality**: Platform Engineering is a transformation, not a project. The principles and strategies outlined in this book provide a roadmap to move from strategy to execution, ensuring sustained impact and enterprise-wide success.

Call to action

As you stand at the threshold of implementing the knowledge and insights gained from this book, we encourage you to take decisive steps toward transforming your organization. Here are actionable steps to guide you on this journey:

Adopt a Platform Engineering mindset: Embrace the principles and strategies discussed in this book. Develop a cohesive plan that aligns with your business objectives and fosters a culture of continuous improvement.

Leverage advanced technologies: Integrate AI, automation, and the platformless approach to enhance operational efficiency and drive innovation. Stay informed about emerging trends and adapt your strategies accordingly.

Empower your teams: Invest in training and development to equip your teams with the skills and knowledge needed to succeed. Foster a collaborative environment that encourages experimentation and learning.

Measure and optimize: Continuously monitor the performance of your platforms and make data-driven decisions to optimize processes. Use metrics to track progress and identify areas for improvement.

Stay agile and forward-thinking: Maintain a forward-thinking mindset, always looking for ways to innovate and stay ahead of the competition. Embrace change and be willing to adapt to new challenges and opportunities.

The future of Platform Engineering holds immense potential for those willing to embrace it. By implementing the insights and strategies discussed in this book, you have the power to transform your organization, drive significant business value, and shape the future of technology. The journey may be challenging, but the rewards are substantial. As pioneers in Platform Engineering, you have the opportunity to lead the way, creating a more efficient, innovative, and successful future for your organization and the industry as a whole.

Great Platform Engineering is more than technology—it's about enabling people, accelerating innovation, and creating thriving ecosystems. The pioneers of this movement will not just react to change; they will define it. You have the tools, the knowledge, and the leadership potential to shape the future—one that is scalable, intelligent, and built for continuous evolution.

The path ahead will require vision, resilience, and an unwavering commitment to excellence. Every step you take toward refining your platforms and embracing new technologies brings you closer to achieving enduring success. The knowledge you've gained from this book is a testament to your commitment to excellence. Now, it's time to put that knowledge into action, drive transformation, and become a catalyst for change in the world of Platform Engineering.

Step forward with confidence, apply what you have learned, and take charge of redefining how platforms power the modern enterprise. The next chapter of Platform Engineering is yours to write—make it extraordinary!

Get This Book's PDF Version and Exclusive Extras

UNLOCK NOW

Scan the QR code (or go to `packtpub.com/unlock`). Search for this book by name, confirm the edition, and then follow the steps on the page.

Note: Keep your invoice handly. Purchase made directly from packt don't require one.

12

Unlock Your Exclusive Benefits

Your copy of this book includes the following exclusive benefit:

- ☁ Next-gen Packt Reader
- 📄 DRM-free PDF/ePub downloads

Follow the guide below to unlock them. The process takes only a few minutes and needs to be completed once.

Unlock this Book's Free Benefits in 3 Easy Steps

Step 1

Keep your purchase invoice ready for *Step 3*. If you have a physical copy, scan it using your phone and save it as a PDF, JPG, or PNG.

For more help on finding your invoice, visit `https://www.packtpub.com/unlock-benefits/help`.

> **Note**
> If you bought this book directly from Packt, no invoice is required. After *Step 2*, you can access your exclusive content right away.

Step 2

Scan the QR code or go to `packtpub.com/unlock`.

On the page that opens (similar to *Figure 12.1* on desktop), search for this book by name and select the correct edition.

Figure 12.1: Packt unlock landing page on desktop

Step 3

After selecting your book, sign in to your Packt account or create one for free. Then upload your invoice (PDF, PNG, or JPG, up to 10 MB). Follow the on-screen instructions to finish the process.

Need help?

If you get stuck and need help, visit
`https://www.packtpub.com/unlock-benefits/help`
for a detailed FAQ on how to find your invoices and more. This QR code will take you to the help page.

Note

If you are still facing issues, reach out to `customercare@packt.com`.

Index

E

‹packt›

Other Books You May Enjoy

If you enjoyed this book, you may be interested in these other books by Packt:

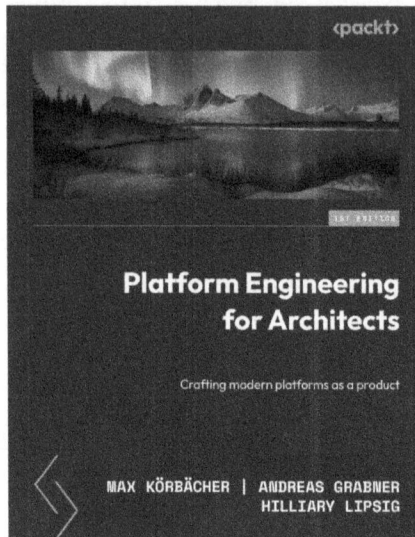

Platform Engineering for Architects

Max Körbächer, Andreas Grabner, Hilliary Lipsig

ISBN: 978-1-83620-359-9

- Make informed decisions aligned with your organization's platform needs
- Identify missing platform capabilities and manage that technical debt effectively
- Develop critical user journeys to enhance platform functionality
- Define platform purpose, principles, and key performance indicators
- Use data-driven insights to guide product decisions
- Design and implement platform reference and target architectures

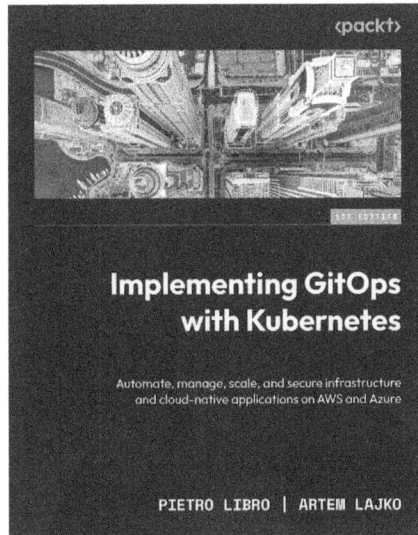

Implementing GitOps with Kubernetes

Pietro Libro, Artem Lajko

ISBN: 978-1-83588-422-5

- Delve into GitOps methods and best practices used for modern cloud-native environments
- Explore GitOps tools such as GitHub, Argo CD, Flux CD, Helm, and Kustomize
- Automate Kubernetes CI/CD workflows using GitOps and GitHub Actions
- Deploy infrastructure as code using Terraform, OpenTofu, and GitOps
- Automate AWS, Azure, and OpenShift platforms with GitOps
- Understand multitenancy, rolling back deployments, and how to handle stateful applications using GitOps methods
- Implement observability, security, cost optimization, and AI in GitOps practices

Packt is searching for authors like you

If you're interested in becoming an author for Packt, please visit authors.packtpub.com and apply today. We have worked with thousands of developers and tech professionals, just like you, to help them share their insight with the global tech community. You can make a general application, apply for a specific hot topic that we are recruiting an author for, or submit your own idea.

Share Your Thoughts

Now you've finished *Mastering Enterprise Platform Engineering*, we'd love to hear your thoughts! Scan the QR code below to go straight to the Amazon review page for this book and share your feedback or leave a review on the site that you purchased it from.

https://packt.link/r/1-835-88049-5

Your review is important to us and the tech community and will help us make sure we're delivering excellent quality content.

www.ingramcontent.com/pod-product-compliance
Lightning Source LLC
Chambersburg PA
CBHW081054220326
41598CB00038B/7094